Profit Measurement During Inflation

Operations Management: A Wiley Series

Arnold Reisman, Editor
Case Western Reserve University
Cleveland, Ohio

Goldschmidt and Admon. Profit Measurement During Inflation: Accounting, Economic, and Financial Aspects

Profit Measurement During Inflation

Accounting, Economic and Financial Aspects

Y. Goldschmidt

Assistant Professor, Faculty of Management, Tel-Aviv University and Department of Agricultural Economics and Management, The Hebrew University

General Director, Heshev - The Inter Kibbutz Economic Advisory Unit

K. Admon

Director, Planning and Control Department,
Koor Chemicals, Ltd.

A Wiley-Interscience Publication

JOHN WILEY & SONS
New York / London / Sydney / Toronto

Library of Congress Cataloging in Publication Data

Goldschmidt, Yaaqov.
Profit measurement during inflation.

(Operations management series)
"A Wiley-Interscience publication."
Bibliography
Includes index.
1. Profit—Accounting. 2. Inflation (Finance) and accounting. 3. Accounting and price fluctuations. I. Admon, K., 1927—joint author. II. Title. III. Series.
HF5681.P8G64 1977 658.1'554 77-4500

ISBN 0-471-01983-6

Printed in the United States of America

10 9 8 7 6 5 4 3 2 1

Foreword

Inflation is a fact of life. Economies that have experienced an annual inflation, no matter how defined, of less than 5% in the last decade are few indeed. Depending on the way inflation is defined and on the country involved, its rate is typically in the range from 6 to 30%. In fact it is not difficult to find economies characterized by inflation rates exceeding 30%.

Management of enterprises in the industrial, retail, service and even the nonprofit sectors requires information that is current and meaningful at the time decisions are made. Such decisions are typically concerned with how to operate in the short term and in the longer range future. Rarely does management make decisions regarding the past. Yet, the higher the rate of inflation, the more quickly does yesterday seem like yesteryear. Accounting, which is said to be one of the older professions, is currently struggling with procedures to cope with inflation—a relatively new phenomenon.

This book is intended to show the reader the ways and the means of processing and displaying the usual accounting and financial reporting information so that it is current and meaningful to decision makers at the upper and middle management levels. It is not intended to replace conventional accounting and reporting procedures, but to supplement them. When the accounting profession and the various tax authorities standardize reporting procedures in inflationary environments, it is hoped that the results will be similar, in principle, to those advocated in this book. The authors have been trained in and are quite knowledgeable about U.S. accounting principles, practices, and procedures, yet they have years of accumulated experience in a more highly inflationary environment—that of the State of Israel. Thus, the methods presented are based on their experience in adapting their training to the realities they have faced for some time.

This book is intended for those who make management decisions in corporations and in institutions and for those who provide the accounting and financial information necessary to make those decisions. Also, the student of accounting or of business or institutional management would benefit from reading this book—a departure from the existing texts in this area.

ARNOLD REISMAN
SERIES EDITOR

Cleveland, Ohio
May 1977

Preface

This book examines the subject of profit measurement under conditions of price level changes, especially during periods of inflation. The approach is based on accounting practices on the one hand, and on economic theory, on the other, and includes some reference to the behavioral sciences as well.

Company profit is a key element in the information on which the functioning of modern economy depends. A reliable profit measure is essential for both company management and external parties. Many economic decisions at different levels—company, industry, and national—rely on profit data. During a period of continuous inflation a correct concept of profit that is measurable in practice, as well as sound theoretically, is therefore indispensable.

Conventional accounting procedures assume a stable monetary unit because the economies of Western developed nations were not, in the past, greatly afflicted by inflation. This attitude is now generally recognized, however, as being inconsistent with the reality of continuous world-wide inflation, and discussions have become extensive in the press, in professional literature, and at conventions. Belatedly, the accounting profession and legal authorities are taking steps to provide adjusted financial data.

Rule 3-17, promulgated by the SEC in March 1976, and the proposed standards of the Cost Accounting Standards Board published in October 1975, are important steps in the direction of adjusting accepted accounting standards to replacement cost and/or price level adjusted accounting in the United States. Similar developments are taking place in other countries. All these make the issues dealt with in this book even more timely. Yet the discussion is not bounded by the many, and sometimes contradictory, pronouncements. Instead, the issues are developed analytically, and illustrated simply.

This book analyzes the distortions that price changes may cause in financial statements. These changes arise from two separate causes: changes in the general price level caused by changes in the purchasing power of the money, and changes in the prices of individual commodities caused by changes in the forces of supply and demand. The book illustrates possible effects of these distortions on decisions by various groups related to the company, and suggests methods of adjustments which can produce meaningful financial statements. Although, for the sake of simplicity, most of the discussion assumes that the prices of all items (except for interest) change simultaneously at the same rate at the same time, attention is given to the more usual situation in which the prices of individual commodities change at different rates.

Most authors concern themselves with the assets of a firm and their effect on profit, assuming (explicitly or implicitly) that companies are financed solely by equity capital. In this book emphasis is placed on the possible effects of financial leverage on profit. Two procedures suggested by opposing schools of thought are integrated into the accounting system: assets can be restated by either their replacement-cost or specific price indices, and equity by a general price index.

During a period of inflation, price level adjustments affect reported profit in two opposite directions: (1) asset restatement or revaluation increases depreciation expenses and the cost of materials used, thereby lowering reported profit; (2) asset restatement or revaluation may be greater than equity restatement, depending on financial leverage, thereby raising reported profit.

The discussion is focused on profit measurement; clearly this implies cost measurement as well. Methods to measure the various effects of price level changes on accounting data are presented. By stating the effects quantitatively, correct estimates for profit, equity, and asset values can be arrived at during periods of price level changes. Two novel techniques are presented for estimating (1) the required adjustment of financial statements by a rule of thumb, and (2) capital erosion by analyzing a series of balance sheets.

This book is intended for various groups of users: (1) managers—by providing guides for corporate inflation management; (2) financial analysts—by developing procedures and rules of thumb for solving real-world problems; (3) accountants—by indicating price level adjustment and replacement-cost accounting procedures; (4) researchers—by exposing a variety of topics and suggesting some provocative solutions; (5) students—by providing a broad coverage of topics, references, ideas, and analytical procedures.

The various topics are presented in a form suitable both for those who supply financial information (accountants) and for those who use it (managers, financial analysts). An important aim is to make the discussion intelligible to readers at different levels of education and experience. The various topics are therefore presented in a simple way, illustrated by a variety of exhibits and summary comparison tables. It is assumed that the reader is acquainted with the basic techniques of financial and managerial accounting, and with introductory economics.

To facilitate comprehension of the underlying processes presented in this book, the variables in the financial statements have been aggregated into major categories: fixed assets, equity, debt, sales, out-of-pocket costs, depreciation, interest expense, and pretax profit. Important elements that have not been included, such as financial assets, inventories, and income tax, are analyzed in separate chapters. The adjustment of financial statements and profit measurement as presented in the first part of the book are formalized in Chapter 6. A numerical example of a hypothetical company illustrates the discussion throughout its stages. References are listed twice for the reader's convenience: at the end of each chapter and at the end of the book.

YAAQOV GOLDSCHMIDT
KURT ADMON

Tel Aviv, Israel
June 1977

Acknowledgments

Valuable comments and suggestions were made by Dr. Leon Shashua. Miss T. Shnipper contributed greatly to this work with her painstaking calculations, proofreading, and valuable comments. Thanks are also due to Mr. E. Blum for his proofreading and comments. Mrs. H. Shashua deciphered the manuscript and typed it intelligently.

Professor Arnold Reisman deserves special acknowledgment. His efforts, suggestions, and stimulation served to improve the book considerably.

Y. G.
K. A.

Contents

Profit Measurement During Inflation

Part One

Introduction

One

Inflation and Measurement Problems in Accounting

During a period of inflation the purchasing power of money decreases; this is expressed by a rise in the general price level (not necessarily the price of particular goods or services). The scale that serves for measuring the economic activities (values, prices) changes in size. This change causes a host of damages, as listed in Exhibit 1.9. Conventional accounting procedures assume, however, that the monetary unit is constant. The contradiction under inflationary conditions between this assumption and actual fact causes biases in accounting reports. Restating recorded items can adjust the accounts, so that the reports will suit their original purposes. This restatement is carried out by inflating recorded data by means of price index numbers.

1.1 Inflation—Shrinkage in the Purchasing Power of Money

There are many theories and explanations of the cause or causes of inflation. Too often an attempt is made to explain the phenomenon by reference to unique factors relevant in the country under consideration. Yet inflation is a worldwide phenomenon, prevailing in all kinds of countries—large and small, developed and developing, socialist and free enterprise—as shown in Exhibit 1.1. It is beyond the scope of this introduction to discuss the possible causes of inflation. Only one explanation is presented here; it provides a sound background for understanding the need to adjust the financial statements of companies operating in an inflationary economy.

> Monetarists contend that all inflations are subject to a common cause even though the institutional setting varies over time as well as between nations. They argue that inflation is inevitably brought on by a rise in the money supply per unit of real output. Since it is difficult to increase output once resources are fully employed, further rapid growth in the money supply is certain to be accompanied by developing in-

Exhibit 1.1. Inflation Rates in Selected Countries: Consumer Price Index (Base: 1960 = 100)

	Year		
Country	1965	1970	1974
Africa			
Kenya	110.5	120.2	149.4
Morocco	121.8	125.2	161.1
America			
Argentina	282.9	648.9	2911.0
Canada	108.4	130.9	168.3
Colombia	178.9	289.0	550.0
United States	106.6	131.3	166.7
Asia			
India	134.5	199.6	329.7
Israel	139.2	171.8	364.1
Japan	134.1	174.8	269.6
Australia	109.3	127.6	180.5
Europe			
Holland	118.1	149.5	205.3
Poland	106.2	113.8	121.2
Sweden	119.6	148.8	198.7
United Kingdom	119.0	148.8	220.8
West Germany	115.3	130.0	165.3
Yugoslavia	189.1	311.5	610.3

Source: International Labor Office, *Bulletin of Labor Statistics,* 1970/III-IV; 1975/I; Supplements I, II, IV, V/75.

> flation.... The view that a rise in the money supply per unit of real output is the major cause of inflation is subject to empirical verification. Although facts cannot prove the correctness of a particular theory, they can be used to disprove it. If a rise in the money supply per unit of output is indeed the major cause of inflation, those countries suffering the most inflation should also record the largest growth in the money supply per unit of output (Sprinkel 1971, p. 11).

There is, in fact, evidence that a correlation exists between these two variables, as illustrated by a sample of countries in Latin America (Exhibit 1.2).

A "test tube" experiment, affirming the monetarist theory, was described by Radford:

> In the little world of a prisoner-of-war camp there developed a trading system surprisingly similar to that prevailing in the business world. The workings of basic economic forces were demonstrated clearly: fluctuations of individual prices; the emergence of a currency unit (cigarettes); general inflationary and deflationary movements in prices [as a result of increased and decreased supply of currency, respectively]; and the difficulties of price-fixing (Radford 1958, p. 69).

Extracts from the detailed description are provided in Appendix A.

Since money is itself a commodity (as cigarettes were in the prisoner-of-war camp), the forces of supply and demand affect it. If the supply of money is increased while the amount of other commodities remains constant, the price of money declines, whereas the prices of the other commodities, expressed in money, go up. The exchange

Exhibit 1.2. Relation between Money Supply and Inflation in Some Latin American Countries, 1965–74

Country	Money Supply/Real Gross Domestic Product (%)*	Consumer Price Index (%)*
Chile	78.2	67.8
Brazil**	24.5	31.2
Peru**	13.6	8.8
Columbia	10.9	11.9
Mexico	6.6	6.1

*The figures are compound annual rates of change.

**1963-72.

Source: International Financial Statistics, May 1976.

ratios (prices) among other commodities may remain stable while the general price level increases.

The forces of supply and demand affect all commodities, causing variation in the ratios of exchange. Over time, the prices of commodities change in different directions and at different rates; a change in the price of one commodity does not necessarily imply a change in the prices of other commodities. For example, while the wholesale price index of all commodities in the United States rose by 16% from 1960 to 1970, the index of plastics prices declined by 16%.[1] Only when the measuring unit has been changed, say by increasing the supply of money and thus causing inflation, will prices in general be changed in one direction at the same relative rate.

> Ordinary language sometimes gets in the way of a clear view of the scene. During an inflation we talk easily of a rise in prices. We should be talking about the shrinkage in the exchange-value of the monetary unit. At the technical or computational level, we can work with either idea—a rise in prices, or a shrinkage in the unit in which prices are expressed. But our thought processes cling to the way we express our ideas. The "money illusion" tells us that the dollar, the pound, or the franc is sound. They have not changed. It is the high prices we must attack, more particularly, the profiteers, monopolists, and special interests who keep pushing those prices up. We focus on the symptom; we tend to treat the symptom. The disease, meanwhile, is likely to go unchecked (Moonitz 1973, pp. 19–20).

1.2 Money as a Scale of Measurement[2]

One of the aims of accounting is to measure the economic results of a company's activities; these activities are recorded in monetary terms, and their effects are also measured in terms of money. When money changes in value, say during a period of inflation, the "scale of measurement" changes.

Measuring an object requires selecting one of its attributes and expressing this attribute in terms of some scale. For example, one may wish to measure the lengths of various objects. This chosen attribute, length, may be expressed in metric units or in traditional English units. If an object is measured as 10 meters long, the same attribute may be expressed as approximately 33 feet. Once measured on a given scale, the attribute may be expressed on other scales; the metric units may be transformed into English units, and vice versa.

Transforming from one scale to another changes the units used to express the measurement, but does not change the measured attribute (length). The length of a given object does not change because the scale has been changed! The increase in numerals from 10 meters to 33 feet has no interpretable meaning. Suppose that two identical objects are measured on two different scales; for example, one object weighs 10 kilograms, and the other weighs 22 pounds (approximately). The total weight, 10 kilograms plus 22 pounds, is not 32 anythings! The numeral 32 is meaningless. The scales must first be transformed to a common base before the measurements can be compared, added, subtracted, and so forth.

In the world of economics and accounting, a major attribute of an object is its exchange ability, that is, its "value in exchange." Value in exchange means the relationship between quantities of two commodities: How many units of commodity A are required in exchange for one unit of commodity B? Expressing exchange value in barter terms requires a ratio for each possible pair of exchanges. If, however, one commodity is selected as a common denominator, and the values of all other commodities are expressed in terms of that one, the number of ratios is reduced to the number of commodities. Trading is simplified by having the exchange value of all commodities quoted in terms of one scale.

One of the functions of money is to serve as the common denominator for exchange. In this way the ratios of exchange become "prices." The meaning of price is how many units of money are required in exchange for one unit of commodity A. Price is thus the measure of a particular attribute of a given object—its exchange value. The price "scale" facilitates comparison of values between different commodities. Each country has its own money scale (e.g., dollars, francs, or marks). Measurements carried out in terms of different currencies must be transformed to make them comparable.

As a medium of exchange, money represents command over goods and services. If one holds 100 units of money, he can exchange them for a set of goods and services, provided that the total exchange value of the set does not exceed 100 units of money. Since money can be exchanged for any good or service, it represents command over "things in general," that is, it provides purchasing power. It can be seen that there is a direct connection between the purchasing power of money and the price scale of things in general.[3]

Measurements using different scales (meters and feet, kilograms and pounds, dollars and francs, etc.) cannot be directly compared, added, or subtracted. The same is true if the exchange ratio of money has changed between two points in time. Although the measurement unit is denoted by the same name as before, its size has changed; it is as different from its namesake as meters are from feet. The results of measurements carried out at two different points in time cannot be meaningfully compared, added, or subtracted unless they are first transformed ("adjusted," "restated").

1.3 Price Indices for Restatement Purposes

A change in the money scale is reflected by a reciprocal change in the general price level. Whereas a change in the money scale itself cannot be measured directly, the reciprocal change in the general price level can easily be measured by the use of index numbers. This is an indirect measure.

Indirect measurements are widespread. For example, measuring temperature requires a medium (mercury) in a tube. The direct measure on the thermometer is of the height of the mercury column. This measurement can represent the temperature of the measured object; the exchange of heat between the object and the thermometer results in the expansion of the mercury, which then rises to a given height in the tube. When thermal equilibrium is reached between the object and the thermometer, the height of the mercury column, by convention, establishes the temperature of the object. Similarly, the general price level index provides an indirect measure of the purchasing power or exchange value of money. For example, suppose that the consumers' price index rose during a given period from 100 to 120 points. This means that the prices of goods and services measured by this index rose by 20%. The index measures the relation of goods to money; the reciprocal of this index measures the relation of money to goods (100:120 = 0.83). The money unit that served as a measuring scale shrank 17% during the given period (from 1.00 to 0.83).

An index is a ratio between two measurements. A price index is the ratio between the price of an object (or a group of objects) on a given date and the price on a base date. It expresses the change in the price level of the object (or group of objects) during the period in question. When the change in price level of a "set" of diversified objects (e.g., consumers' goods) is measured, the relative weight of each object in the set must be taken into account. There are several methods for calculating the index number in such a case. One of them (that of Paasche) uses current period quantities for weighing purposes; another (that of Laspeyres), base period quantities.[4] Usually, the price index is provided as a series of measurements, expressed as percentages, of the weighted average price of a group of objects at a succession of dates related to a base date.

The index is a sophisticated tool for measuring and expressing changes in prices. The index is easy to understand and simple to use. Since it is a ratio (of two price levels), it is independent of the scale on which the original measurements were carried out. If the consumers' price index for a given date is 120, it indicates that the price level of consumers' goods is 20% above that of the base date, irrespective of whether the prices are measured in dollars or francs. Thus the price index makes it possible to compare both time-series data (price changes over time) and cross-section data (price changes in products, services, etc., among countries). There are, of course, some deficiencies and arbitrariness in constructing price indices and in collecting the relevant data, which reduce, to some extent, the reliability of the index numbers.[5]

The best measure of changes in the purchasing power of money is an index number of price change in all goods. (Recall that this is an indirect measure). Therefore a general price index is best suited for restating historical costs in terms of "new" money with different (lower) purchasing power. Restating historical costs to adjust for the new purchasing power of money does not contradict accounting principles; it only corrects the assumption of a constant-value monetary unit on which conventional accounting is based.[6] The Financial Accounting Standards Board (1974, p. 12) has stated:

> Changing the measuring unit does not change the attribute being measured. Regardless of whether the historical cost of an asset is expressed in terms of the number of units of money invested in the asset or the number of units of general purchasing power invested in the asset, it is the cost of the asset that is being measured.

The general price indices are available in the United States (1) the GNP implicit price deflator (gross national product in current prices divided by the current GNP expressed in base period prices), and (2) the consumers' price index. The argument in favor of the former is that it is more broadly based. The argument for the latter rests on technical grounds; it is more carefully constructed and its measurements are more accurate.[7] However, the two indices seem to move in tandem and there are no significant differences between them, as depicted in Exhibit 1.3.[8]

The general price index is a tool for the restatement of accounting items in accordance with the current purchasing power of money; price indices for individual goods, on the other hand, measure the change in price levels of particular items. Therefore, specific indices can be applied to obtain a close estimate of replacement costs. Ap-

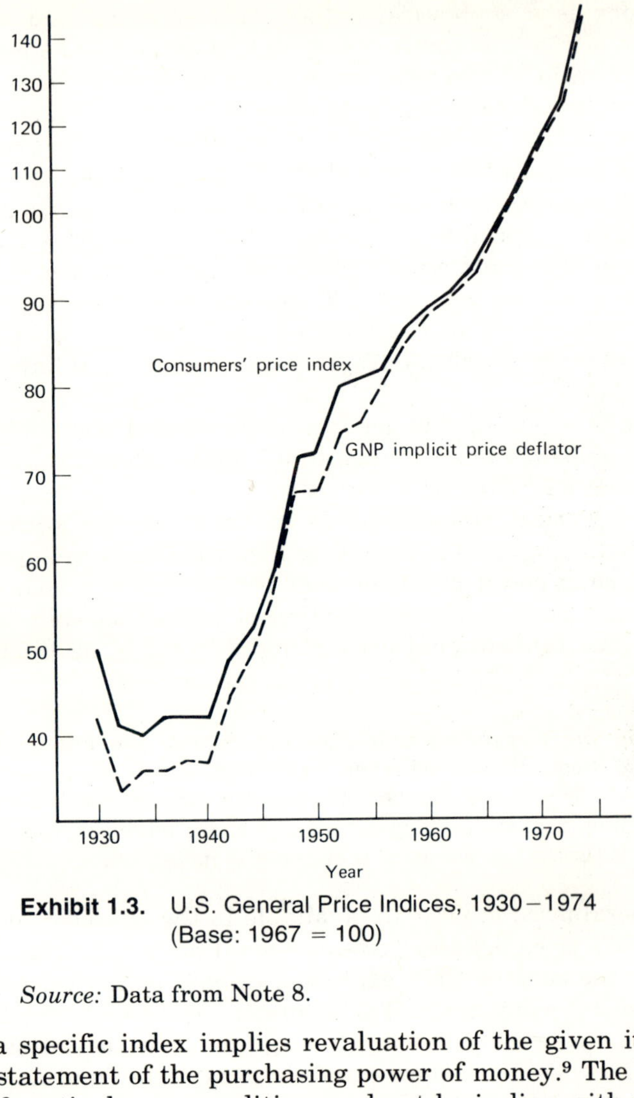

Exhibit 1.3. U.S. General Price Indices, 1930–1974 (Base: 1967 = 100)

Source: Data from Note 8.

plying a specific index implies revaluation of the given item rather than restatement of the purchasing power of money.[9] The changes in prices of particular commodities need not be in line with the change in the general price level. Moreover, during a period of inflation, the prices of some goods may decline. For example, the average price of a black and white television set declined in the United States from \$222 in 1960 to \$124 in 1972. This price level decline of 44% occurred while the consumers' price level rose by 41%.

Specific price indices may be used for revaluation purposes. Since it is not practical to use an index for each commodity, indices for specific groups of commodities are available. A selected group of such indices is provided in Exhibit 1.4.

In summary, a general price index can be used to restate historical costs (e.g., assets at acquisition cost) in terms of the current purchasing power of money. Applying a specific price index translates the historical costs into current replacement costs.

1.4 Distortions of Accounting Data during Inflation

The economic activities of a company are recorded by an accounting system that applies money as the common scale for measuring all the activities. As the scale of measurement (the purchasing power of money) changes, conventional accounting reports distort figures. Profit and loss statements, balance sheets, budgets, and standard costs and prices are all distorted and cannot be used correctly to manage the company. The main types of information supplied by the accounting system that are used by company management are summarized in Exhibit 1.5. When this information is distorted, management activities may be distorted as well.

The change in the purchasing power of money (the scale of measurement) during a period of inflation causes considerable distortions in the financial statements. The magnitude of these distortions for an industry can be seen from a study of nine U.S. steel companies during the 1940s, as shown in Exhibit 1.6.[10] The magnitude of the distortions on a national scale in the United States is shown in Exhibit 1.7.[11]

Exhibit 1.4. Specific Price Indices of Selected Groups of Commodities in the United States, 1960–1974* (Base: 1967 = 100)

Commodity	Year			
	1960	1965	1970	1974
Industrial commodities	95.3	96.4	110.0	153.8
Farm products	97.9	99.4	111.0	187.7
Machinery and equipment	92.0	93.9	111.4	139.4
Household furniture	90.1	94.1	111.6	136.6
House electronic equipment	117.9	103.3	93.6	93.1
Motor vehicles and equipment	98.9	98.6	108.5	129.2
Composite construction cost	81.1	90.6	119.7	173.1

*Wholesale price indices except for the last group.

Source: U.S. Department of Commerce and U.S. Department of Labor publications.

Exhibit 1.5. Managerial Purposes in Accounting Information

Type of Information	Purpose of Information	
Cost and profit	Operational decisions	Make or buy Expand or contract Input mix Product mix
	Price decisions	
	Performance evaluation	Comparison to: Standards Previous periods Other units
	Tax considerations	
Profit	Dividend decisions Wage policy Income tax considerations Investment decisions	
Asset values	Operational decisions	Lease or buy Asset mix Inventory management Replacement policy
	Performance evaluation	Return on capital
	Property tax considerations Insurance decisions	
Equity	Financial decisions	Finance mix Type of debt
	Performance evaluation	Return to equity

Davidson and Weil (1975, pp. 43, 44) found that the interquartile range of adjusted net income as a percentage of the 1974 reported net income of 75 U.S. companies is as follows:

Depreciation adjusted only	0.5 – 84%
Depreciation adjusted and gains on monetary items	63–115%

Restating some items in the balance sheet and, in turn, adjusting cost items in the profit and loss statement can correct accounting measurements that have been distorted by a change in the purchasing power of money. These adjustments are then reflected in the

Exhibit 1.6. Illustration of Discrepancies between Reported and Adjusted Accounting Data (Nine U.S. Steel Companies, 1941–1947)

	Reported Data	Adjusted Data
Dividends	Earned every year	Not earned in any year
Income for 1946 in million $	200	88
Net income available to investors in 1947	356	91
Percentage by which working capital increased during 7-year period	51	2
Percentage to which fixed assets decreased during 7 years	6	19
Percentage by which preferred stock decreased during 7 years	12	48

Source: Jones (1949, p. 13).

reported profit, as recorded in the price level adjusted (PLA) statements. In this book several profit measures are developed and used, as summarized in Exhibit 1.8.[12]

The Report of the Inflation Accounting Committee in the United Kingdom (Sandilands 1975, p. 7) stated:

> Current Cost Accounting will indicate more clearly than existing accounting conventions the effect of inflation on a company's affairs and that it is urgent that it should be introduced as soon as possible. However, it should not be assumed that accounting for inflation is in itself a panacea for the difficulties of companies during a time of inflation. By demonstrating the effect of past inflation on profits, Current Cost Accounting will provide companies with more useful information than existing conventions on the amounts they can distribute in the form of dividends, or pay in increased wages and other costs without eroding the capital required to carry on their business. Moreover, in providing information about the past in a more useful form, Current Cost Accounting may help a company to make an assessment of the possible effects of future inflation.

Management in an inflationary environment requires more plan-

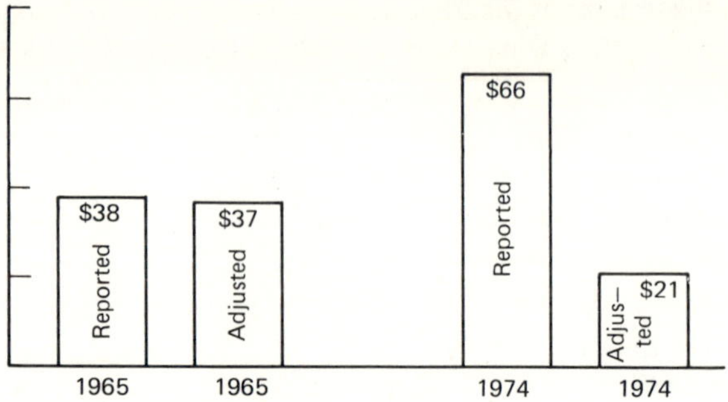

Exhibit 1.7. Distortion of After-Tax Profit of Nonfinancial Corporations in the United States (billions of dollars)

Source: Adapted from Jones (1975, p. 51). Data from William E. Simon, U.S. Secretary of the Treasury, in testimony before the Joint Economic Committee, February 5, 1975. Copyright © 1975 by the President and Fellows of Harvard College; all rights reserved; permission granted.

Exhibit 1.8. Definitions of Profit Measures

Sales − Historical costs = Conventional Profit

Sales − Adjusted costs = PLA operating profit

Conventional profit = PLA operating profit + Realized restatement gains

Under 100% equity conditions:
PLA total profit = PLA operating profit
Under financial leverage conditions:
PLA total profit = PLA operating profit + Net restatement gains
PLA total profit = Inflationfree profit + Inflationary leverage returns

ning because an additional variable—price level change—must be considered. Furthermore, planning is based, to some extent, on *ex post* data, usually those related to several years. *Ex post* accounting data can be used intelligently only if they are adjusted and updated.

A summary of the main damaging effects that inflation imposes on companies and on the economy as a whole is presented in Exhibit 1.9 (the last column indicates the chapter in which each one is discussed).

1.5 Acceptance of Inflation Accounting Procedures

In the United States, application of PLA or replacement-cost accounting procedures to published financial statements is, to a large extent, dependent on tax laws and Securities and Exchange Commission (SEC) rulings.[13] Tax legislation has had a negative effect on the acceptability of current value reporting in the United States. The Internal Revenue Code specifies that the "basis for property acquired by purchase generally is cost."[14] Inventory valuation is also regulated so as to reflect cost (or market if this is lower than cost). Some recognition of the divergence between current value and historical cost has been given through the allowance of the last in, first out (LIFO) inventory method and the accelerated depreciation of fixed assets.

The U.S. Supreme Court established the original cost theory in the 1930s and has continued on this basis up to the present day. This, of course, has had great influence on accounting practice, delaying the development of current-value methods.

Although the SEC, in special cases, required disclosure of current values,[15] the general rule was to require historical-cost reporting, with departures from this branded as potentially misleading.[16] The SEC's attitude in this matter, as in most others, was based on its reliance on generally accepted accounting standards; in Release No. 4 it stated, "Financial statements prepared in accordance with accounting principles for which there is no authoritative support will be presumed to be misleading or inaccurate despite disclosures contained in the certificate of the accountant or in footnotes to the statement."

The burden of initiating change was thus placed on the accounting profession. As inflation became an almost permanent phenomenon, the American Institute of Certified Public Accountants (1963), the American Accounting Association (1966), the Accounting Principles Board (1969), and the Financial Accounting Standards Board (1974), took steps in this direction.

A major turning point toward the introduction of current value accounting came in March 1976, when the Securities and Exchange Commission (1976a), in a complete reversal of its previous position, published Rule 3-17. This rule, which amends Rule S-X, requires that information on the replacement costs of assets and on the costs of sales in terms of replacement costs must accompany the audited financial statements of companies over which the SEC has jurisdiction. Rule 3-17 and sections of the appended explanatory note (Securities and Exchange Commission 1976b) are reproduced in Appendix B.

The Cost Accounting Standards Board (1975), which sets standards for cost computations in contracts that fall under the regulation of the Defense Production Act of 1950, published, in October 1975, a proposed standard that would recognize price level adjustment of depreciation expense. Sections of the proposal are reproduced in Appendix B.

Exhibit 1.9. Damaging Effects of Inflation

Subject	Possible Results of Inflation	Implications: For Company	Implications: For Economy	Chapter in Which Effect is Discussed
Damages Resulting from Biased Accounting Data				
1. Overall policy	Overoptimism	Waste, higher consumption	Misallocation of resources, higher consumption, procycle effect	
2. Dividend decisions	Overpayment	Inflated stock prices, capital erosion, future increased leverage	Decreased productive capacity, increased consumption	13, 15
3. Wage policy	Overpayment	Capital erosion	As for Point 2	2, 15
4. Operational decisions	Misallocation of resources	Lower profit	Waste	3, 7
5. Replacement decisions	Downward tendency	Future loss	Decreased productive capacity	3, 4, 16
6. Performance evaluation	Lower efficiency	Lower profit	Waste	7, 8, 12
	Overpayment of bonuses	As for Point 2	As for Point 2	
7. Pricing decisions	Downward tendency	Lower profit	Increased consumption	3, 7
8. Insurance decisions	Downward tendency	Possible loss	—	
9. Income tax				
On equity	Overtaxation	As for Point 2	Countercycle effect	14
On debt	Undertaxation	Benefit	Inequitable income distribution	
10. Property tax	Undertaxation	Benefit	Inequitable income distribution	

		Damages Resulting from Environmental Situation		
1. Economic orientation	Loss of orientation due to money illusion	Nonconcious wealth and price changes, benefit from implicit price change	Misallocation of resources, inequitable income distribution	
2. Investment decisions	Tendency to increase	Overinvestment	Waste	9, 16
3. Financial decisions	Tendency to high leverage	Increased risk	Future increased bankruptcy	4, 15, 16
4. Foreign trade	Increased price of foreign currency	Decreased sales	Decreased export	
5. Planning	Greater complexity	Additional cost, lower profit	Waste	9, 16
6. Price level adjustment	Required	Additional cost	Waste	2

These pronouncements by two important U.S. government agencies are experimental and do not integrate current-cost adjustments into audited financial statements. Nevertheless, they are important steps in the direction of adjusting accepted accounting standards to replacement-cost and/or PLA accounting in the United States.

In other countries as well, various forms of current-value accounting are gaining acceptance. In England, mention must be made of the outstanding Report of the Inflation Accounting Committee (Sandilands 1975), which in September 1975 proposed incorporation of replacement cost into financial statements. Earlier, in May 1974, the Institute of Chartered Accountants in England and Wales (1974), published a provisional statement urging the inclusion of price level adjustments in audited financial reports.

It is interesting to note that some price level adjustments for income tax purposes are compulsory in four Latin American countries (Argentina: since 1972, Brazil: since 1964, Chile: since 1963, Uruguay: since 1958); in three countries it was compulsory once (France: 1959, Japan: 1954, Peru: 1971); and in six countries it was permitted once (Austria: 1954, Belgium: 1946, Germany: 1948, France: 1947–1958, Israel: 1964, Italy: 1952). In other countries (Australia, Canada, Denmark, the Netherlands, Norway, Sweden), professional accounting bodies have permitted the introduction of some adjustments into financial statements.[17]

Notes

1. The respective wholesale price indices (1967 = 100) are as follows:
   all commodities: 1960 = 94.9; 1970 = 110.4
   plastic resins and materials: 1960 = 108.2; 1970 = 90.6
2. The discussion in this section and the next one relies heavily on Moonitz (1973, Chapter II).
3. "...Money is general purchasing power, and is sought as a means to all kinds of ends" (Marshall 1910, p. 22).

   "A man does not hold money for its own sake, but for its purchasing power—that is to say, for what it will buy. Therefore his demand is not for units of money as such, but for units of purchasing power" (Keynes 1971, p. 47).
4. The respective formulas for the price index calculated in these ways are as follows:

$$\text{Paasche: } \frac{\sum p_t\, q_t}{\sum p_o\, q_t}$$

$$\text{Laspeyres: } \frac{\sum p_t\, q_o}{\sum p_o\, q_o}$$

where p is the price per unit,
q is the quantity of object (commodity, service),
0, t denote the base date and a given date, respectively, and
Σ is the sign for summation.

For a detailed discussion of index numbers, including a bibliography, see the American Institute of Certified Public Accountants (1963, pp. 81-117) and Clarke (1975).

5. For a brief examination of the deficiencies of price indices see, for example, Stickney and Green (1974, pp. 28–30) and Stigler and Kendahl (1970).
6. The claim that adjusted costs maintain the accounting criterion of objectivity is supported by many authors, for example, Edwards and Bell (1961, pp. 283–284), Wright (1966, pp. 63–65), and Revsine (1973, pp. 75–81). Moreover, empirical studies (McDonald 1968, Parker 1975), although limited in scope, indicate that market-based values are, in some cases, more objective than book values. It should be noted, in comparison, that

> historical-cost accounting permits considerable scope for the exercise of subjective judgment and alternative bases of accounting.... These include the assessment of bad debt provisions, the valuation of goodwill, the valuation of assets in the event of a merger or acquisition, the treatment of research and development expenditure, and the method of conversion of amounts expressed in overseas currencies when accounts are consolidated (Sandilands 1975, pp. 73–74).

Furthermore, the claim that historical-cost accounting is objective is questionable on the grounds that objectivity has meant different things to different authors (Hendriksen 1970, p. 114).

7. It is interesting to note the ruling of rabbinical courts in the sixteenth century *(Responsa Ma'aseh Hiya,* 17) that the purchasing power of money be calculated in relation to "basic commodities," like wheat, oil, and wool, and not general "goods." This shows that the "consumers' price index" was considered rather

than the "price index of the national product." E. Blum and A. Shmu'eli drew our attention to this source.

8. U.S. Consumers' Price Index (CPI) and GNP Implicit Price Deflator (GNP IPD), 1930–1974 (Base 1967 = 100)

Year	CPI	GNP IPD	Year	CPI	GNP IPD	Year	CPI	GNP IPD
1930	50.1	41.9	1945	53.9	50.8	1960	88.7	87.8
1931	45.6	38.1	1946	58.5	56.7	1961	89.6	88.9
1932	40.9	34.2	1947	66.9	63.4	1962	90.6	90.0
1933	38.8	33.4	1948	72.1	67.7	1963	91.7	91.2
1934	40.1	35.9	1949	71.4	67.3	1964	92.9	92.6
1935	41.1	36.2	1950	72.1	68.2	1965	94.5	94.3
1936	41.6	36.3	1951	77.8	72.8	1966	97.2	97.1
1937	43.0	37.8	1952	79.6	74.4	1967	100.0	100.0
1938	42.2	37.3	1953	80.2	75.1	1968	104.2	104.0
1939	41.6	36.7	1954	80.5	76.2	1969	109.8	109.0
1940	42.0	37.3	1955	80.2	77.3	1970	116.3	115.0
1941	44.1	40.1	1956	81.4	79.9	1971	121.3	120.4
1942	48.9	45.1	1957	84.3	82.9	1972	125.3	124.2
1943	51.9	48.3	1958	86.6	85.0	1973	133.1	131.2
1944	52.7	49.5	1959	87.3	86.4	1974	147.7	144.7

Source: U.S. Department of Commerce and U.S. Department of Labor Publications.

9. Restatement by specific price index does not provide exact revaluation (or replacement cost), as will be shown in Sections 3.4 and 7.2.
10. For additional case studies see, for example, American Institute of Certified Public Accountants (1963), Backer (1973, Chapters 11, 12, 13), Cutler and Westwick (1973), and Kirkman (1974, Chapter 9).
11. Earlier data on the extent of distortion of reported profit in the United States are provided by Ray (1960). The following condensed data are from Edwards and Bell (1961, pp. 138, 164):

		Percentage of Profit Overstatement	
Year	Reported Corporate Profits before Taxes (million $, rounded)	Due to Inventory Adjustment	Due to Depreciation Adjustment
1929	9,400	– 4.8	10.1
1930	3,200	– 50.6	20.6

Year	Reported Corporate Profits before Taxes (million $, rounded)	Percentage of Profit Overstatement: Due to Inventory Adjustment	Percentage of Profit Overstatement: Due to Depreciation Adjustment
1931	– 800	–147.4	20.0
1932	–3,000	– 54.1	– 3.7
1933	150	107.7	–40.0
1934	1,650	60.6	13.7
1935	3,000	8.2	8.2
1936	5,650	15.1	4.4
1937	6,100	0.5	8.5
1938	3,050	– 24.0	17.2
1939	6,200	13.0	7.8
1940	9,100	2.3	6.0
1941	16,750	17.3	4.5
1942	20,650	6.2	4.8
1943	24,300	3.3	4.3
1944	23,050	1.3	4.5
1945	18,750	3.1	5.8
1946	22,150	31.2	7.4
1947	28,850	25.7	10.2
1948	32,150	7.2	11.3
1949	25,550	– 6.8	13.4
1950	39,650	14.3	
1951	40,950	3.0	
1952	35,550	– 2.7	
1953	37,200	2.8	
1954	32,650	0.1	
1955	43,300	4.2	
1956	43,750	6.2	
1957	41,500	3.9	
1958	37,700	0.5	
1959	47,000	1.1	

12. Graphical comparisons of the various profit measures are presented in Exhibits 2.5, 4.6, and 7.6.
13. For a survey of this subject see Backer (1973, Chapters 5, 13) and Trienens (1973).

14. Internal Revenue Code, Section 1012.
15. SEC Amicus Curiae, *Speed* v. *Transamerica,* 99 F. Supp. 8085; SEC Amicus Curiae, *Gerstle* v. *Gamble–Skogmo,* 298 F. Supp. 66.
16. Securities and Exchange Commission, Accounting Series Releases No. 4 and No. 8.
17. Source of data: Scapens (1973, App. 1) and Kollaritsch (1961). For additional surveys see Institute of Chartered Accountants in England and Wales (1972), and Price Waterhouse International (1973).

References

Accounting Principles Board, *Financial Statements Restated for General Price Level Changes,* Statement No. 3, American Institute of Certified Public Accountants, New York, 1969.

American Accounting Association, *A Statement of Accounting Theory,* Evanston, Ill., 1966.

American Institute of Certified Public Accountants, *Reporting the Financial Effects of Price Level Changes,* Accounting Research Study No. 6 by the Staff of the Accounting Research Division, New York, 1963.

Backer, M., *Current Value Accounting,* Financial Executive Research Foundation, New York, 1973.

Clarke, F. L., "Some Observations on the Indexation of Accountants," *Abacus,* December 1975, pp. 107–121.

Cost Accounting Standards Board, "Adjustment of Historical Depreciation Costs for Inflation," Proposed Rules, *Federal Register,* Vol. 40, No. 197, October 9, 1975, pp. 57,517–57,519.

Cutler, R. S. and C. A. Westwick, "The Impact of Inflation Accounting on the Stock Market," *Accountancy,* March 1973, pp. 15–24.

Davidson, S. and R. L. Weil, "Impact of Inflation Accounting on 1974 Earnings," *Financial Analyst Journal,* September–October 1975, pp. 42–54.

Edwards, E. O. and P. W. Bell, *The Theory and Measurement of Business Income,* University of California Press, Berkeley and Los Angeles, 1961.

Financial Accounting Standards Board, *Financial Reporting in Units of General Purchasing Power,* Exposure Draft, Stamford, Conn., December 1974.

Hendriksen, E. S., *Accounting Theory,* Irwin, Homewood, Ill., 1970.

Institute of Chartered Accountants in England and Wales, *Accounting Principles and Practices in European Countries,* London, 1972.

———, *Accounting for Changes in the Purchasing Power of Money,* Provisional Statement of Standard Accounting Practice No. 7, May 1974.

Jones, R. C., "The Effect of Inflation on Capital and Profits: The Record of Nine Steel Companies," *Journal of Accountancy,* January 1949, pp. 9–27.

Jones, R. H., "Why Business Must Seek Tax Reform," *Harvard Business Review,* September-October 1975, pp. 49-55.

Keynes, J. M., *A Treatise on Money,* Vol. 1, Macmillan, London, 1971.

Kirkman, P. R. A., *Accounting under Inflationary Conditions,* Allen & Unwin, London, 1974.

Kollaritsch, F. P., "Replacement Values in Practice—The Example of Austria," *Management Accounting,* August 1961 (reproduced in National Association of Accountants, *Management Reporting under Inflation,* 1975, pp. 146–157).

Marshall, A., *Principles of Economics* (6th ed.), Macmillan, London, 1910.

McDonald, D. L., "A Test Application of the Feasibility of Market Based Measures in Accounting," *Journal of Accounting Research,* Spring 1968, pp. 38–49.

Moonitz, M., *Changing Prices and Financial Reporting,* Occasional Paper No. 3, International Center for Research Accounting, University of Lancaster, England, 1973.

Parker, J. E., "Testing Comparability and Objectivity of Exit Value Accounting," *Accounting Review,* July 1975, pp. 512–524.

Price Waterhouse International, *Survey of Accounting Principles and Reporting Practices in 38 Countries,* Price Waterhouse & Co., London, 1973.

Radford, R. A., "The Price System in Microcosm: A P.O.W. Camp," in C. L. Harris (ed.), *Selected Readings in Economics,* Prentice-Hall, Englewood Cliffs, N.J., 1958, pp. 69–79.

Ray, D. D., *Accounting and Business Fluctuations,* University of Florida Press, Gainesville, 1960.

Revsine, L., *Replacement Cost Accounting,* Prentice-Hall, Englewood Cliffs, N.J., 1973.

Sandilands, F. E. P., *Inflation Accounting,* Report of the Inflation Accounting Committee, Her Majesty's Stationery Office, London, 1975.

Scapens, R. W., *The Treatment of Inflation in the Published Accounts of Companies in Overseas Countries,* Institute of Chartered Accountants in England and Wales, 1973.

Securities and Exchange Commission, "Release No. 190," *Accounting Series,* Bureau of National Affairs, Washington, D. C., March 1976, pp. E-1–4.(a)

———"Interpretations of Accounting Series Release No. 190," *Staff Accounting Bulletin,* No. 7, SEC DOCKET, March 1976, pp. 295–300. (b)

Sprinkel, B. W., "Inflation—Its Cause and Cure," *Financial Analyst Journal,* May–June 1971, pp. 11–16.

Stickney, C. P. and D. O. Green, "No Price Level Adjusted Statements, Please (Pleas)," *CPA Journal,* January 1974, pp. 25–31.

Stigler, G. J. and J. K. Kendahl, *The Behavior of Industrial Prices,* National Bureau of Economic Research, General Series, No. 90, 1970.

Trienens, H. J., "Some Legal Implications of Current Value Accounting," in M. Backer, *Current Value Accounting,* Financial Executive Research Foundation, 1973, pp. 77–109 (also in *Financial Executive,* September 1972).

Wright, F. K., "Accounting and Price Changes," in R. J. Chambers, L. Goldberg, and R. L. Mathews (eds), *The Accounting Frontier,* Cheshire, Melbourne and London, 1966.

Part Two

Profit Measurement

Two

Profit Measurement under Inflationary Conditions

According to economic theory, profit is the amount of money that may be drawn from a company and leave its real capital untouched. Profit as calculated by conventional accounting procedures is more or less in line with the economic definition as long as the purchasing power of the money (the price level) is stable. During a period of inflation the conventional accounting profit also includes some realized restatement (holding) gains, which originate from the change in the measurement scale. Price level adjustment of lagged cost items (depreciation and materials drawn from inventory) corrects the inflationary distortion of reported profit.

2.1 Profit Concept in Economics and Accounting

The profit of a going concern can be defined as the increase in net worth during a given period or, alternatively, as the sum that may be withdrawn from the company without impairing its net worth position in comparison with the beginning of the period. This definition holds in both economic and accounting disciplines. The economic concept of profit was defined by Hicks (1950, p. 172) as follows:

> A person's income is the maximum value which he can consume during a week and still expect to be as well off at the end of the week as he was at the beginning.

In popular terms, the fruit (income) may be picked but the tree (capital) may not be felled. Being "as well off" means that the owner's wealth in terms of discounted future net receipts, measured in base purchasing power currency, is intact (Chapter 3).[1]

Similarly, the accounting profit concept involves calculation of net worth from the position statements of two successive periods. Accounting theory assumes that the future earning capabilities of assets are fairly represented by their historical prices. Debt value, representing external obligations, is "objective." The difference between asset value and debt value, net worth, is the owner's wealth; if this is unimpaired, he is "as well off." This approach is methodologically illustrated by drafting balance sheets before income statements (as is done in this book). The similarity of the profit concept in both disciplines is illustrated numerically for a normal period—in which no inflation exists.

Consider a going concern that is maintaining overall stability, that is, stability in physical assets, real income, and expenses. The company is housed in a rented building. Its assets consist of two machines, each of which cost (installed) $50. The machines are depreciated using the straight-line depreciation method over 2 years. At the end of 2 years, each machine is removed from the premises with a scrap value of zero (i.e., depreciation period equals economic life of the asset). The machines are bought in a stagger system, so that at the beginning of each year one machine is new and one machine is half depreciated. The outgoing machine is scrapped on December 31, and the new machine is bought and installed on the same day.[2] The machines are equal in productive ability during both years. Therefore the acquisition cost (gross value) can serve as a measure of productive capacity. For the sake of simplicity, it is assumed that the company does not keep inventories of raw materials, goods in process, and finished goods, nor does it hold financial assets. (These assumptions will be relaxed in Chapters 5 and 4, respectively.) Since the company aims to maintain stability, after-tax profit is distributed as dividends (i.e., "consumed") each December 31. All transactions are on a cash basis.

The opening balances in the company books are as follows:

Assets:	Machine 1	$ 50
	Machine 2	50
	Total acquisition cost	100
	Accumulated depreciation	25
	Assets, at cost	75
Equity		75

Throughout the year 19X1, all prices were constant, just as in previous years. Sales for the year totaled 100 units at $2 each, that is, $200. Out-of-pocket costs were $130, and the depreciation expense was, of course, $50. The financial statements are presented in Exhibit 2.1

Depreciation ($50) charged to operations exactly equaled the cost of the new machine that will maintain productive capacity at its previous level. This is so because historical costs, which are matched against revenue, accurately represent the replacement values of the inputs used in production. Total profit ($20) is taxed and distributed as dividends, and the equity of $75 is intact.

Exhibit 2.1. Manufacturing Equity Company
Financial Statements for the Year 19X1
(No Inflation, 100% Fixed Assets, 100% Equity)
Conventional and PLA Accounting

Balance Sheet as of December 31, 19X1

Assets			Liabilities and Equity		
12.31.19X0		12.31.19X1	12.31.19X0		12.31.19X1
$50.00	Machine 1	—	$75.00	Equity	$75.00
50.00	Machine 2	$50.00			
—	Machine 3	50.00			
100.00	Assets, at cost	100.00			
(25.00)	Accum. depr.	(25.00)			
75.00		75.00	75.00		75.00

Profit and Loss Statement for the Year 19X1

Sales, 100 units		$200.00
Out-of-pocket costs	$130.00	
Depreciation	50.00	
		180.00
Profit = tax and dividend		20.00

Sources and Uses Statement for the Year 19X1

Sources		Uses	
Depreciation	$50.00	Machine 3	$50.00
Profit	20.00	Tax and dividend	20.00
	70.00		70.00

The illustration indicates that under certain conditions conventional accounting procedures measure profit in accordance with the economic concept as defined by Hicks (1950). This, in fact, is what accountancy has set out to do. It is successful as long as (1) prices are stable and historical costs serve as accurate proxies for replacement costs, and (2) all income has been realized. This profit measure, correct from both the economic and the accounting points of view, is used in practice for decision making and control (in the firm at large and in its segments)[3] and for determining the sum that may be taxed and distributed as dividends.

2.2 Effect of Inflation on Conventional Profit Measurement

During a period of inflation, the prices of most inputs and outputs rise. This, by itself, does not necessarily impair conventional profit measurement. Consider a very short production process for which all inputs are bought shortly before the output is sold. If the profit from this process, as computed by conventional accounting procedures, is currently withdrawn from the company, the company will be as well off at the end of the period as it was at the beginning. As long as profit is calculated by matching current (i.e., replacement) cost with current income, accounting profit is consistent with the Hicksian economic profit concept.

In real life, however, companies utilize not only inputs that are bought currently, but also inputs that were bought in the past when prices were different from present ones. There are delays of various lengths between acquisition of inputs and realization of outputs, and the time lag between acquisition and realization causes these transactions to be measured by monetary units of different purchasing power. The convention of charging historical costs of inputs against current sales distorts the magnitude of "consumable income," which conventional accounting profit purports to represent.[4]

To see this, consider the example in Section 2.1. After the financial statements for the year 19X1 were completed, a sudden change in the price level occurred on January 1, 19X2. All prices rose 10% and stayed at the new level throughout the year. (This assumption will be relaxed in Chapter 5.)

Sales were again 100 units, but now at $2.20 each, so that total sales were $220. Out-of-pocket costs also rose 10% to $143. The new machine bought on December 31, 19X2, cost $55, 10% above the price of previous years. Financial statements for the year 19X2 are presented in Exhibit 2.2.

Pretax profit in 19X2 ($27) was higher than that in 19X1 ($20), although in real (physical) terms no change in the company activity level occurred. Profit ratios increased as well. For example, profit to sales rose from 10% in 19X1 to 12.3% in 19X2, and returns on equity increased from 26.67% to 33.8%.[5]

After the shareholders happily received their increased dividends (based, as in the past, on 100% payout of after-tax profit), it was discovered that insufficient cash was available for purchasing the new machine. Additional shares to the amount of $5 had to be subscribed and paid for to permit continuation of the company on a stable basis.

The balance sheet records two machines at different prices ($50 and $55), although the machines are technically and economically identical.

Exhibit 2.2 illustrates that during a period of inflation conventional accounting procedures produce a profit figure that is not consistent with its economic counterpart; it includes a fictitious element.[6] The profit is biased upward; thus it should not serve for decisions or control purposes. Furthermore, the conventional balance sheet does not show the true current value of the company's set of assets.

2.3 Claimants to Profit

The numerical illustrations in this book assume that total after-tax profit is distributed as dividends to shareholders. In reality, however, several other parties seek to benefit from the profit.

Cyert and March (1963) suggest viewing a business organization as a "coalition" whose "members include managers, workers, stockholders, suppliers, customers, lawyers, tax collectors, regulatory agencies, etc." (p. 27). The coalition divides the "booty" that is produced by the organization among its members (p. 29). In most companies there are four major parties that lay claims to a share of the profit: (1) shareholders through dividends, (2) managers through bonus grants, (3) labor through wage claims, and (4) government through income tax. A fifth party, the creditors, also has some claims (this is shown in Section 15.4). Fulfillment of labor and management claims on profit is usually recorded as costs (increases in wages, salaries, benefits, etc.). Only part of the remuneration takes the form of open participation in profit.

During a period of inflation, the upward-biased reported profit produced by conventional financial statements may cause an unjustified withdrawal of resources from the company by the various claimants. In Exhibit 2.2 it was shown that the upward bias of conventional accounting profit reported during an inflationary period

Exhibit 2.2. Manufacturing Equity Company
Financial Statements for the Year 19X2
(10% Inflation, 100% Fixed Assets, 100% Equity)

Balance Sheet as of

Assets

12.31. 19X1 Conventional and PLA		12.31.19X2 Conventional	12.31.19X2 PLA*
$50.00	Machine 2	—	—
50.00	Machine 3	$50.00	$55.00 ^{r}
—	Machine 4	55.00	55.00
100.00	Assets, at cost	105.00	110.00
(25.00)	Accum. depr.	(25.00)	(27.50)
75.00		80.00	82.50

Profit and Loss Statement

19X1 Conventional and PLA		
$200.00	Sales, 100 units	
(130.00)	Out-of-pocket costs	
(50.00)	Depreciation	
20.00	PLA operating profit	
	Asset restatement gains:	
—		Realized
—		Nonrealized
—	Less equity maint. adjustment	
—	Net restatement gains	
20.00	Profit = tax and dividend	

Sources and Uses Statement

Sources	Conventional	PLA
Depreciation	$50.00	$55.00
Profit	27.00	22.00
New shares	5.00	—
Equity maint.	—	7.50
	82.00	84.50

*The letter *r* indicates restated figure.

December 31, 19X2

Liabilities and Equity

12.31.19X1 Conventional and PLA		12.31.19X2 Conventional	12.31.19X2 PLA
$75.00	Equity	$75.00	$75.00
—	New shares	5.00	—
—	Equity maint. reserve	—	7.50
75.00		80.00	82.50

for the Year 19X2

19X2 Conventional		19X2 PLA	
	$220.00		$220.00
$143.00		$143.00	
50.00		55.00	
	193.00		198.00
—			22.00
—		5.00	
—		2.50	
		7.50	
—		(7.50)	
	—		—
	27.00		22.00

for the Year 19X2

Uses	Conventional	PLA
Machine 4	$55.00	$55.00
Tax and dividend	27.00	22.00
Asset restatement	—	7.50
	82.00	84.50

may cause declaration of dividends beyond the real earnings of the company. Income tax may also withdraw some of the "profit," which is in fact only equity maintenance.

Managers and labor demand, and often receive, higher remuneration, based on illusory profit figures, which may in the long run endanger the company.[7] Whereas income tax is proportional to reported profit and will drop as inflationary profits decrease, the other claimants to profit sharing display varying degrees of downward rigidity. Having received higher remuneration during the period of inflation, they resist downward adjustments of their income when prices stabilize.[8] The major claimants to profit and the main characteristics of their claims are listed in Exhibit 2.3.

Under financial leverage conditions (Chapter 4), PLA total profit includes net restatement gains. These gains are profit in the Hicksian sense and are therefore distributable. But if the current rate of inflation is a short-run phenomenon, these inflationary gains cannot be considered as long-run profit in the Hicksian sense. With the lessening or disappearance of inflation (let alone the appearance of deflation) these gains will also drop off. Because of the downward rigidity of claims on income it may be prudent to "neutralize" these inflationary gains to avoid raising income expectations and, in a way, company obligations that cannot be fulfilled during later, noninflationary years.

Just as the analysis of a single department is partial and should be considered within the framework of the company at large, the annual analysis of a company is partial and should be considered within the framework of several years. In this context the "period" in the Hicksian definition of profit should be a cycle of several years. The behavioral aspects of the claimants to profit should be taken into account when long-run income policy is considered.

Exhibit 2.3. Claimants to Profit and Characteristics of the Claims

Claimants	Type of Claim	Claims Recorded as Cost	Downward Flexibility
Shareholders	Dividend	No	Partial
Managers	Bonuses	Yes	Yes
	Salaries, benefits	Yes	No
Laborers	Wages, benefits	Yes	No
Government	Income tax	No	Yes
Creditors	Interest	Yes	Partial

2.4 Decomposing Income into Operating Profit and Holding Gains

The upward bias of profit, as measured by conventional accounting procedures during inflation, stems from the fact that inputs are charged against income at historical cost. Thus the reported profit figure is composed of (1) profit that originates from operations, and (2) gains originating from the difference between the historical and current costs of inputs whose realization is significantly later than their acquisition.

The classical theory explaining the reasons for these two profit components was developed by Edwards and Bell (1961).[9] They pictured the two profit components as two dimensions of the inputs flow: (1) operations, represented by the vertical dimension by which inputs enter the company and exit from it, and (2) holding, represented by the horizontal dimension by which inputs enter the "period" and exit from it; this is depicted in Exhibit 2.4. The company begins each period with an "inherited" stock of asset inputs, which enable the production process to take place. At the end of the period, asset inputs are "bequeathed" to the next period.[10] Growth of asset inputs during the given period in Exhibit 2.4 may be due to one of two reasons: (1) some of the current inputs do not exit from the company as output, but rather exit from the period as assets (inventories or durables); or (2) the price level of assets increases, as occurs in a period of inflation.

During a period of inflation the two-dimensional motion causes two types of gains: (1) "operating profits" resulting from the combination or transformation of inputs into products whose sale value exceeds their input value, and (2) "holding gains," resulting from a price rise of the inputs in possession. The two types of income should be analyzed separately because they result from two different types of decisions and events. In addition, holding gains should not be distributed (or taxed) if the company is to be as well off at the end of the period as it was at the beginning, assuming that it is financed wholly by equity. (This assumption is relaxed later on.)

2.5 Price Level Adjusted Profit Measurement

Distortions in financial statements that are caused by changes in the purchasing power of currency should be corrected. This is done by price level adjusted (PLA) accounting procedures. Asset values should be restated, and lagged costs adjusted. The restatement or adjustment is carried out by applying a general price index to the relevant recorded historical costs.

Exhibit 2.4. Two-dimensional Flow of Inputs in a Firm*

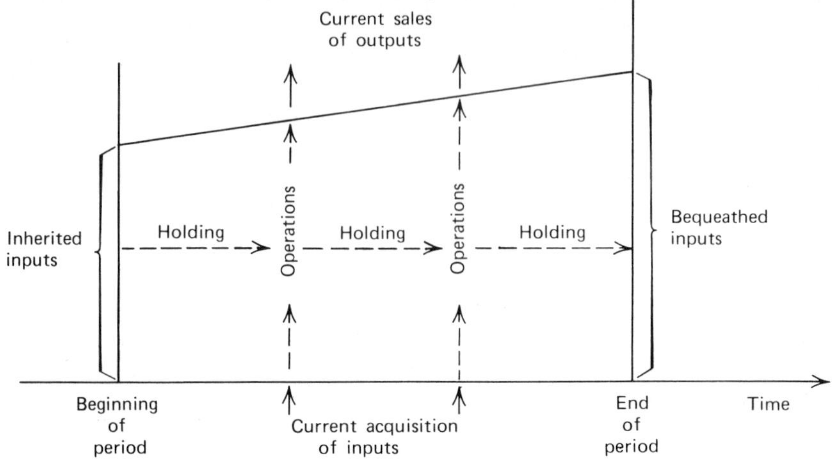

*Copyright © 1961 by the Regents of the University of California; reproduced by permission of the University of California Press.
Source: Based on Edwards and Bell (1961, p. 72).

Consider the former example for the year 19X2. The current market value for a new machine on January 1, 19X2, was $55, although one day earlier a machine of the same kind (Machine 3) had been bought for $50. The value, therefore, was restated at $55, and Machine 2, whose net value was 50% of a new machine, was restated at $27.50. The total restatement gain was $7.50. Depreciation calculated on the new asset value was $55. Relevant PLA financial statements are presented in Exhibit 2.2, along with the conventional statements.

The figures in Exhibit 2.2 result from applying price level adjustment (PLA) accounting procedures. Each side of the balance sheet has been treated separately. Assets have been restated to arrive at their PLA values. Equity has been restated as well, to maintain its value in current monetary terms. As a result of these restatements, assets value "rose" by $7.50 ("asset restatement gains") and equity by $7.50 to provide "equity maintenance adjustment." Since the two adjustments are equal, the balance—"net restatement gains"—is zero [under different assumptions this balance could be positive (Chapter 4) or negative (Sections 3.5 and 15.4)].

Under PLA accounting procedures adjusted depreciation ($55) rather than historical expense ($50) is charged to income. This causes the PLA pretax profit to be lower by $5 than the conventional profit. A graphical comparison of the two profit measures is presented in Exhibit 2.5.

The reported PLA pretax profit for 19X2 ($22) is equal in real terms to that for 19X1 ($20 + 10% PLA). As a result of price level adjustment, the profit reported for 19X2 remained 10% of sales ($22:$220) and 26.67% of equity

Exhibit 2.5. Comparison of Profit Measurement
Equity Manufacturing Company

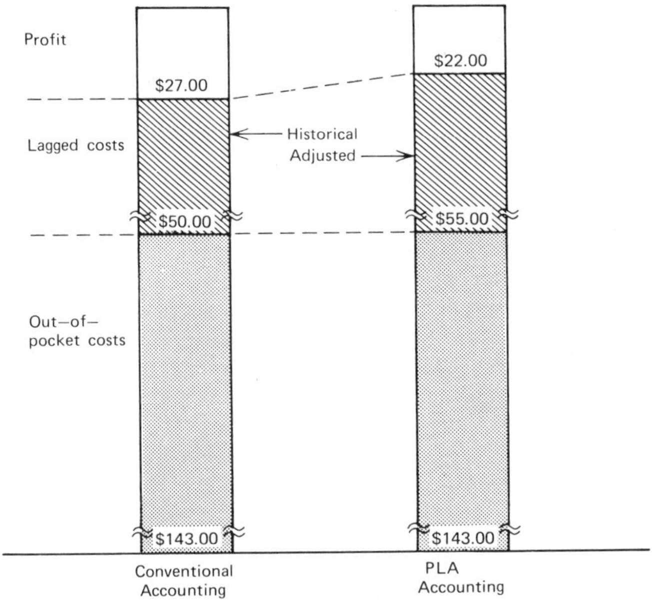

Source: Data from Exhibit 2.2.

($22:$82.50), as in 19X1. This is consistent with the fact that both production efficiency and sales remained at the previous year's levels.

Depreciation expenses exactly equal the acquisition cost of the new machine (bought at a higher price); the expense charged to production for use of the asset equals the cost of replacing the asset. The physical asset position of the company was maintained. It was unnecessary to rely on cash raised by additional shares (as in the case with conventional accounting procedures), and the real value of equity was maintained. The balance sheet provides information on the current cost of replacing the company's set of assets.

By computing profit on the basis of current cost (in the illustration, based on asset restatement and PLA depreciation), the inflationary distortion of conventional profit is eliminated. The PLA profit figure is conceptually equivalent to the conventional profit figure calculated under stable price conditions.

2.6 Measuring and Meaning of Holding Gains

Holding gains, by definition, represent an increase in asset values caused by a rise in prices. The increase in asset values can be computed by appraisal or on balance sheet data by inflating the recorded values by the appropriate price index. In other words, the difference between asset values computed according to prices at the beginning of the period and asset values computed according to prices at the end of the period represents the holding gains for the period.

Restatement in the numerical illustration for 19X2 increased the stated asset values from $75 to $82.50 (Exhibit 2.2). This increase stemmed from the 10% rise in the price level ($75 + $7.50). Holding gains of $7.50 for the year 19X2 were offset by an "equity maintenance reserve" on the equity side.

Holding gains represent the numerical difference resulting from a change in the measure used for valuing assets. In 19X1 the measure was based on dollars with a given purchasing power, and in 19X2 on dollars with another, lower purchasing power: $82.50 of asset values on December 31, 19X2 (Exhibit 2.2) is equivalent to $75 on December 31, 19X1; the measure changed, but not the real asset values.[11]

Holding gains of assets (durables and inventories) that have been bought for speculative purposes (i.e., over and above current production requirements), because management anticipates specific price rises, provide income from a special (speculative) activity which should be analyzed separately, as is done in Section 8.3.

Holding gains during a given period are computed by PLA accounting on balance sheet data; they are not included in the PLA operating profit of the period. Profit as measured by conventional accounting procedures, on the other hand, includes a portion of holding gains—the part that has been realized during the period through depreciation expenses and the charging to operations at historical costs of materials from inventories. These are termed "realized holding gains." Realized holding gains can be measured by deducting the operating profit, as measured by PLA accounting, from the conventional profit figures.

Consider again the numerical illustration for 19X2. The different profit figures result from different depreciation expenses under the two accounting systems. The difference between these figures is equal to realized holding gains, as shown below using data from Exhibit 2.2:

	Conventional Accounting		PLA Accounting		Realized Holding Gains
Sales		$220		$220	
Out-of-pocket costs	$143		$143		
Depreciation	50		55		$5
		193		198	
Profit		27		22	5

The $5 realized holding gain (which is only a part of the $7.50 total holding gain for the period) should have been directed to renewal of the machines in order to assure stable production capability. Since total conventional profit was taxed and distributed as dividends, a deficiency in cash had to be compensated for by subscription for $5 of new shares. Obviously, these holding gains are not profit in the Hicksian sense. By basing its dividend decision on conventional accounting reports, management did not preserve the capital of which it was custodian.

In summary, holding gains reported by PLA accounting are a by-product of restating the company's assets. Therefore these gains are termed here "asset restatement gains." Restatement gains are the "output" of the holding activity during inflation. The asset restatement gains of a going concern's basic set of assets (assuming 100% equity) are illusory since the physical inventory of assets has not been increased. Such a gain merely records a change in the measuring unit of asset and equity value. Profit as computed by conventional accounting procedures includes a portion of the period's restatement (holding) gains, and thus the figure is misleading.

Notes

1. The subject of income determination is widely discussed in the literature; see, for example, Alexander et al. (1950), Backer (1966), Bedford (1966), Parker and Harcourt (1969), and Sterling (1970, 1971).
2. The discussion is based on a stagger assumption, but holds also for a set of assets of "one-horse shay" character, given that annual depreciation expenses are charged against production and the cash generated is invested in "price level linked" assets.
3. To make the accounting profit measure suitable for decisions and control, two adjustments should be introduced: (1) realizable income should be included in profit, and (2) interest on equity should be charged, as suggested by Anthony (1973). The conventional profit figure includes not only the excess of sales over total costs but also implicit interest on equity capital.
4. Consumption, from the company's point of view, includes all distribution of its added value among various claimants—owners, employees, and government. From the company's viewpoint wages, dividends, income tax, bonuses, and other forms of profit sharing (in cash) are all "consumption."

5. Even had there been a decline in performance, resulting from reduced efficiency, the inflationary effect might have concealed this. The operational turn for the worse could go unnoticed.
6. This extra profit has been labeled "fool's profit" (Cotter 1940) and "paper profit" (Bullers and Niland 1949).
7. On the other hand, there is a possibility that the increased renumeration will attract high-level employees, who in turn will increase profits. Behavioral scientists, however, would not always agree with such a claim (see, e.g., Herzberg 1968).
8. For further discussion of this subject see Ray (1960, Chapter 6).
9. For a short elaboration of this subject see Parker and Harcourt (1969, pp. 6–25); for a critical discussion see Drake and Dopuch (1965). This type of analysis had been suggested in 1927 by F. Schmidt (Ray 1960, p. 1) and in 1929 by C. R. Rorem (Revsine 1973, p. 58).
10. This procedure can be depicted as follows:

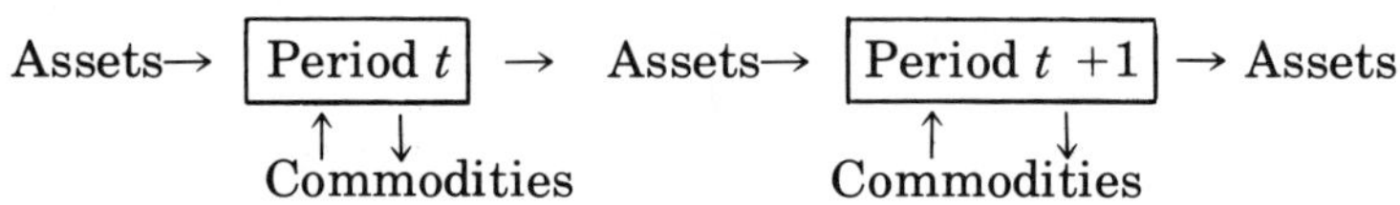

Note that each period (1) "buys" assets (durables and inventories) from the preceding period, (2) "sells" assets to the next period, and (3) buys and sells commodities (inputs, outputs, and sometimes assets) on the market (Goldschmidt 1970, pp. 63–65, 204–206).

11. The company's set of assets, which may be viewed as a pool of capital, can be compared to a pool of liquids. Holding gains are analogous to the difference resulting from a change in the measure used (e.g., instead of cubic yards, as in the past, cubic feet now are employed). The difference in the measured volume of this pool is the result of changing the measure; its physical volume did not change.

References

Alexander, S.S., M. Bronfenbrenner, S. Fabricant, and C. Warburton, *Five Monographs on Business Income,* American Institute of Certified Public Accountants, New York, 1950.

Anthony, R. N., "Accounting for the Cost of Equity," *Harvard Business Review,* November–December 1973, pp. 88–102.

Backer, M. (ed.) *Modern Accounting Theory,* Prentice-Hall, Englewood Cliffs, N.J. 1966.

Bedford, N. M., *Income Determination Theory: An Accounting Framework,* Addison-Wesley, Reading, Mass., 1966.

Bullers, J. K. and P. Niland, *Effects of Taxation–Inventory Accounting and Policies,* Riverside Press, Cambridge, Mass., 1949.

Cotter, A., *Fool's Profits,* Barron's New York, 1940.

Cyert, R. M. and J. G. March, *A Behavioral Theory of the Firm,* Prentice-Hall, Englewood Cliffs, N.J., 1963.

Drake, O. F. and N. Dopuch, "On the Case for Dichotomizing Income," *Journal of Accounting Research,* Autumn 1965, pp. 192–205.

Edwards, E. O. and P. W. Bell, *The Theory and Measurement of Business Income,* University of California Press, Berkeley and Los Angeles, 1961.

Goldschmidt, Y., *Information for Management Decisions–A System for Economic Analysis and Accounting Procedures,* Cornell University Press, Ithaca and London, 1970.

Herzberg, F., "One More Time: How Do You Motivate Employees?" *Harvard Business Review,* January–February 1968, pp. 53–62.

Hicks, J. R., *Value and Capital,* Clarendon Press, Oxford, 1950.

Parker, R. H. and G. C. Harcourt, *Readings in the Concept and Measurement of Income,* Cambridge University Press, London, 1969.

Ray, D. D., *Accounting and Business Fluctuations,* University of Florida Press, Gainesville, 1960.

Revsine, L., *Replacement Cost Accounting,* Prentice-Hall, Englewood Cliffs, N.J., 1973.

Sterling, R. R., *Theory of the Measurement of Enterprise Income,* Kansas University Press, 1970.

——— (ed.), *Asset Valuation and Income Determination,* Scholars Book Co., Lawrence, Kan., 1971.

Three

Asset Valuation and Replacement Costing

Three approaches to asset valuation—accounting, managerial, and economic—depend on three different types of data: past, present, and future, respectively. The accounting approach, which is based on historical cost, leads to price level adjusted (PLA) accounting. The managerial approach advises revaluation of assets by appraising their current replacement cost. This procedure provides the basis for replacement-cost accounting. The economic approach calculates the present value of projected cash flow; it cannot provide relevant data for accounting purposes.

Price level adjusted and replacement-cost accounting procedures are integrated in this chapter by applying both general and specific price indices in one set of financial statements. This procedure is used again in Chapter 8; for the sake of simplicity, the other illustrations in this book deal with one price index only.

3.1 Asset Valuation in Economics and Accounting

According to economic theory, the value of an asset is calculated by discounting the estimated future net cash flow (receipts less payments) that will be generated by the asset.[1] This approach to asset valuation has two serious limitations. First, it requires estimating four variables: the useful life of the asset, the annual cash flows in constant dollars, the discount factor (the cost of capital), and the inflation rate. The values that these variables will assume in the future are uncertain and must be estimated by subjective judgment. Second, the cash flows are often generated by a group of assets, and there is no objective way to estimate the specific portion generated by each asset in a group. Although it is possible to estimate the value of the group, individual asset values are not always objectively determinable.

The discounted cash flow provides the present (economic) value of an asset (or a group of assets). This figure provides a basis for decisions regarding the profitability of (1) investing in a new asset (when the economic value exceeds the acquisition cost), or (2) selling an existing asset (when its economic value is lower than its selling price).[2]

The value of an asset as determined by conventional accounting procedures is based on its actual acquisition cost in the past. This value, less accumulated depreciation charges (the portion of the original cost that has been charged to the users of the asset's services in the past), represents the net book value of the asset. The annual depreciation expense, which is one of the variables that determines this value, is, in turn, computed by means of three variables that must be estimated under conditions of uncertainty: the estimated life span of the asset, its salvage value, and the depreciation method. Thus, although the gross value of the asset is based on an historically objective fact, its computed net value is relatively arbitrary.

The values determined by the accounting approach do not necessarily indicate the service potentials of the assets. This approach may lead to absurdities: an asset that provides useful services may be valued at zero because it is fully depreciated (it lives on beyond its expected time). The opposite may occur when a "young" asset does not provide the services anticipated. Furthermore, it is conceivable that the original price of an asset does not indicate its true value at the time of purchase because of a special discount, inefficiency or mistakes in construction, or other factors.

In summary, whereas the economic approach to asset valuation is based on future net receipts, the accounting approach is based on past cost, as depicted schematically in Exhibit 3.1. The economic approach provides a value figure that indicates the company's wealth, whereas the accounting approach provides a cost figure. The figures arrived at by the economic approach cannot serve for asset valuation in an accounting framework for three reasons: (1) the calculations are

Exhibit 3.1. Asset Valuation by Economic and Accounting Approaches at the End of Year 1 (Assets Life: Two Years; Zero Scrap Value)

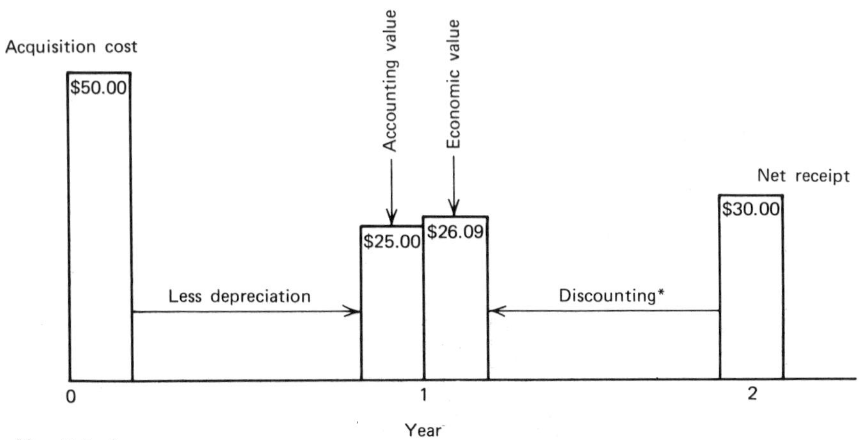

*See Note 1.

based on subjective judgment, (2) usually this method does not provide data on individual assets, and (3) it contradicts the main objective of the accounting system—to provide cost and income data for judging performance and determining wealth (value). Economic value is computed from projections of accounting data; using this value as an "input" for the accounting system (which provides data for determining value) represents circular reasoning.

3.2 A Managerial Approach to Asset Valuation

The value of an asset from the managerial point of view is its replacement cost, which indicates the opportunity cost of the asset.[3] To remain a going concern, a firm must replenish the goods sold, and therefore renew the inputs consumed in production. It follows that the costs of inputs to the production process (materials used, depreciation, interest, etc.) must be based on their replacement costs during the period in which they were employed.

The valuation of assets by this approach necessitates (1) inspection of each asset to determine its service potential (i.e., checking whether the asset is active and what services it can provide), (2) collecting relevant market prices, and (3) estimating the operating costs (repairs, etc.) of the asset in comparison to the figures for similar assets on the market. This valuation procedure, also called "appraisal," is discussed further in Section 7.2.

Applying this approach is difficult in practice; there may not be a market price for a given asset because of technological developments in general or special modifications performed on the existing asset. Even when no technological developments and/or changes have occurred, an asset similar in type and condition to the existing one is often difficult to locate on the market. Estimating comparative operating costs presents another hurdle to be overcome.

Replacement cost provides important information for managerial purposes, in regard to both decisions and control. It is of special importance within a managerial cost accounting system (see Chapters 7 and 8). The replacement cost of an asset (or a group of assets) in conjunction with its economic value provides a basis for decisions on retention versus replacement by a new asset.[4] Replacement cost also provides a basis for calculating the cost of an asset's services to the firm; if the current cost is prohibitive (i.e., the production process suffers a loss), the question of a change in the production process, including stoppage, becomes acute. Replacement costs should serve as a basis for determining standard costs, which are used in performance evaluation.

Compared with the economic approach, the managerial method requires fewer subjective estimates and is simpler to apply, since the necessary estimates concern present market prices rather than future cash flow. Although market prices for many assets can be collected, the asset values arrived at are more subjective than those obtained by the accounting approach. Nevertheless, the managerial approach, like the accounting approach, is based on cost, whereas the economic approach is based on value.

The managerial approach can be viewed as intermediate between the economic and the accounting approaches with regard to (1) the time consideration (present prices vs. future values and past costs, respectively); (2) the level of subjective judgment and precision of the estimates; and (3) the quantity of data required for valuation. The amount of work and the cost expended in the valuation process may be greater than for the other methods.

3.3 A Comparative Illustration of the Three Approaches

Consider a machine that costs \$50. Its expected economic life is 2 years with zero scrap value. The machine can produce 50 units per year of a commodity having a net sales value of $2 each—that is, a total of $100. The productive ability of the machine is equal during the first and the second years. Out-of-pocket costs, in constant money, are $60 during the first year and $70 during the second year. The rise in these costs is due to higher repair costs. To simplify, it is assumed that all transactions take place at the end of the respective year, and that uncertainty does not exist. The cost of capital is 15% per annum. Income tax is ignored, again for simplicity.

The three approaches to asset valuation are applied to these data in Exhibit 3.2. According to the accounting approach, the value of the machine is $50 and $25 at the beginning of the respective years, using straight-line depreciation.

According to the managerial approach, the value of the asset is determined by its productive potential, taking into account its operating costs; these include recovery of the original investment and current expenditure to maintain the productive potential. Because of the higher repair costs in the second year, the depreciation charge in this year should be lower than that in the first year by $10; in this way, total asset service costs are equal over the 2 years, just as is the productive potential. Asset service cost per potential unit of production is also equal in both years; similarly, asset service costs of a new machine with equal productive potential would be the same as asset service costs of this machine. Thus depreciation charges will be $30 and $20 in the respective years rather than $25 and $25, as calculated by the accounting approach.[5] Since asset valuation by the managerial approach is based on current asset acquisition cost, the machine's net value at the begin-

Exhibit 3.2. Machine Valuation and Profit Calculation, Years 1 and 2 (Higher Repair Costs in Year 2, 15% Cost of Capital, No Tax)

Machine Value

	Year 0	Year 1	Year 2
Accounting approach	$50.00	$25.00	$0
Managerial approach	50.00	20.00	0
Economic approach	57.47*	26.09*	0

Profit and Loss Statements

	Accounting Approach		Managerial Approach	
	Year 1	Year 2	Year 1	Year 2
Sales	$100.00	$100.00	$100.00	$100.00
Out-of-pocket costs	(60.00)	(70.00)	(60.00)	(70.00)
Depreciation	(25.00)	(25.00)	(30.00)	(20.00)
Profit	15.00	5.00	10.00	10.00

*See Note 1.

ning of the second year is $20 ($50 – $30).

The economic values ($57.47 and $26.09) of the machine are determined by discounting the expected net receipts, as forecast in the profit and loss projections, using the 15% cost of capital as the discount factor. Depreciation and, accordingly, profit and loss statements are not calculated from the values arrived at by the economic approach because this approach provides value figures, rather than cost figures, in contrast with both the accounting and the managerial approaches. (See the end of Section 3.1.)

Suppose that the price of machines identical with the one under consideration increased at the start of Year 2 by 7%. This does not affect the accounting valuation of the existing machine (neither the historical cost nor the general price level has changed). Its economic value is also unaffected (the future net receipt is not changed). However, this change in price affects the managerial valuation, which is based on current replacement cost. The existing machine's replacement cost increased by 7% (from $20 to $21.40),[6] and, accordingly, depreciation charges rise, as shown in Exhibit 3.3. As a result of this revaluation, profit in Year 2 decreased from $10 to $8.60.

Suppose now that the product sales price increased by 10% in Year 2 (rather than the machine cost by 7%). As a result, income increased from $100 to $110. This change affects neither the accounting nor the managerial valuation. However, it does increase the asset's economic value from $26.09 to $34.78 (Exhibit 3.3) since higher income is imputed to it ($40 is discounted rather than $30).

In summary, the three approaches to asset valuation provide different results since different types of data are taken into account. Although all the approaches provide important information, only the results of the accounting and the managerial approaches can be incorporated into the accounting system. The characteristics of the three approaches are summarized in Exhibit 3.4.

3.4 Replacement-Cost Accounting

For a company to survive in the long run, its output value (current sales) must at least equal the renewal value (current costs) of the inputs used in generating this output.[7] Therefore only the income that is in excess of replacement requirements is real profit.[8] The replacement cost of inputs used in producing a given product includes current out-of-pocket costs, replacement costs of inventories, and service costs, which are computed from the replacement values of fixed assets.

According to this reasoning, in a period of inflation the historical costs of asset inputs should be continuously adjusted to replacement

Exhibit 3.3. Machine Revaluation, Year 2
(Higher Repair Costs in Year 2, 15% Cost of Capital,
No Tax, Increase in Either Machine or Sale Index)

	Original Data (Exhibit 3.2)	Increase in Price: Machine, 7%	Increase in Price: Sales, 10%
	Machine Value		
Accounting approach	$25.00	$25.00	$25.00
Managerial approach	20.00	21.40*	20.00
Economic approach	26.09	26.09	34.78
	Profit and Loss Statements		
Accounting Approach			
Sales	$100.00	$100.00	$110.00
Out-of-pocket costs	(70.00)	(70.00)	(70.00)
Depreciation	(25.00)	(25.00)	(25.00)
Profit	5.00	5.00	15.00
Managerial Approach			
Sales	$100.00	$100.00	$110.00
Out-of-pocket costs	(70.00)	(70.00)	(70.00)
Depreciation	(20.00)	(21.40)	(20.00)
Profit	10.00	8.60	20.00

*Approximated figure. For the correct one, see Note 6.

values. If this is done, current sales are matched with real current costs, and this bias of conventional profit calculation is eliminated. In other words, the managerial approach to asset valuation (Section 3.2) should be applied.

Revaluation of each asset input to its replacement value, that is, to reflect current costs, will provide information on (1) the amount the company would have to pay (at present) to replace the set of assets it holds, and (2) costs for correct profit computation—depreciation expenses, and inventory costs and changes.[9] Both revaluation purposes will be best served if asset replacement costs are appraised.

Appraising the actual replacement cost of a company's existing asset is cumbersome and difficult; indeed, often it is not feasible in practice (see Sections 3.2 and 7.2). A close estimate of replacement cost, which is feasible, can be obtained by using specific price indices

Exhibit 3.4. Comparison of Three Approaches to Asset Valuation

	Approach		
Criterion	Accounting	Managerial	Economic
Time considered	Past	Present	Future
Based on:	Acquisition cost	Replacement cost	Future income
Provides:	Cost data	Cost data	Value data
Source of data	Cost and date of acquisition	Market and inspection	Accounting system and expectations
Items determined subjectively	Asset life span Depreciation	Market price Service potential	Asset life span Cash flow Discounting factor
Amount of valuation work	Low	High	Medium
Main use	Dividend decisions and company performance evaluation	Decisions and departmental performance evaluation	Decisions on resource allocation
Suitability for accounting purposes	For external reports	For internal reports	Not feasible

for asset revaluation. Revaluation by a general price level index would provide a poorer estimate, because of the divergence of individual price changes from the general one.

Replacement cost represents the cost, in current dollars, of replacing the productive capacity of an existing asset. It does not represent its sale value. In some cases replacement and sale values are very close, as for liquid assets having negligible transfer costs (dismantling, erection, etc.).[10]

Replacement is justified only if the economic value (present value of all future cash flows) of an asset exceeds its replacement cost. Thus, to maintain long-run viability of the firm, replacement cost should be less than economic value.[11] However, firms do hold and use assets whose replacement is unwarranted (economic value, although positive, is lower than replacement cost). This situation can arise if, for example, asset prices have risen without a corresponding rise in the prices of outputs produced by such assets. As a result the given production process will earn less than normal profit (which is based on replacement cost); in the long run this will lead to curtailment or abandonment of the process. Recording the replacement costs of assets will reflect this reduction of profitability.[12] For example, the rise in the machine's market price in Exhibit 3.3 caused a decrease (from \$10 to \$8.60) in the "managerial" profit, which is based on replacement cost.

3.5 Integrating Price Level Changes and Specific Price Changes

During a period of inflation, there are two feasible methods of adjusting asset values: (1) restating the historical costs of the assets, and (2) revaluing their replacement costs.[13] The PLA accounting procedure is based on restating historical costs (in terms of current dollars) by means of a general price index. This procedure is recommended by some financial accounting organizations;[14] it is reconcilable with the objectivity principle of financial accounting and therefore is suitable for preparing financial statements for external purposes.[15] Replacement-cost accounting procedures, on the other hand, are based on estimating the current cost of duplicating assets with equal productive capacity and operating costs; the estimate is often made by means of specific price indices. This procedure is recommended by some authors[16] and recently by the Inflation Accounting Committee in the United Kingdom (Sandilands 1975). It provides important managerial information, but is more difficult to reconcile with the objectivity principle of financial accounting. Some authors recommend preparing two corresponding versions of financial statements.[17]

Changes in the relative values of assets constitute a problem of changes in terms of trade—a phenomenon that occurs in the absence, as well as the presence, of inflation (Chapter 8). Therefore the use of specific price indices is not necessarily a problem related to PLA profit measurement during a period of inflation. Nevertheless, the change in the general price level during inflation results from price changes in most products, each at a different rate. Hence the problem of which index to use in asset revaluation during a period of inflation still holds.

In Chapter 2 a general price level index was used for restating both assets and equity. The use of this index makes sense from the shareholders' point of view, since they are interested in preserving the purchasing power of their capital; ultimately their interest lies in purchasing power as measured by a general price level index.[18] Another advantage of such an index for asset restatement (rather than specific indices) is that it may be considered "objective" (in accounting terminology), since one unique index is used for all purposes by everyone. Furthermore, applying only one index is simpler than applying several indices, each for a given group of assets.

A possible contradiction might arise from the application of a general index for asset revaluation. Two equivalent assets, one acquired in the past and one acquired recently, might be tagged with different values.

Consider the following numerical illustration. Suppose that the price index level of machines increased in 19X2 by 7% compared to the 10% rise in the general price level. Thus the new machine (No. 4 in Exhibit 2.2) costs $53.50, while the old machine (No. 3) is restated at $55 ($50 inflated by 10%).

This contradiction results from two different changes: (1) the change in specific prices, indicating a change in the supply and demand forces affecting assets (and other commodities), and (2) the change in the general price level, indicating a change in the supply of money with respect to all commodities other than money. Both changes should be evaluated and incorporated in the PLA accounting system.

In fact, there are two separate restatement objectives, and the means for accomplishing these objectives are different. Assets are restated in order to provide a close estimate of their replacement value (and service costs), whereas equity is restated in order to present its value consistently with current purchasing power. Therefore assets should be restated by specific price indices (for arriving at estimates of their current replacement costs), whereas equity should be restated by a general price level index (for adjusting the shareholders' nominal value of capital to the current price level).[19] Both methods of restatement should be applied together, as illustrated in the following example, and reconciled in the profit and loss statement.[20]

Consider the Manufacturing Equity Company (as illustrated in Exhibit 2.2). In 19X2 the general price level increased by 10%, while the machine price level rose by only 7%. This means that a new machine costs $53.50

rather than $55, and the adjusted depreciation expenses are also $53.50 rather than $55; this is illustrated in Exhibit 3.5. Restatement of assets by their specific index records $5.25 of restatement gains (7% of $75). Restatement of equity by the general index requires a maintenance adjustment of $7.50 (10% of $75). Because the company's assets increased in value less than the general price level ($5.25 and $7.50, respectively), there was a net restatement loss of $2.25. In other words, the company's real profit in 19X2 consists of $23.50 PLA operating profit and a net restatement loss of $2.25.[21] Total PLA profit, in this case, is only $21.25

The equity maintenance reserve ($7.50) covered asset restatement gains ($5.25), with the balance ($2.25) allocated to a "new investment." In this way all of the original equity capital (in real terms) remains invested in assets.

The fact that the specific index differs from the general one affects profit unequally in two opposite directions. The effect of a specific index that is lower than the general one can be seen by comparing the figures in Exhibit 3.5 with those in Exhibit 2.2. The PLA operating profit is higher (because of lower depreciation expense), and the restatement gains are lower. A graphical illustration of this analysis is presented in Exhibit 3.6.

The application of specific indices for asset revaluation is of special importance for cost accounting purposes at the departmental level because each department (or product) may use different types of assets. When the specific index diverges considerably from the general one, revaluation of a given asset (which is used by the department) by a general index will provide significantly distorted information. If the adjustments are made only on aggregate company figures, it may be practical to apply the same general index to asset restatement as is employed for equity restatement. On a company-wide level this is more convenient; furthermore, the bias will certainly be less than at the department level and may in fact be insignificant.

In summary, price level adjustment has one purpose when applied to assets, and another when applied to equity. It follows that PLA and replacement-cost procedures should be incorporated into one system. The characteristics of the PLA and replacement-cost accounting procedures are summarized in Exhibit 3.7. Explicit application of replacement-cost accounting (asset restatement by means of specific price indices) in this book is restricted to Chapter 8. In all other illustrations, the presentation has been simplified, and only one (general) index has been applied to all restatements.

Exhibit 3.5. Manufacturing Equity Company
PLA Financial Statements for the Year 19X2
(10% Inflation, 100% Fixed Assets, 100% Equity)
Integration of Specific (7%) and General (10%) Price Indices

Balance Sheet as of December 31, 19X2

Assets			Liabilities and Equity		
12.31.19X1		12.31.19X2*	12.31.19X1		12.31.19X2
$50.00	Machine 2	—	$75.00	Equity	$75.00
50.00	Machine 3	$53.50r	—	Equity maint. reserve	7.50
—	Machine 4	53.50			
100.00	Assets, at cost	107.00			
(25.00)	Accum. depr.	(26.75)			
—	Investment	2.25			
75.00		82.50	75.00		82.50

Profit and Loss Statement for the Year 19X2

19X1			
200.00	Sales, 100 units		$220.00
(130.00)	Out-of-pocket costs	$143.00	
(50.00)	Depreciation	53.50	
			196.50
20.00	PLA operating profit		23.50
—	Asset restatement gains	5.25	
—	Less equity maint. adjustment	(7.50)	
—	Net restatement loss		(2.25)
20.00	Profit = tax and dividend		21.25

Sources and Uses Statement for the Year 19X2

Sources		Uses	
Depreciation	$53.50	Machine 4	$53.50
Profit	21.25	Tax and dividend	21.25
Equity maint.	7.50	Asset restatement	5.25
		New investment	2.25
	82.25		82.25

*The letter *r* indicates restated figure.

Exhibit 3.6. Comparison of Profit Measures
Manufacturing Equity Company

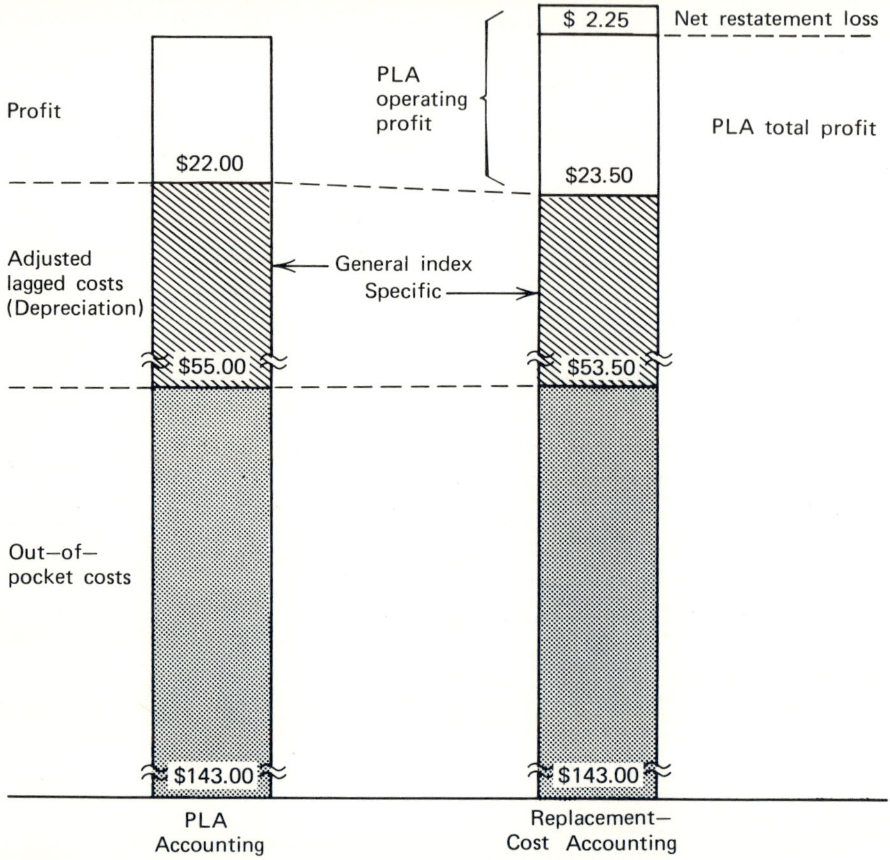

Source: Data from Exhibits 2.2 and 3.5.

Exhibit 3.7. Comparison of PLA and Replacement-Cost Accounting

Criterion	PLA Accounting	Replacement-Cost Accounting
Asset valuation approach	Accounting	Managerial
Base for resultant value	Historical cost	Current cost
Treatment of values	Restated	Revalued
Procedure of valuation	Inflating by a general index	Appraisal, or inflating by specific indices
Valuation provides data in terms of:	Current money	Current prices

Notes

1. Stated formally, the present (economic) value of an asset is

$$\text{P.V.} = \sum_{t=1}^{T} \frac{R_t}{(1+r)}$$

where P.V. is the present value,
R_t is the net receipts (income less costs) in year t,
r is the discounting factor (cost of capital), and
t is a given year, starting at 1 and ending at T.

Suppose that $R_1 = 40$, $R_2 = 30$, $r = 0.15$, and $T = 2$.

Then

$$\text{P.V at } t = 0 \quad \frac{40}{1 + 0.15} + \frac{30}{(1 + 0.15)^2} = 57.47$$

$$\text{P.V at } t = 1 \quad \frac{30}{1 + 0.15} = 26.09$$

2. This subject is discussed extensively in the engineering economy literature; see, for example, Grant and Ireson (1960), Morris (1960), and Reisman (1971).
3. There is another type of asset opportunity cost—its sale value. Using the sale value as a basis for valuation, Chambers (1966, Chapter 10), implies liquidation, whereas the use of replacement cost for this purpose implies continuity.

   From the legal aspect, "the value of a property to its owner is identical in amount with adverse value of the entire loss, direct and indirect, that the owner might expect to suffer if he were to be deprived of the property" (Bonbright 1937, Vol. I, p. 71).
4. See, for example, Reisman (1971, Chapter 6).
5. This valuation procedure simulates the implicit pricing of used assets on a second-hand market. The only difference is that the cost of capital is also taken into consideration in real-life valuation of used assets.
6. This is an approximation but not a correct computation. The machine's replacement cost increased to \$21.75 (rather than to \$21.40). The new asset now costs \$53.50 (\$50 plus 7%). To arrive at equal service costs in both years, depreciation in Year 1 will be

$31.75, and in Year 2 $21.75 (the difference of $10 is due to additional repairs in Year 2). As a result of the correct revaluations, profit in Year 2 would be $8.25 instead of $8.60.

7. As early as 1770 Turgot stated that "before there is any net produce there must be deducted that wherewith to replace annually the wear and tear of the property employed in their undertaking" (quoted from Ray 1960, p. 58).
8. Economists would say that in the long run profit disappears. The normal return on capital investment and risk, which business men call profit, is in this view payment for capital, risk, and entrepreneurship. Whereas accountants view profit as a residual, economists view it as a cost.
9. There are other reasons for asset revaluation, such as insurance, taxation, and purchase or sale decisions.
10. Comparing the sale value to the replacement cost provides an index of asset liquidity (Goldschmidt and Smidt 1969).
11. These arguments are based on Revsine (1973, pp. 68–69).
12. Vos (1970, p. 133) claims that an asset's economic value is relevant if it is lower than the replacement value; this is in correspondence with the principle "cost or market, whichever is lower."
13. For a review of this subject see, for example, American Institute of Certified Public Accountants (1963) and Gynther (1966, Chapter 8).
14. For example, the Accounting Principles Board (1969), the Financial Accounting Standards Board (1974), and the Institute of Chartered Accountants in England and Wales (1974).
15. Price level adjusted financial statements should be published officially by a company only if this procedure is practiced by the industry as a whole (see Section 16.6).
16. For example, Edwards and Bell (1961), Mathews (1965), Gynther (1966), and Revsine (1973). The first author recommending this procedure was, probably, Limperg (Burgett 1972).
17. For example, American Accounting Association (1966), Backer (1969), and Ross (1969). It is interesting to note that one-half century ago authors sided with either approach (e.g., Middleditch 1918 and Bauer 1919).

    The Talmud (third till sixth century) rules that, in the case of a change in the purchasing power of money, the debt is restated accordingly (*Bava Kamma,* 97, 98). The Talmud also recognizes the problem of variations in the exchange rates between different groups of coinage, but gives no definite ruling (*Bava Metzi'a,* 60). E. Blum and A. Shmueli drew our attention to these sources.

18. Some supporters of replacement-cost accounting regard equity as the capital of the company rather than of the shareholders (Sandilands 1975, p. 140). As such, equity should be maintained at the level that enables replacement of the company's assets, but does not necessarily maintain its purchasing power.
19. For a similar procedure see Gray (1973).
20. It is interesting to note that Philips Electrical Industries of Holland apply a similar procedure in practice. For a description of Philips PLA accounting procedures see American Institute of Certified Public Accountants (1963), Gynther (1966), Rosen (1972), and Burgett (1972). The last-named author includes an extensive bibliography.
21. Kirkman (1974, p. 168), suggests that the term "holding gain (loss)" could be applied to this item.

References

Accounting Principles Board, *Financial Statements Restated for General Price Level Changes,* Statement No. 3, American Institute of Certified Public Accountants, New York, 1969.

American Accounting Association, *A Statement of Basic Accounting Theory,* Evanston, Ill., 1966.

American Institute of Certified Public Accountants, *Reporting the Financial Effects of Price Level Changes,* Accounting Research Study No. 6 by the Staff of the Accounting Research Division, New York, 1963.

Backer, M., *Financial Reporting for Security Investment and Credit Decisions,* National Association of Accountants, 1969.

Bauer, J. "Renewal Costs and Business Profits in Relation to Rising Prices," *Journal of Accountancy,* December 1919, pp. 413–419.

Bonbright, J. C., *The Valuation of Property,* McGraw-Hill, New York, 1937.

Burgett, R., "Reservations about 'Replacement Value' Accounting in the Netherlands," *Abacus,* December 1972, pp. 111–126.

Chambers, R. J. *Accounting, Evaluation and Economic Behavior,* Prentice-Hall, Englewood Cliffs, N.J., 1966.

Edwards, E. O. and P. W. Bell, *The Theory and Measurement of Business Income,* University of California Press, Berkeley and Los Angeles, 1961.

Financial Accounting Standards Board, *Financial Reporting in Units of General Purchasing Power,* Exposure Draft, Stamford, Conn., December 1974.

Goldschmidt, Y. and S. Smidt, "Valuing the Firm's Durable Assets for Managerial Information," *Accounting Review,* April 1969, pp. 317–329.

Grant, E. L. and W. G. Ireson, *Principles of Engineering Economy* (4th ed.), Ronald Press, New York, 1960.

Gray, S. J., "ED-8: Its Defects and an Alternative," *Accountancy,* September 1973, pp. 40–41.

Gynther, R. S., *Accounting for Price Level Changes—Theory and Procedures,* Pergamon Press, Oxford, 1966.

Institute of Chartered Accountants in England and Wales, *Accounting for Changes in the Purchasing Power of Money,* Provisional Statement of Standard Accounting Practice No. 7, May 1974.

Kirkman, P. R. A., *Accounting under Inflationary Conditions,* Allen & Unwin, London, 1974.

Mathews, R. L., "Price Level Changes and Useless Information," *Journal of Accounting Research,* Spring 1965, pp. 133–155.

Middleditch, L., Jr., "Should Accounts Reflect the Changing Value of the Dollar?" *Journal of Accountancy,* February 1918, pp. 114–120.

Morris, W. T., *Engineering Economy,* Irwin, Homewood, Ill., 1960.

Ray, D. D., *Accounting and Business Fluctuations,* University of Florida Press, Gainesville, 1960.

Reisman, A., *Managerial and Engineering Economics,* Allyn & Bacon, Boston, 1971.

Revsine, L., *Replacement Cost Accounting,* Prentice-Hall, Englewood Cliffs, N.J., 1973.

Rosen, L. S., *Current Value Accounting and Price Level Restatements,* Canadian Institute of Chartered Accountants, Toronto, Canada, 1972.

Ross, H., *Financial Statements: A Crusade for Current Values,* Pitman, New York, 1969.

Sandilands, F. E. P., *Inflation Accounting,* Report of the Inflation Accounting Committee, Her Majesty's Stationery Office, London, 1975.

Vos, J., "Replacement Value Accounting," *Abacus,* December 1970, pp. 132–143.

Four

Effects of the Financial Mix

Companies employ financial leverage to increase the rate of return on equity capital. During a period of inflation, debt capital can be a source of additional returns: because of institutional restrictions on the rate of interest, the lenders do not receive full compensation for the loss in purchasing power of the contractual repayments; the difference is retained by the company. This difference is called "inflationary leverage returns."

The lender recoups some of the loss in purchasing power of debt repayment through increased interest charges. These are recorded by the company as a cost. However, the corresponding loss regarding equity capital is not recorded in conventional accounting, so that reported profit is upward biased. Therefore, the larger the financial leverage, the less biased is the conventional profit figure. The effect on profit of financial assets that are not "price level linked" is symmetrically opposite to that of "nonlinked" debt.

4.1 Maintaining Equity Investment Value

In Chapters 2 and 3 accounting procedures that restate the real value of a company's assets were outlined. Price level adjusted valuation of assets on one side of the balance sheet was accompanied by an equity maintenance reserve on the other side. Depreciation was calculated on the restated assets, and thus the economic (Hicksian) profit figure was calculated. In this chapter the subject is viewed from the investors' viewpoint. In other words, whereas the discussion above analyzed the position of the users of capital, the discussion below analyzes the position of the suppliers of capital.

We follow Anthony (1973) in claiming that the company should be

> viewed as an entity that is entirely separate from its proprietors. This entity obtains capital from two principal sources; it obtains its debt capital from creditors and equity capital from the investors who purchase its stock. Management decides on the best mix of debt capital and equity capital. Under the entity concept, then, both creditors and equity investors are viewed as outsiders (p. 89).

During a period of inflation both types of capital suppliers make efforts to preserve the real value of their investments in the given entity—the corporation.

To simplify the discussion, two extreme (and artificial) cases are first analyzed: (1) assuming that there is only equity capital, and (2) assuming that there is only debt capital (Section 4.2). A more realistic case, in which a company is financed by a mix of equity and debt capital, is discussed in Section 4.4.

If the investors' equity is to be preserved in terms of real purchasing power, an increment should be added to the equity. Under PLA accounting procedures this increment is recorded as an equity maintenance reserve and added to the opening equity figure.[1] Although conventional accounting procedures do not present the facts in this manner, many institutions have found a practical remedy; some of the profit is appropriated through issuance of bonus shares, thereby reducing the profit available for cash dividends.

Suppose that the equity investors conditioned their share subscription by a clause requiring management to record equity in terms of real purchasing power. Then the accountant would periodically have to restate the equity and record it in new terms; recorded profit would be consistent with PLA accounting procedures.

Consider the conventional balance sheet of the numerical illustration used earlier (Exhibit 2.2). Restatement of \$75 equity by a 10% increase in price level (to maintain real value) results in \$82.50. To maintain balance between both sides of the balance sheet, the corresponding total asset value will also be \$82.50 and depreciation expenses will change from \$50 to \$55. Accordingly, pretax profit will be \$22 rather than \$27. These results are exactly as those in PLA accounting in the case of 100% equity (Exhibit 2.2).

In summary, restating equity and accordingly restating asset value reflects the preservation of equity value in real terms and is consistent with the measurement of PLA profit (in the case of 100% equity). Although this method can be used for calculating the profit of the company as a whole, it does not provide necessary data for computing the PLA profits of the various segments within the company. This is so because the PLA depreciation of each asset should be charged to the user of the asset, as will be shown later on.

4.2 Maintaining Lenders' Investment Value

Assume another artificial case in which a company is financed completely by debt capital. The same numerical illustration is used; however, instead of $75 equity capital the company is financed by loans only, granted and repaid in parallel with acquisition and depreciation of the assets of the company. The bank grants a loan for each machine (using that machine as collateral), on terms calling for repayment of the principal 50% after 1 year and 50% at the end of the second year. Interest of 26.67% per annum is paid in yearly installments on the outstanding balance.[2] Financial statements for the year 19X1 are presented in Exhibit 4.1. Since it is assumed that in 19X1 there was no inflation, conventional accounting and PLA accounting provide equivalent data. These statements are presented for comparison with both Exhibit 2.1 and Exhibit 4.2.

The bank, anticipating that previous stable price conditions might not continue, inserted a new "linkage" clause into the loan agreements (both Loan 2 and Loan 3). This clause, based on current common practice in Brazil, Israel, and other countries and likely to be adopted more generally, "links" both principal and interest to changes in a generally accepted price level index.[3] On December 31, 19X1 the index stood at 100.

Alternatively, the bank could have demanded a higher nominal rate of interest. From the standpoint of indemnification, it is irrelevant whether the loss of purchasing power of the outstanding debt is compensated for through a higher nominal interest rate or through some form of adjustment of payments on the principal. The formal linkage clause achieves the compensatory effect with less uncertainty. It assures, formally, complete correlation between loan repayments (principal and interest) and price level changes. A higher nominal interest rate, based on inflation expectations, will probably not give exact price level compensation.[4] In Section 4.4 the effects of this will be demonstrated.

On January 1, 19X2, prices in fact rose 10%, thereby raising the price index by 10%. This situation remained in force until December 31, 19X2. Corresponding conventional financial statements are presented in Exhibit 4.2.

As can be seen, without restatement and without the increased depreciation costs that would result therefrom, profit has remained stable at zero (as in 19X1, before inflation). There is no need for restatement of assets since economically they do not belong to the company. Nor is there need for

Exhibit 4.1. Manufacturing Debt Company
Financial Statements for the Year 19X1
(No Inflation, 100% Fixed Assets, 100% Debt at 26.67%)
Conventional and PLA Accounting

Balance Sheet as of December 31, 19X1

Assets			Liabilities and Equity		
12.31.19X0		12.31.19X1	12.31.19X0		12.31.19X1
$50.00	Machine 1	—	$25.00	Loan 1	—
50.00	Machine 2	$50.00	50.00	Loan 2	$25.00
—	Machine 3	50.00	—	Loan 3	50.00
100.00	Assets, at cost	100.00			
(25.00)	Accum. depr.	(25.00)			
75.00		75.00	75.00		75.00

Profit and Loss Statement for the Year 19X1

Sales, 100 units		$200.00
Out-of-pocket costs	$130.00	
Interest	20.00	
Depreciation	50.00	
		200.00
Profit = tax and dividend		—

Sources and Uses Statement for the Year 19X1

Sources		Uses	
Depreciation	$50.00	Machine 3	$50.00
Loan 3	50.00	Loan repayment	50.00
	100.00		100.00

restatement of equity that does not exist. Therefore the conventional balance sheets of both years (Exhibits 4.1 and 4.2) are equivalent to those prepared by conventional accounting for the case of 100% equity (Exhibits 2.1 and 2.2). On the other hand, interest cost as recorded in the profit and loss statement (Exhibit 4.2) equals operating profit as computed by PLA accounting (Exhibit 2.2). In both cases the lender and the investor preserve the value of their capital investments, through linkage differences in one case and through a maintenance reserve in the other.

Increased financing costs have absorbed the nominal difference resulting from price level changes. If debt capital is linked to a price level index, conventional accounting procedures provide correct profit and loss statement even in a period of inflation (assuming 100% debt financing).

To make the case of zero equity (Exhibit 4.2) comparable to that of 100% equity under PLA accounting (Exhibit 2.2), price level adjustments are carried out as presented in Exhibit 4.2.

Asset restatement gains were $7.50; of this $5 was realized through increased depreciation ($55 instead of the original $50). Similarly, the loans outstanding were adjusted by $7.50, and $5 was actually paid out with the installments due. As can be seen, the inflationary gain in assets was offset by the inflationary increase in financial costs.[5]

Profit has remained stable at zero (as in 19X1), comparable to stability of profit under conventional accounting. Income before interest and taxes (IBIT) has also remained stable at 10% of sales ($20 in 19X1, and $22 in 19X2). Similarly, interest on lenders' invested capital has remained stable (26.67% in both years).

In summary, in an artificial case in which a company is financed only by debt and all loans are price level linked, conventional accounting procedures provide profit and loss statements consistent with PLA statements (the profit figures under both procedures in Exhibit 4.2 are identical).

4.3 Financial Leverage Returns

It is well known that financial leverage, if properly applied, provides returns to the equity investors. During a noninflationary period, these returns are compensation for the equity investors, who assume total company risk while assuring the creditor of his return. During inflation there is another possible source for gain from financial leverage, resulting from a depressed interest rate. Although inflation

Exhibit 4.2. Manufacturing Debt Company
Financial Statement for the Year 19X2
(10% Inflation, 100% Fixed Assets, 100% Debt at 26.67%)

Balance Sheet as of December 31, 19X2

Assets				Liabilities and Equity			
12.31.19X1		12.31.19X2		12.31.19X1		12.31.19X2	
Conventional and PLA		Conventional	PLA*	Conventional and PLA		Conventional	PLA
$ 50.00	Machine 2	—	—	$25.00	Loan 2	—	—
50.00	Machine 3	$50.00	$55.00 r	50.00	Loan 3	$25.00	$27.50
—	Machine 4	55.00	55.00	—	Loan 4	55.00	55.00
100.00	Assets, at cost	105.00	110.00				
(25.00)	Accum. depr.	(25.00)	(27.50)				
75.00		80.00	82.50	75.00		80.00	82.50

Profit and Loss Statement for the Year 19X2

19X1		19X2			
Conventional and PLA		Conventional		PLA	
$200.00	Sales, 100 units		$220.00		$220.00
(130.00)	Out-of-pocket costs	$143.00		$143.00	
(20.00)	Interest†	22.00		22.00	
—	Linkage difference	5.00		—	
(50.00)	Depreciation	50.00		55.00	
			220.00		220.00

—	PLA operating profit		—		—
—	Asset restatement gains	—		7.50	
—	Less debt linkage expense	—		(7.50)	
—	Net restatement gains		—		—
—	Profit = tax and dividend		—		—

Sources and Uses Statement for the Year 19X2

Sources	Conventional	PLA	Uses	Conventional	PLA
Depreciation	$50.00	$55.00	Machine 4	$55.00	$55.00
Loan 4	55.00	55.00	Loan repayment	50.00	50.00
Loan appreciation	—	7.50	Linkage paid	—	5.00
			Asset restatement	—	7.50
	105.00	117.50		105.00	117.50

*The letter r indicates restated figure.

†The calculations regarding loan repayments were as follows:

Loan	Index Base	Index 12.31.X2	Principal 1.1.X2	Adjusted Principal 12.31.X2	Installment Due 12.31.X2	Adjusted Installment 12.31.X2
2	100	110	$25.00	$27.50	$25.00	$27.50
3	100	110	50.00	55.00	25.00	27.50
			75.00	82.50	50.00	55.00

Interest on adjusted principal = \$82.50 × 26.67% = \$22.00

and expectations of inflation have the effect of raising the price of money, as of other goods, often institutional restrictions do not allow an increase in the interest rate to compensate fully for the rise in the price level.[6] Institutional restrictions on the rate of interest cause (1) a lag in changing the rate of interest, and (2) a lag in changing the terms of outstanding loans. These terms are usually not renegotiable when price level conditions change. The latter effect is ignored here in order to simplify the illustrations; it is assumed that all outstanding loans bear floating interest rates (this assumption is relaxed in Section 15.4). Obviously, nonfloating interest rates will result in higher financial leverage returns.

Consider again the artificial case of Section 4.2 in which the company is financed completely by debt capital. Assume now, however, that the company is financed, in one case, by linked loans at 8% interest per annum (compared to 26.67% in Section 4.2) and, in another case, by nonlinked loans at 8% interest. Profit and loss statements for the years 19X1 and 19X2 for both cases are presented in Exhibit 4.3.

The $14 pretax profit recorded for the year 19X1 is due to the fact that the interest rate on loans is lower than the return on capital (8% and 26.67%, respectively). This profit, termed "rent" in economics, is appropriated by equity capital, in compensation for assuming company risk while guaranteeing the debt. Consider now the profit for the year 19X2. On the assumption that the loans are price level linked, the $15.40 profit represents "rent," which is equivalent (in real terms) to that in 19X1 ($14 + 10% PLA). In the case of nonlinked loans, the profit is composed of three components: (1) $15.40 of "rent," (2) $0.60 of underpaid interest due to understated nonlinked loans, and (3) $7.50 of asset restatement gains, partly realized and partly nonrealized.

The asset restatement gains should have been allocated as price level compensation to all the capital owners. Since the lender did not request this compensation under the terms of the nonlinked loan, they have been left to the use of the borrower. In this case asset restatement gains are not merely the result of a change in the scale of measurement (change in the purchasing power of the dollar); they are also real returns. If this sum were taxed or distributed as dividends, the company would still be as well off as it was at the beginning of the year. This holds true, however, only if the company is assured of obtaining the same volume of loans (in real terms) in the future as in the past.

Therefore the $23.50 PLA profit is "profit" in the Hicksian sense. The operating profit of $16 plus the realized restatement gains of $5 ($21) is

Exhibit 4.3. Manufacturing Debt Company
Profit and Loss Statement for the Year 19X2
(10% Inflation, 100% Fixed Assets, 100% Debt at 8%)

19X1 Conventional and PLA		Conventional		PLA	
Linked Loans					
$200.00	Sales, 100 units		$220.00		$220.00
(130.00)	Out-of-pocket costs	$143.00		$143.00	
(6.00)	Interest	6.60		6.60	
—	Linkage difference	5.00		—	
(50.00)	Depreciation	50.00		55.00	
			204.60		204.60
14.00	PLA operating profit				15.40
	Asset restatement gains	—		7.50	
	Debt linkage expense	—		(7.50)	
			—		—
14.00	Profit = tax and dividend		15.40		15.40
Nonlinked Loans					
$200.00	Sales, 100 units		$220.00		$220.00
(130.00)	Out-of-pocket costs	$143.00		$143.00	
(6.00)	Interest	6.00		6.00	
(50.00)	Depreciation	50.00		55.00	
			199.00		204.00
14.00	PLA operating profit				16.00
	Assets restatement gains:				
—	Realized	—		5.00	
—	Nonrealized	—		2.50	
—	Net restatement gains		—		7.50
14.00	Profit = tax and dividend		21.00		23.50

recorded by conventional accounting procedures; the nonrealized restatement gains are not recognized.

In summary, profits resulting from financial leverage are consistent with the Hicksian definition of profit. Since PLA compensation for debt capital is usually not required under the terms agreed to by the capital owners (lenders), conventional accounting procedures provide a satisfactory (but not necessarily complete) profit measure in the artificial case of zero equity.

4.4 Profit Measurement When Financial Leverage Exists

In Sections 4.1 through 4.3 two artificial cases (100% equity, zero equity) were analyzed to illustrate the conceptual problems and solutions of profit measurement in an inflationary situation. A more realistic case is described in this section with a company financed partly by equity and partly by loans.

It is assumed here that the company is able to obtain necessary debt capital up to 40% of its total financing requirements at a cost of 8% interest per annum. Conventional and PLA financial statements for the year 19X1 are presented in Exhibit 4.4.

Because of $2.40 interest expense, pretax profit is $17.60, as compared to $20 when only equity financing is used (Exhibit 2.1). However, because of financial leverage the company was able to earn 39.1% pretax profit on equity ($17.60 : $45.00), as compared to 26.67% for the case of 100% equity. In other words, "rent" of the leverage mix is appropriated by equity.

Leverage returns ($5.60) are calculated by allocating the total returns of $20 proportionally between equity and debt, as follows:

	Equity, 60%	Debt, 40%	Total, 100%
Returns as actually distributed	$17.60	$2.40	$20.00
Returns allocated proportionally	12.00	8.00	20.00
Leverage returns (balance)	5.60	(5.60)	—

At the end of 19X1 the bank anticipated that previous stable price conditions would not continue. Therefore it renegotiated the loan agreements and succeeded in raising the nominal interest rate. To keep the accounting simple, it is assumed that the increase affected both Loan 3 and the outstanding balance of Loan 2. The new rate of interest, as of January 1, 19X2, was 14%. Relevant financial statements are presented in Exhibit 4.5.

The figures in Exhibit 4.5 result from applying PLA accounting procedures to a more realistic situation in which it is assumed that the company has managed its financing in accordance with PLA procedures. Each side of the balance sheet has been treated separately, and assets have been restated to arrive at their PLA values. Equity has also been restated, adding $4.50 to maintain its original value in terms of current dollars; a $1 additional loan (No. 3a) has been taken to keep up 40% debt in financing Machine 3. As a result of restatements, asset values "rose" by $7.50 (asset restatement gains).

Exhibit 4.4. Manufacturing Leverage Company
Financial Statements for the Year 19X1
(No Inflation, 100% Fixed Assets, 60% Equity)
Conventional and PLA Accounting

Balance Sheet as of December 31, 19X1

Assets			Liabilities and Equity		
12.31.19X0		12.31.19X1	12.31.19X0		12.31.19X1
$50.00	Machine 1	—	$10.00	Loan 1	—
50.00	Machine 2	$50.00	20.00	Loan 2	$10.00
—	Machine 3	50.00	—	Loan 3	20.00
100.00	Assets, at cost	100.00	30.00	Total liabilities	30.00
(25.00)	Accum. depr.	(25.00)	45.00	Equity	45.00
75.00		75.00	75.00		75.00

Profit and Loss Statement for the Year 19X1

Sales, 100 units		$200.00
Out-of-pocket costs	$130.00	
Interest	2.40	
Depreciation	50.00	
		182.40
Profit = tax and dividend		17.60

Sources and Uses Statement for the Year 19X1

Sources		Uses	
Depreciation	$50.00	Machine 3	$50.00
Profit	17.60	Tax and dividend	17.60
Loan 3	20.00	Loan repayment	20.00
	87.60		87.60

Exhibit 4.5. Manufacturing Leverage Company
Financial Statements for the Year 19X2
(10% Inflation, 100% Fixed Assets, 60% Equity)

Balance Sheet as of December 31, 19X2

Assets				Liabilities and Equity			
12.31.19X1		12.31.19X2		12.31.19X1		12.31.19X2	
Conventional and PLA		Conventional	PLA*	Conventional and PLA		Conventional	PLA
$50.00	Machine 2	—	—	$10.00	Loan 2	—	
50.00	Machine 3	$50.00	$55.00 r	20.00	Loan 3	$10.00	$10.00
				—	Loan 3a	—	1.00
—	Machine 4	55.00	55.00	—	Loan 4	22.00	22.00
100.00	Assets, at cost	105.00	110.00	30.00	Total liabilities	32.00	33.00
(25.00)	Accum. depr.	(25.00)	(27.50)	45.00	Equity	45.00	45.00
				—	New shares	3.00	—
				—	Equity maint. reserve	—	4.50
75.00		80.00	82.50	75.00		80.00	82.50

*The letter r indicates stated figures.

Exhibit 4.5 (continued)

Profit and Loss Statement for the Year 19X2

19X1 Conventional and PLA		19X2 Conventional		19X2 PLA	
$200.00	Sales, 100 units		$220.00		$220.00
(130.00)	Out-of-pocket costs	$143.00		$143.00	
(2.40)	Interest	4.20		4.20	
(50.00)	Depreciation	50.00		55.00	
			197.20		202.20
17.60	PLA operating profit				17.80
—	Asset restatement gains			7.50	
—	Less equity maint. adjustment			(4.50)	
—	Net restatement gains				3.00
17.60	Profit = tax and dividend		22.80		20.80

Sources and Uses Statement for the Year 19X2

Sources	Conventional	PLA	Uses	Conventional	PLA
Depreciation	$50.00	$55.00	Machine 4	$55.00	$55.00
Profit	22.80	20.80	Tax and dividend	22.80	20.80
Loan 3a	—	1.00			
Loan 4	22.00	22.00	Loan repayment	20.00	20.00
New shares	3.00	—			
Equity maint.	—	4.50	Asset restatement	—	7.50
	97.80	103.30		97.80	103.30

These gains may be allocated proportionally between equity and debt as follows:

Equity, 60%	\$4.50
Debt, 40%	3.00
Total, 100%	7.50

Asset restatement (holding) gains (\$7.50) have been decomposed into equity maintenance (\$4.50) and leverage gains (\$3.00); the latter are termed "net restatement gains." These gains are added to the PLA profit and loss statement.

The PLA profit and loss statement provides two profit figures: PLA operating profit (\$17.80) and PLA total profit (\$20.80). The first is computed after charging PLA depreciation expense to income (in contrast with historical depreciation in the conventional profit and loss statement). The second is computed after adding net restatement gains to the former profit figure. The PLA operating profit is consistent with conventional accounting principles. It is based on historical-cost data, with lagged costs restated to current dollar figures. The PLA total profit, on the other hand, violates the realization principle of financial accounting; yet it is consistent with economic principles.[7] A graphical comparison of these profit measures is presented in Exhibit 4.6.

Since the debt share of the restatement gains (\$3) is not paid to the creditors (they received their compensation through increased interest payment), it is left in the company as a profit. This sum is considered profit in the Hicksian sense. If it is distributed as dividends, the company will still be as well off as it was at the beginning of the year,[8] assuming that it can preserve its optimal mix of finance, in both volume and repayment schedule. (In Exhibit 4.5 debt increased from \$30 in 19X1 to \$33 in 19X2 to keep 60% equity.) It should be noted, however, that cash distribution of net restatement gains by taking a corresponding loan increases the company's risk in regard to the possibility of a future decline in price level (as shown in Section 15.4).

4.5 Inflationary Leverage Returns

Profit in 19X1 was \$17.60; it is expected to rise in 19X2 by 10% to \$19.36 (given that physical assets, production, and sales are stable). Exhibit 4.5 indicates that the PLA operating profit is below the expected sum (\$17.80). This is so because of increased interest expense, paid as partial price level compensation to the lender. The PLA total profit, on the other hand, is higher than the expected sum ($20.80) because the price level compensation paid to the lender did not provide full compensation.

The company employed $30 of bank financing at the beginning of the year. Had the bank ensured preservation of the real value of this sum, it would have required a $3 restatement payment. Having been compensated for price level changes, the bank would have required 8% interest (as in the preceding year) on the $33 restated loan, that is, $2.64. Thus the bank should have been paid $5.64 in 19X2. Actually, the company paid $4.20 interest, keeping the balance of $1.44 for itself.[9] Because of institutional restrictions the bank raised the interest rate by 6 percentage points (from 8% to 14%) rather than requiring full PLA compensation as in "linked" loans. If this sum, termed "inflationary leverage returns," is subtracted from $20.80 (pretax profit), the resulting profit of $19.36 is exactly the same percentage of sales and of equity as was achieved in the preceding year.[10]

Exhibit 4.6. Comparison of Profit Measures
Manufacturing Leverage Company

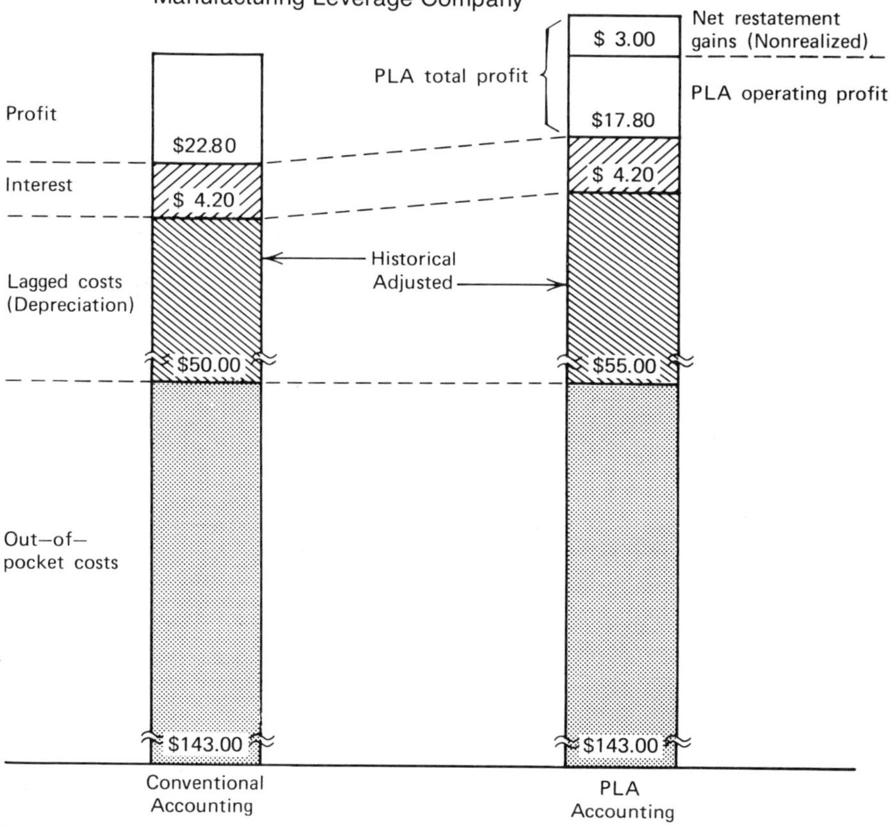

Source: Data from Exhibit 4.5.

Profit for 19X1 was decomposed into two components: direct returns on equity ($12) and leverage returns ($5.60). Returns for 19X2, as computed in Exhibit 4.5, can be decomposed into three components, as follows:

Direct returns ($12 in 19X1 plus 10% PLA)	$13.20
Leverage returns ($5.60 in 19X1 plus 10% PLA)	6.16
Inflationary leverage returns	1.44
Total returns	20.80

In summary, to arrive at a conceptually correct profit figure for a company with mixed financing, both equity and assets must be restated. Equity restatement is required for maintaining the equity investment value. Asset restatement is required for estimating the value of the company's present assets and for computing PLA depreciation. Profit, as computed by PLA accounting procedures, is composed of direct returns to equity, leverage returns, and inflationary leverage returns. The PLA total profit figure is consistent with the Hicksian definition.

4.6 Treatment of Financial Assets

Usually companies hold financial assets (cash, accounts receivable, investment, etc.) in addition to fixed assets. The inflationary effect on most financial asset items differs from that on real assets. Whereas the value of most real assets is, more or less, "price level linked," the value of most financial assets is usually not "linked." Assets are price level linked to the extent that they are realizable in output sold at the new price level. One type of financial asset, equity shares, however, "behaves" similarly to real assets; these should be revalued to their market levels. The price of financial assets, except for stock, is usually not affected by inflation, and therefore their historical value, as recorded in conventional financial statements, equals the PLA value, even during a period of inflation. For the sake of simplicity, the discussion and numerical illustration below deal only with financial assets whose monetary value is not affected by price level changes.

For example, suppose that a debt of $100 for a product delivered a year ago to a customer still stands as receivable. The company will be paid only $100 even though this sum now represents less purchasing power; the financial asset is realized at its historical value.

Since financial assets are not price level linked, during inflation they do not endow the company with restatement gains, as is the case with real assets. Thus, the larger the share of financial assets in the balance sheet, the fewer restatement gains accrue to the company during a period of inflation.[11]

Financial assets (on the asset side of the balance sheet) are the mirror image of debt finance (on the liabilities and equity side of the balance sheet). On one side there are real assets and financial assets; on the other side, equity and debt (including payables that are in effect interest-free loans). On each side only the first item (real assets and equity, respectively) is restated; the other items (financial assets and debt) are not.

Consider a financial company holding its $75 of equity capital in cash and in various investments. In the year 19X1 it earned $20 net returns (26.67%).[12] In 19X2 net returns remained at the 19X1 level (i.e., $20) despite the 10% rise in price level. To restate the value of equity capital it has to be inflated by 10%. Thus equity will be increased by a maintenance reserve of $7.50, as shown in Exhibit 4.7. This sum is charged to the profit and loss statement, reducing profit from the $20 shown by conventional accounting to $12.50 under PLA procedures.

Exhibit 4.7. Financial Equity Company
PLA Financial Statements for the Year 19X2
(10% Inflation, Zero Fixed Assets, 100% Equity)

Balance Sheet as of December 31, 19X2

Assets 12.31.19X1		Assets 12.31.19X2	Liabilities and Equity 12.31.19X1		Liabilities and Equity 12.31.19X2
$75.00	Investment	$75.00	$75.00	Equity	$75.00
—	New investment	7.50	—	Equity maint. reserve	7.50
75.00		82.50	75.00		82.50

Profit and Loss Statement for the Year 19X2

19X1		19X2
$20.00	Returns on investment	$20.00
—	Less equity maint. adjustment	(7.50)
20.00	Profit = tax and dividend	12.50

Sources and Uses Statement for the Year 19X2

Sources		Uses	
Profit	$12.50	Tax and dividend	$12.50
Equity maint.	7.50	New investment	7.50
	20.00		20.00

The numerical illustration assumed that returns on the financial assets did not rise when inflation occurred. It can be expected, however, that these returns will rise, just as the interest rate on debt finance rose, as assumed above. If such a rise lags behind the rise in the general price level, the company will suffer losses. These are analogous to the returns that the borrowing company enjoys from institutional restrictions on the interest rate. Since the method of analysis is the same as illustrated for the case of debt, it is not repeated here. It is, however, incorporated in the illustration in Appendix D.

The case discussed here is representative of the situation of financial institutions, such as banks, during a period of inflation. Bank profits, as computed by conventional accounting, usually increase during inflation because of rises in the rate of interest set by the bank on loans it grants. In fact, increases in the interest rate are (partial) compensation for the loss in capital value due to inflation; yet conventional accounting procedures report as profit sums that are actually required for equity maintenance. In practice, consumption of these funds is prevented by appropriating portions of reported profits to various reserves.

In summary, price level changes affect most financial assets in the same way as they affect debt finance; the effect on both is treated alike in PLA accounting. Just as financial debt (which is not price level linked) may increase a company's profit during inflation, so may the existence of financial assets (which are not price level linked) reduce the company's real profits. Stock and other securities whose monetary values are affected by price level changes, on the other hand, should be restated in PLA accounting in the same manner as real assets.

On the assumption that neither financial assets nor debt finance is price level linked, the former may be deducted from the latter to provide an aggregated figure called "net debt." For simplicity the discussion and illustrations in the remaining chapters (except Chapter 6) ignore financial assets. The implications regarding debt should therefore be considered as referring to net debt.

Notes

1. For a discussion of equity maintenance see, for example, Gynther (1970), Bak (1974), and Gak (1974).

2. As will be seen, interest cost equals profit in this example. This assumption will be relaxed in the next section. The high interest rate could be explained by the fact that the total financial risk of the company is being borne by the lender. Managerial remuneration, included in out-of-pocket costs, covers entrepreneural remuneration as well.
3. For a detailed exposition of this practice and its accounting implications see Aharoni and Ophir (1967).
4. In both cases, returns to the lender are composed of two components: inflation-free interest and price level compensation. This is analogous to decomposing the conventional profit figure into operating profit and holding gains.
5. Under PLA accounting, loan linkage difference is a balance sheet account, whereas under conventional accounting it is a profit and loss account.
6. For example, Cargill and Meyer (1974, p. 470) discovered instability in the relationships between prices and interest rates.
7. It is interesting to note that Sweeney (1964, p. 21), as long ago as 1936, suggested providing this kind of profit and loss statement:

   > The practical way of overcoming the artificiality caused by classifying income into realized and unrealized is...first, in using a realized-income section the contents of which are identical with those in the ordinary profit and loss statement. Second, an unrealized-income section is added because of the helpful information that it contains. Finally, at the very bottom of the profit and loss statement the total of the realized and unrealized income is shown.

   Davidson and Weil (1975) suggested adding the year's net restatement gains to the PLA profit.
8. Cash for distributing dividend on the nonrealized gains would be available only if a corresponding loan was taken. However, distribution of nonrealized profit is not accepted as legal in most countries.
9. If the rise in the interest rate overcompensates for the rate of inflation (as may occur because of erroneous expectations, or as an uncertainty premium set by the lender), the balance will be negative.
10. For a similar procedure see Bradford (1974).
11. Often it is said that there is a loss from holding financial assets (that are not "price level linked") during a period of inflation. It is

an economic loss stated in opportunity (not in accounting) terms. The loss stems from the fact that capital was not invested in price level linked assets.

12. This case is a mirror image of the Manufacturing Debt Company as illustrated in Exhibit 4.1. Here the company holds 100% financial assets; there, 100% debt finance.

References

Aharoni, Y. and T. Ophir, "Accounting for Linked Loans," *Journal of Accounting Research,* Spring 1967, pp. 1–26.

Anthony, R. N., "Accounting for the Cost of Equity," *Harvard Business Review,* November–December 1973, pp. 88–102.

Bak, G. G. M., "Financial Reporting under Inflationary Conditions—The Netherlands," in Institute of Certified Public Accountants in Israel, *Critical Problems of External Financial Reporting,* Proceedings of the 2nd Jerusalem Conference on Accountancy, 1974, pp. B-IV-1–11.

Bradford, W. D., "Price Level Restated Accounting and the Measurement of Inflation Gains and Losses," *Accounting Review,* April 1974, pp. 296–305.

Cargill, T. F. and R. A. Meyer, "Interest Rates and Prices since 1950," *International Economic Review,* June 1974, pp. 458–471.

Davidson, S. and R. L. Weil, "Inflation Accounting," *Financial Analyst Journal,* January–February 1975, pp. 27–31, 70–84.

Gak, A. L., "Financial Reporting under Inflationary Conditions—Argentine," in Institute of Certified Public Accountants in Israel, *Critical Problems of External Financial Reporting,* Proceedings of the 2nd Jerusalem Conference on Accountancy, 1974, pp. B-I-1–15.

Gynther, R. S., "Capital Maintenance, Price Changes, and Profit Determination," *Accounting Review,* October 1970, pp. 712–730.

Sweeney, H. W., *Stabilized Accounting,* Harper, New York, 1936 (renewed, Holt, Rinhart & Winston, New York, 1964).

Five

Creeping Inflation and Inventories

The discussion and illustrations in the preceding chapters and in all the chapters that follow this one assume, for the sake of simplicity, that (1) inflation occurred in the form of a sudden price level change (on January 1), and (2) the company in question holds only fixed assets. This chapter analyzes the effect of inflation when it is, as usual, gradual and when companies hold inventories as well as fixed assets. The basic data of the illustrations used earlier also serve the discussion here.

The main conclusion from the analysis in this chapter is that the preparation of PLA interim financial statements overcomes the problems caused by the facts that (1) prices creep up gradually, (2) investment is carried out gradually over time, and (3) the inventory life cycle is usually relatively short.

5.1 Effect of Creeping Inflation on Profit and Loss

Inflation is usually gradual, with prices changing continuously during the year. Therefore the sales values and out-of-pocket costs, as recorded in the annual report, are given in terms of dollars characterized by various purchasing powers. The year's totals are actually the year's weighted average (purchasing power) dollars.

The PLA depreciation expenses should also be computed on the basis of creeping price level changes, consistently with the market changes in sales values and out-of-pocket costs.[1] Thereby all data in the profit and loss statement will be stated in terms of the given year's average (purchasing power) dollars. The PLA balance sheet (which includes the new, acquired machine), on the other hand, represents values in year-end dollars. There is a discrepancy between the "sizes" of the dollars that state the depreciation expense and those measuring the asset values. To analyze and reconcile this discrepancy, interim financial statements must be prepared.

Suppose that prices creep up during 19X2 by 2.41% quarterly (10% for the whole year). Thus both sales value and cost of acquisition are creeping up during 19X2, as shown in Exhibit 5.1. Since prices are rising gradually over the year (rather than jumping 10% January 1, 19X2, as assumed earlier), the average price level of 19X2 is 6.17% above the average level of 19X1. Although in both cases year-end prices are 10% above those of January, the gradual rise assumed here caused the average prices of the year to be below the average prices of previous examples.

Exhibit 5.1. Manufacturing Equity Company
Interim Profit and Loss Statement for the Year 19X2
(10% Creeping Inflation, 100% Fixed Assets, 100% Equity)

12.31.X1	Date:	3.31.X2	6.30.X2	9.30.X2	12.31.X2	Total
100.00	Price index:	102.41	104.88	107.41	110.00	106.17*
	Conventional Accounting					
$50.00	Sales	$51.20	$52.44	$53.71	$55.00	$212.35
32.50	Out-of-pocket costs	33.28	34.09	34.91	35.75	138.03
17.50	Net cash inflow	17.92	18.35	18.80	19.25	74.32
12.50	Depreciation	12.50	12.50	12.50	12.50	50.00
5.00	Profit (pretax)	5.42	5.85	6.30	6.75	24.32
	PLA Accounting					
17.50	Net cash inflow	$17.92	$18.35	$18.80	$19.25	$74.32
12.50	Depreciation	12.80	13.11	13.43	13.75	53.09
5.00	Profit (pretax)	5.12	5.24	5.37	5.50	21.23

*Average for the year.

The cash flow data—sales values and out-of-pocket costs (Exhibit 5.1)—are identical under conventional and PLA accounting procedures. This illustrates an important fact: data representing current cash transactions, as recorded in conventional financial statements, need not be price level adjusted. Price level adjustment is required only to take into account changes in the monetary measuring unit caused by the time lag between input acquisition and output realization. However, if the sales and out-of-pocket costs data are to be stated in currency equal in value to that used in the balance sheet, these items need be updated to year-end dollars. The updating procedure is explained and illustrated in Chapter 12.

The preinflation quarterly depreciation expense (in 19X1) was $12.50 ($50:4). Using this figure in the conventional accounting statements for 19X2 (all machines were acquired at 19X1 prices) causes the quarterly profit figure to be biased upward; this bias increases as the year progresses (upper section in Exhibit 5.1). Under PLA accounting, on the other hand, the $12.50 quarterly depreciation figure is inflated by the corresponding quarterly price indices (lower section of Exhibit 5.1). The resulting PLA interim cost and profit figures are based on dollars of equal purchasing power in the given quarter.

The sum of the quarterly PLA depreciation figures for the whole year is $53.09, compared to the $55 obtained if depreciation expense is calculated on the basis of year-end restated assets.[2] The difference arises from the discrepancy between two scales of measurements: one is based on year-end dollars; the other, on four quarterly dollars of different values. The last quarterly depreciation charge of $13.75, calculated in year-end dollars, is in fact at the rate of $55 per annum ($13.75 x 4 = $55).

To reconcile the average purchasing power figure of $53.09 and the year-end purchasing power figure of $55, each quarterly PLA depreciation sum must be updated by the corresponding price level index number, as follows:

$$\$12.80 \times 1.0741 + \$13.11 \times 1.0488 + \$13.43 \times 1.0241 + \$13.75 \times 1.000 = \$55.00$$

If the quarterly sales and out-of-pocket costs are also updated to year-end dollars, the updated profit for the year is $22. This figure equals that in the illustration of Exhibit 2.2, where the price level jumped at the beginning of the year rather than creeping up gradually.

5.2 Effect of Creeping Inflation on the Balance Sheet

The preceding discussion showed that, if quarterly PLA depreciation expenses (and materials used) are computed, the yearly PLA profit and loss statement is stated in the year's average dollars. The balance sheet data, on the other hand, are given in year-end dollars. This is true if assets are acquired at the end of the year, as assumed in the preceding numerical illustrations. However, investment in assets usually occurs throughout the year. As a result, part of the balance sheet data (that which refers to assets acquired during the current year) is stated in the year's average dollars, just as are sales and out-of-pocket costs (in the profit and loss statement). Gradual investment is illustrated by the following example.

Suppose that the Manufacturing Equity Company's assets consist of eight machines, each of which cost $12.50 (before inflation started), rather than of two machines at $50 each. This assumption of eight machines makes it possible to illustrate smoother periodical replacement than the simpler case of two machines. In both cases the total acquisition cost is $100. This value represents the productive capacity of the machines, assuming, as before, that their productive ability is equal over their life span. The machines are depreciated using the straight-line method over 2 years. They are bought in a stagger system, so that each quarter begins with one new machine.

The balance sheet of a company with eight machines differs, of course, from that of a company with two machines; whereas the acquisition cost (gross value) is equal ($100 in 19X1), the net value of assets is lower for the former company ($56.25 compared to $75 in 19X1), as shown in Exhibit 5.2. Despite the differences in the balance sheets the two companies produce and sell at the same level because it is assumed here that the acquisition cost of the assets determines their productive capacity. Depreciation charges in the two companies are equal as well; during a period of stable prices the respective annual depreciation charges are as follows:

($50.00:2 years) x 2 machines = $50
($12.50:2 years) x 8 machines = $50

The quarterly depreciation charges are also equal ($12.50). During a period of price level changes, conventional quarterly depreciation charges differ because of the difference in investment policy between the two companies, whereas in one company assets are replaced once a year, in the other company replacement of assets occurs quarterly. For the two machines quarterly conventional depreciation in 19X2 is $12.50 (Exhibit 5.1); for the eight machines the respective quarterly conventional charges are $12.50, $12.54, $12.62, and $12.74.[3] The PLA depreciation, on the other hand, is equal in the two companies. Whereas for the company with two machines (and year-end renewal) the quarterly PLA depreciation expense represents quarterly restatement, for the company with eight machines it can be seen that each quarterly depreciation expense sets aside exactly enough funds to buy one new machine, as required for maintaining productive capacity at a stable level.[4]

The fact that prices are creeping up continuously rather than jump-

Exhibit 5.2. Manufacturing Equity Company (Eight Machines)

Balance Sheet as of December 31, 19X2

Assets								Liabilities and Equity			
12.31.19X1			12.31.19X2								
Conventional and PLA			Conventional			PLA		12.31.19X1		12.31.19X2	
Net Value	Accumulated Depreciation	Machine	Net Value	Accumulated Depreciation	Index at Acquisition	Net Value*	Accumulated Depreciation	Conventional and PLA		Conventional	PLA
$ 1.56	$10.94	1						$56.25	Equity	$56.25	$56.25
3.12	9.38	2							New equity	2.70	—
4.69	7.81	3							Equity maint.	—	5.63
6.25	6.25	4									
7.81	4.69	5	$ 1.56	$10.94	100.00	$ 1.72^r	$12.03				
9.38	3.12	6	3.12	9.38	100.00	3.44^r	10.31				
10.94	1.56	7	4.69	7.81	100.00	5.16^r	8.59				
12.50		8	6.25	6.25	100.00	6.88^r	6.87				
		9	8.00	4.80	102.41	8.59^r	5.16				
		10	9.83	3.28	104.88	10.31^r	3.44				
		11	11.75	1.68	107.41	12.03^r	1.72				
		12	13.75	—	110.00	13.75	—				
56.25		Total net value	58.95			61.88		56.25		58.95	61.88
43.75			44.14			48.12					
100.00		Assets, at cost	103.09			110.00					

*The letter r indicates restated figure.

ing on certain dates does not affect PLA profit if the cash flow of the depreciation fund is reinvested in "price level linked" assets. This is parallel to the continuous renewal of material inventories.

To arrive at a precisely correct PLA balance sheet, stated in year-end dollars, the fact that assets are acquired during the year should be taken into account. Each set of assets should be inflated by the price index number corresponding to the relevant date: the "old" assets, recorded in the opening PLA balance sheet, should be inflated by the total rise in the price index for the year; newly acquired assets should be inflated by the indices relevant to the acquisition dates.

In summary, to provide PLA financial statements in which all the data are recorded in year-end dollars, two alternatives are available: one is to prepare interim financial statements, which can then be updated; the other, to inflate every transaction or group of transactions by the price index pertinent to the date of transaction. The latter procedure can be easily implemented when the accounting system is computerized.[5]

5.3 Treatment of Raw Material Inventories

Inventories are affected by price level changes in a manner identical to that for fixed assets. There is, however, an important difference between inventories and fixed assets, due to the different length of their life cycles. Fixed assets are by definition bought to serve for more than 1 year, whereas inventories are usually turned over several times during the year. If the first in, first out (FIFO) method of recording inventories is assumed, inventory prices at year's end represent acquisitions made relatively close to the date of the financial statement. Hence restatement serves to compensate for a rise in price level during this relatively short period.

Consider a commercial company that bought 180 units of a commodity in the year 19X1 for $180 and sold them for $200, earning $20 profit. Suppose, for the sake of simplicity, that there are no operating costs. The company holds 75 units in inventory (i.e., for 5 months' sales), financed by $75 equity. During 19X2 prices crept up by 2.41% quarterly (10% compounded for the whole year), as in Section 5.2. Again assuming the FIFO method of inventory records, the cost of goods sold for the quarterly sale of 45 units is taken from historical inventory costs of one and two quarters ago. The cost of goods sold, as computed by conventional accounting procedures, therefore lags behind the current price rise.

Under PLA accounting, however, inventories are restated, with the difference credited to a "restatement gains" account. Thereby the costs of units entering, remaining, and leaving inventory at any given point in time are equal. As a result both the cost of goods sold and the inventory value are higher than those under conventional accounting during a period of inflation, as shown in Exhibit 5.3.

Here, as in Exhibit 5.1, the yearly totals of both sales values and out-of-pocket costs are lower than in former illustrations because prices crept upward (rather than jumping up 10% on January 1, 19X2). Profit for the year 19X2 (Exhibit 5.4), as computed by conventional accounting procedures ($27.96), is higher than the operating profit computed by PLA procedures ($21.24). The difference of $6.72 is due to gains realized from holding inventories during a period of inflation.

Most of the restatement gains ($7.50) are realized ($6.72) in the case of raw material inventories (Exhibit 5.4). In the case of the machine (Exhibit 2.2) a smaller portion of the total gains ($7.50) was realized ($5.00).

Conventional accounting procedures record these realized restatement gains as part of current profit; PLA procedures credit them to a special restatement gains account. The longer the life of the asset, the larger is the nonrealized portion of the restatement gains.

According to the FIFO method, inventory recorded in the December 31, 19X2, balance sheet consists of two batches that were acquired at different dates. (Exhibit 5.3). Restatement of these batches, according to the time they have been in storage, is as follows:

Units	Date of Acquisition	Cost of Acquisition	Time in Storage (Quarters)	Price Index	Restatement Factor	Restatement Value
30	9.30.X2	$32.22	1	107.41	1.0241	$33.00
45	12.31.X2	49.50	0	110.00	1.0000	49.50
75		81.72				82.50

The $0.78 difference in inventory value between acquisition cost and restatement ($82.50—$81.72) is the nonrealized fraction of total restatement gains ($7.50) from holding the inventories during the year 19X2.

The total restatement gains ($7.50, $6.72 realized and $0.78 nonrealized) are identical with those obtained from holding fixed assets. In the case of 100% equity financing these gains are completely offset by the equity maintenance reserve, and so do not affect profit. In the case of a leverage financed company, however, only a portion equal to the equity share (60% above) is offset by the equity maintenance reserve; the rest (40%) remains as profit in the Hicksian sense.

Exhibit 5.3. Commercial Equity Company Interim Profit and Loss Statements for the Year 19X2 (10% Creeping Inflation, 100% Raw Materials Inventory, the FIFO Method)

12.31.X1	Date:	3.31.X2	6.30.X2	9.30.X2	12.31.X2	Total
100.00	Price Index:	102.41	104.88	107.40	110.00	106.17*
	Profit Calculation					
	Conventional Accounting					
$ 50.00	Sales	$51.21	$52.44	$53.70	$55.00	$212.35
45.00	Cost of goods sold	45.00	45.36	46.45	47.58	184.39
5.00	Profit	6.21	7.08	7.25	7.42	27.96
	PLA Accounting					
50.00	Sales	51.21	52.44	53.70	55.00	212.35
45.00	Cost of goods sold	46.08	47.20	48.33	49.50	191.11
5.00	Profit	5.13	5.24	5.37	5.50	21 24
	Inventory Cost Calculation					
	Conventional Accounting					
	Opening	75.00	76.08	77.92	79.80	
	Use	45.00	45.36	46.45	47.58	184.39
	Balance	30.00	30.72	31.47	32.22	
	Buy	46.08	47.20	48.33	49.50	191.11
	Closing	76.08	77.92	79.80	81.72	
	PLA Accounting					
	Opening	75.00	76.81	78.66	80.55	
	Restatement gains	1.81	1.85	1.89	1.95	7.50
	Restated value	76.81	78.66	80.55	82.50	
	Use	46.08	47.20	48.33	49.50	191.11
		30.73	31.46	32.22	33.00	
	Buy	46.08	47.20	48.33	49.50	191.11
	Closing	76.81	78.66	80.55	82.50	

*Average for the year.

Raw material inventories are usually composed of many items, each remaining in store for a different duration. For detailed cost accounting computations, the procedure illustrated should be carried out for every major inventory item. For PLA profit computations of the company as a whole, however, weighted average time in store may be used.

5.4 Treatment of Finished Goods Inventories

Inventories of goods in process and of finished goods are composed of several cost elements (raw materials, labor, depreciation, etc.). Price level adjustment should take into account (1) the fact that each cost element was acquired on a different date, and (2) that some elements are already price level adjusted (e.g., raw materials in stores), so as to avoid double adjustment.

Consider an industrial company for which the following profit and loss statement for the year 19X1 holds:

Sales, 120 units			$200
Expenses:	Materials	$90	
	Labor	40	
	Depreciation	50	
			180
Profit			20

The monthly material usage is $7.50 ($90:12 months), and the monthly cost of goods sold is $15 ($180:12 months). The company holds $75 of inventories: $30 of raw materials (i.e., for 4 months' production) and $45 of finished goods (i.e., for 3 months' sales). Interim cost calculations under both conventional and PLA accounting procedures are shown in Exhibit 5.5.

The treatment of raw materials is the same as that illustrated in Exhibit 5.4. Price level adjustment of raw materials that are included in finished goods, however, takes into consideration the previous adjustment (of raw material inventory). Since labor is paid on a current basis, this cost item needs no adjustment, and it is identical under both conventional and PLA accounting.

Inventory cost calculations under the two accounting procedures, as illustrated in Exhibit 5.5, result in different increases in inventory value during the year 19X2, as follows:

	PLA	Conventional (Realized)	Nonrealized (PLA) − Conventional)
Raw materials	$3.00	$2.80	$0.20
Finished goods	4.50	2.48	2.02

Exhibit 5.4. Commercial Equity Company
Financial Statements for the Year 19X2
Inventory Restatement Gains

Balance Sheet as of

Assets

12.31.19X1 Conventional and PLA		12.31.19X2 Conventional	12.31.19X2 PLA*
$75.00	Inventory	$81.72	$82.50 ^{r}
75.00		81.72	82.50

Profit and Loss Statement

19X1 Conventional and PLA		
$200.00	Sales, 100 units	
180.00	Cost of goods sold	
20.00	PLA operating profit	
	Asset restatement gains:	Realized
		Nonrealized
	Equity maint.	
—	Net restatement gains	
20.00	Profit = tax and dividend	

Sources and Uses Statement

Sources	Conventional	PLA
Profit	$27.96	$21.24
New shares	6.72	—
Equity maint.	—	7.50
	34.68	28.74

*The letter *r* indicates restated figures.

December 31, 19X2

Liability and Equity

12.31.19X1 Conventional and PLA		12.31.19X2 Conventional	12.31.19X2 PLA
$75.00	Equity	$75.00	$75.00
	New shares	6.72	—
—	Equity maint. reserve	—	7.50
75.00		81.72	82.50

for the Year 19X2

19X2 Conventional		19X2 PLA
$212.35		$212.35
184.39		191.11
—		21.24
—	$6.72	
—	0.78	
	7.50	
—	(7.50)	
—		—
27.96		21.24

for the Year 19X2

Uses	Conventional	PLA
Tax and dividend	$27.96	$21.24
Inventory increase	6.72	—
Asset restatement	—	7.50
	34.68	28.74

Exhibit 5.5. Industrial Equity Company
Interim Cost Calculation for the Year 19×2
(10% Creeping Inflation, 100% Raw Materials and Finished Goods Inventories, 100% Equity)

Date:	12.31.X1		3.30.X2
Price Index:	100.00		102.41
			Conventional
Raw materials			
Opening			$30.00
Use (transfer to production)			(22.50)
Buy			23.04
Closing			30.54
Finished goods			
Opening			45.00
Use (sell)			(45.00)
Buy: Raw materials		22.50	
Labor		10.24	
Depreciation		12.50	
			45.24
Closing			45.24
			PLA
Raw materials			
Opening			30.00
Restatement			0.72
			30.72
Use			(23.04)
Buy			23.04
Closing			30.72
Finished goods			
Opening			45.00
Restatement			1.08
			46.08
Use			(46.08)
Buy: Raw materials		23.04	
Labor		10.24	
Depreciation		12.80	
			46.08
Closing			46.08

*Average for the year
†Rounded figure.

	6.30.X2		9.30.X2		12.31.X2	Total
	104.88		107.40		110.00	106.17 *
Accounting						
	$30.54		$31.28		$32.03	
	(22.86)		(23.41)		(23.98)	$92.75
	23.60		24.16		24.75	95.55
	31.28		32.03		32.80	
	45.24		45.85		46.65	
	(45.24)		(45.85)		(46.65)	182.74
22.86		23.41		23.98		92.75
10.49		10.74		11.00		42.47
12.50		12.50		12.50		50.00
	45.85		46.65		47.48	185.22
	45.85		46.65		47.48	
Accounting						
	30.72		31.46		32.22	
	0.74		0.76		0.78	3.00
	31.46		32.22		33.00	
	(23.60)		(24.17) †		(24.75)	(95.56)
	23.60		24.17		24.75	95.56
	31.46		32.22		33.00	
	46.08		47.20		48.33	
	1.12		1.13		1.17	4.50
	47.20		48.33		49.50	
	(47.20)		(48.33)		(49.50)	191.11
23.60		24.16 †		24.75		95.55
10.49		10.74		11.00		42.47
13.11		13.43		13.75		53.09
	47.20		48.33		49.50	191.11
	47.20		48.33		49.50	

Since the time lag embodied in the two types of inventory differs (because of differences in cost composition and in length of storage), the nonrealized fraction of PLA restatement gains is also different.

For practical purposes, price level adjustment of inventories in the balance sheet may not be of major importance. But PLA costs of goods drawn from inventories are often significant in size and may have a marked effect on the profit and loss statement.[6] If the last in, first out (LIFO) method is practiced, the effect on profit and loss is reduced, but the inventory value shown in the balance sheet is meaningless and can be revalued only by appraisal methods.[7]

These conclusions hold for all types of inventories (raw materials and spare parts, goods in process, and finished goods). The difference between current (or PLA) and historical costs of goods drawn from inventories is expected to be larger the more rapidly prices are rising, because (1) for a given time lag between acquisition and realization prices will rise more, and (2) the inflationary conditions may lengthen the time lag itself since larger inventories are carried for speculative purposes.[8]

Notes

1. See Moonitz (1970, p. 473) on this subject.
2. The use of the $55 figure in cost accounting or interim profit calculations would result in an "unfair" cost penalty, causing profit to be biased downward; this bias decreases as the year progresses. Suppose that revaluation is estimated in advance to provide standard costs to be applied during the year for allocation of depreciation and overhead. The upward bias of these standards will decrease during the year. Thus production will show lower performance in earlier than in later months.
3. The quarterly conventional depreciation charges are computed from detailed schedules, as illustrated in Appendix D.
4. There is an erroneous approach to depreciation expense that identifies yearly and accumulated depreciation with each specific asset, rather than as a pool that sets aside funds for maintaining the company's productive capacity. Following this approach, it is claimed that there would be a backlog of PLA depreciation expenses as illustrated below:

	Year 1	Year 2
Replacement cost at end of year	$50.00	$55.00
PLA depreciation charges	25.00	27.50
Accumulated depreciation		52.50
Backlog (replacement cost minus, accumulated depreciation)		2.50

This approach is erroneous since seldom are the depreciation funds used for the specific item on whose account they were accumulated. Furthermore, if the cash generation earmarked as depreciation expenses is invested currently in price level linked assets, there will not be any backlog. The discussion here, as well as throughout the book, assumes that the part of internal cash generation that has been designated as depreciation expense is promptly invested in replacing assets. As shown, this enables the company to maintain its productive capacity, thus proving that a backlog does not exist.

5. This solution was suggested by Mr. A. Kedem in an unpublished seminar paper.
6. See Note 9, Chapter 11.
7. If constant purchase of materials is assumed, the LIFO method will also equalize the cost of units entering and leaving inventory. However, the value of units remaining in stock becomes completely unrelated to current costs since these units remain at their historical purchasing costs. The major difference between PLA and LIFO treatment of inventories lies in this: whereas with PLA accounting inventories are recorded at current prices, with LIFO accounting inventories are recorded at a random collection of historical prices that have no meaning.

   The various methods of recording inventory value by average cost (moving, yearly, etc.) fall between FIFO and LIFO; the cost of goods taken from inventory is closer to current cost than with FIFO, and the value of goods remaining in inventory is closer to current value than with LIFO. Yet neither withdrawal cost nor inventory value reflects actual current prices.
8. Edwards (1975, p. 237).

References

Edwards, E. O., "The State of Current Value Accounting," *Accounting Review,* April 1975, pp. 235–245.

Moonitz, M., "Price Level Accounting and Scales of Measurements," *Accounting Review,* July 1970, pp. 465–475.

Six

Formal Presentation of Profit Measurement

Profit measurement during a period of inflation is summarized in this chapter. The formal development here which follows the numerical examples in the preceding chapters, presents a simplified abstract of reality. Only important categories of the various financial statements have been included; the simplifying assumptions that have been made allow emphasis of the major effects of general and specific price changes on financial statements.

The formal expressions employed here to represent the financial statements, under conventional, PLA, and replacement-cost accounting procedures, are presented in Exhibit 6.1 at the end of the chapter. Income tax effects are presented formally in Chapter 14.

6.1 Notations and Simplifying Assumptions

The following notation is used:

A	Real assets, gross value on day X, which opens period j
$\Sigma A/L$	Accumulated depreciation to day X
F	Financial assets on day X
E	Equity on day X
D	Debt on day X
$D - F$	Net debt (i.e., financial debt less financial assets)

I	Profit for period j, following day X
S	Sales for period j, following day X
C	Out-of-pocket costs for period j, following day X
L	Asset life span
i	Preinflation interest rate on D and F
p	Inflation rate in period j = general price level change
$i + h$	Actual interest rate during inflation
h	Compensation in interest rate for inflation
N.R.G.	Net restatement gains
I.L.R.	Inflationary leverage returns

The formal model is constructed with a number of simplifying assumptions. It has been assumed that the company in question maintains stability in real terms. As shown in (6.7), this assumption can be relaxed by adding relevant terms to the model to represent real changes during period j. Real assets have been aggregated into one group (A) with an average life span L, and salvage value is assumed to be zero. In practice, these assets should be defined in smaller groupings, such as buildings, machinery, and raw material inventory, each represented by $A_1, A_2, \ldots, A_n$ with life spans $L_1, L_2, \ldots, L_n$. Financial assets (F) bear the same average interest rate $(i + h)$ as that paid on debt (D). Again, in practice, this would be unlikely, and F would bear an interest rate differing from that of debt; these could probably be split into relevant subgroups. Annual depreciation is computed according to the straight-line method, which is the simplest and most commonly used in practice.

In Sections 6.2 to 6.4 it is assumed that all price changes in goods sold (S) and in out-of-pocket costs (C) are the result of inflationary change only and do not reflect any changes in the terms of trade, that is, specific price changes. This assumption is relaxed in Section 6.5, which deals with specific price changes. In practice the abstract situation presented in Sections 6.2 to 6.4 is unlikely to occur, and adjustments for specific price changes will be necessary in most cases.

As can be seen, relaxation of the simplifying assumptions can add considerable bulk to the algebraic expressions. In practical applications these technical encumbrances can be overcome. In theoretical exposition unnecessary complexity may obscure basic patterns without imparting additional information.

6.2 Adjusted Accounting Profit Measurement

The balance sheet of a company for day X which summarizes a period of price level stability can be represented by

$$(A - \Sigma A/L)\,F = E + D \tag{6.1}$$

that is, gross fixed assets (A) less accumulated depreciation (ΣAL) plus financial assets (F) equal equity (E) plus debt (D). Inventories are, like fixed assets, "real" assets, and the effect of price level changes is the same as with fixed assets; for the sake of simplicity they have not been included here. Financial assets, on the other hand, are usually not "price level linked" and therefore are represented here.

The profit and loss statement for Period j preceding Day X can be represented by

$$I = S - C - A/L - i\,(D - F) \tag{6.2}$$

that is, profit (I) equals sales (S) less out-of-pocket costs (C), less depreciation expense (A/L), and less interest (i) on net debt $(D - F)$, assuming, for the sake of simplicity, that the average interest rate (i) on debt (D) is the same as the rate on the company's financial assets (F).

After publication of the financial statements expressed by (6.1) and (6.2), the general price level rose by p and remained at level $1 + p$ during the whole period under analysis. In line with the presentation in the preceding chapters, it is assumed that the company is stable in terms of real activity (assets, production, and sales). This makes the analysis of quantitative changes unnecessary, and the effects of price level changes on the financial statements can be more easily isolated.

As a result of the rise in the general price level, the interest rate rose from i to $i + h$. Applying this rate to the net debt $(D - F)$ provides actual interest expenses:

$$(i + h)\,(D - F) \tag{6.3}$$

The conventional profit and loss statement for the period is

$$I_{\text{con}} = (1 + p)\,S - (1 + p)\,C - A/L - (i + h)\,(D - F) \tag{6.4}$$

Conventional profit equals sales (which, although assumed to be equal in units to those of the previous period, have increased in dollar value by p, the rise in the general price level); less out-of-pocket costs (which have also risen in dollar value comparison to those of the preceding period); less depreciation, which is stated in historical-cost terms (and therefore remains unchanged); less interest on net debt (which has now risen from rate i to rate $i + h$ as compensation to the lenders for the loss in purchasing power of the loan principal and interest).

To price level adjust the profit and loss statement, depreciation expense must be adjusted to $(1 + p)(A/L)$. Thus the PLA operating profit is

$$I_{op} = (1 + p)(S - C) - (1 + p)(A/L) - (i + h)(D - F) \tag{6.5}$$

Both conventional and PLA operating profit figures are based on historical costs, the latter resulting from adjustment of lagged costs (depreciation and materials drawn from inventory). The difference between these figures:

$$I_{con} - I_{op} = (1 + p) A/L - A/L = p\,(A/L) \tag{6.6}$$

depends on the inflation rate (p) and the life span of assets (L); the greater p and smaller L, the larger is the difference. This difference equals the upward bias in conventional profit during a period of inflation if the company is financed by equity only. If net debt exists, and it is not "price level linked," the company reaps additional benefits during a period of inflation. This effect is considered in the following section.

6.3 Economic Profit Measurement

The balance sheet at the end of the period is not necessarily equal to the one that existed at the beginning of the period. Fixed assets, financial assets, equity, and debt have been added or removed. The closing balance sheet can be symbolized by

$$(A - \Sigma A/L) + (A' - A/L') + F + F' = E + E' + D + D' \tag{6.7}$$

with the prime (′) indicating the addition or subtraction that occurred during the period in the relevant item. Equation 6.7 can be separated into two equations:

$$(A - \Sigma A/L) + F = E + D \tag{6.7a}$$

$$(A' - A/L') + F' = E' + D' \tag{6.7b}$$

The first of these is merely a repetition of (6.1); the second is obviously equivalent in form. The two equations can now be dealt with separately.

The treatment will be identical, except that, whereas (6.7a), which is in fact (6.1), will be inflated by p, the inflation rate of period j, the items in (6.7b) will be inflated by the p', p'', and so on relevant to subperiods of period j. During a period of creeping inflation this p

will depend on the date on which the item entered the balance sheet, since the price level on each date is different. To shorten the discussion, only the first equation (6.7a) will be dealt with.

The net fixed asset value should be restated as follows:

$$(1 + p)\,(A - \Sigma\, A/L)$$

To express the original value of equity in terms of current purchasing power, it should also be restated as follows:

$$(1 + p)\,E$$

If it is assumed, for the sake of simplicity, that neither financial assets nor debt is price level linked, the resulting PLA balance sheet is

$$(1 + p)\,(A - \Sigma\, A/L) + F = (1 + p)E + D + p\,[(A - \Sigma\, A/L) - E] \tag{6.8}$$

The balancing term is:

$$p\big[(A - \Sigma\, A/L) - E\big] = \text{Net restatement gains} = \text{N.R.G.} \tag{6.9}$$

It can be seen that

$$\text{N.R.G.} = p[(A - \Sigma\, A/L) - \mathrm{E}\,] = p(D - F) \tag{6.10}$$

In other words, net restatement gains can be expressed by the difference between asset restatement gains, $p[A - \Sigma\,(A/L)]$, and equity maintenance adjustment, $p(E)$, or by the imputed price level increase of net debt.

$$\text{If} \qquad (A - \Sigma\ \ A/L) > E \qquad \text{or} \qquad D > F$$

there is a positive net restatement gain during a period of inflation. (The reverse holds true during deflation.)

Since the real value of equity has been maintained by $p(E)$, in (6.8) the net restatement gain (N.R.G.) is an addition to net worth. Thus the N.R.G. is profit in the economic (Hicksian) sense. The N.R.G. can remain in the balance sheet, thereby increasing the share of equity financing, or, if a loan is available, can be distributed without harming the equity position of the company. The distribution of the N.R.G. may affect the company's liquidity position in the future if the payback period of the loan is shorter than the life span of the assets. It also increases the company's risk in regard to the possibility of a future decline in price level.

Since the N.R.G. is profit, economic profit is calculated as follows:

$$I_{\text{tot}} = (1 + p)\,(S - C - A/L) - (i + h)\,(D - F) + \text{N.R.G.}$$

$$= (1 + p)\,(S - C - A/L) - (i + h)\,(D - F) + p\,[(A - \Sigma\, A/L) - E] \tag{6.11}$$

Using (6.10),

$$I_{tot} = (1 + p)(S - C - A/L) + [p - (i + h)](D - F) \tag{6.12}$$

The difference between PLA total and operating profit:

$$I_{tot} - I_{op} = p(D - F) = \text{N.R.G.} \tag{6.13}$$

is the imputed price level compensation of net debt. The difference between conventional and PLA total profit is

$$I_{con} - I_{tot} = p(A/L) - p(D - F) = p[A/L - (D - F)] \tag{6.14}$$

This difference is called the "bias of conventional profit" during a period of inflation. It depends on the inflation rate *(p),* the asset life span *(L),* and the net debt *(D – F).* Since the inflation rate *(p)* affects both net debt and depreciation *(A/L),* the bias of conventional accounting profit depends on the relative sizes of *A/L* and *D – F*. If *A/L* is larger than *D – F,* the bias is positive.

It should be recalled here that the term *p(A/L)* includes both restatement of fixed assets depreciation and realization of materials drawn from inventory. If the company is highly leveraged, the PLA total profit (economic profit) may be higher than the conventional profit. In ordinary circumstances $A/L > (D - F)$, and the conventional accounting profit will be higher than the PLA total profit.

Two types of PLA profit have been defined: (1) PLA operating profit, which is based on historical adjusted costs and therefore is in line with conventional accounting principles; and (2) PLA total profit, which includes the net restatement gain. This gain is profit in the economic sense; although it has accrued during the period, it is not recognized by conventional accounting procedures until realization during later periods. The difference between PLA and conventional profit figures depends on (1) the rate of inflation, (2) the asset life span, and (3) the relative size of the net debt, which depends in turn, on the composition of both assets and capital.

Companies can benefit from inflation to the extent that their non-linked net debt (net financial leverage) is significant. On the other hand, companies lose as a result of inflation because the depreciation adjustment is not recognized as an expense; thus profits are overstated, and income tax (and other profit-sharing payments) are levied on fictitious profit. The balance between these two factors determines the final effect that inflation has on a company.

6.4 Measuring Financial Leverage Returns

The sum required for full price level compensation of net debt is composed of (1) price level compensation *(p)* on the net debt $D - F$, and (2) interest expense at the preinflation rate on the restated net debt, that is,

$$i\,(1 + p)\,(D - F) \tag{6.15}$$

In other words, if net debt were price level linked, as it should be to receive full PLA compensation, the cost of borrowing for the period would be

$$[i + p\,(1 + i)]\,(D - F) \tag{6.16}$$

When debt is not price level linked, the actual interest expense during an inflationary period, $(i + h)\,(D - F)$ is usually less than the sum required for full PLA compensation (relation 6.16), that is,

$$p(1 + i) > h \qquad \text{when } p > 0$$

The difference is called the "inflationary leverage returns" (I.L.R.):

$$\begin{aligned} \text{I.L.R.} &= [i + p\,(1 + i)]\,(D - F) - (i + h)\,(D - F) \\ &= [p\,(1 + i) - h]\,(D - F) \end{aligned} \tag{6.17}$$

This difference is usually positive during a period of inflation because of institutional restrictions on the rate of interest (lag in the adjustment of interest rates and "rigidity" in the terms of outstanding loans).

An alternative procedure for measuring I.L.R., is to deduct required PLA compensation from actual compensation paid to net debt through the increased interest rate (relation 6.3 less relation 6.15), that is,

$$(i + h)\,(D - F) - i\,(1 + p)\,(D - F) \tag{6.18}$$

from net restatement gains (relation 6.9 or 6.10):

$$\begin{aligned} \text{I.L.R.} &= \text{N.R.G.} + i\,(1 + p)\,(D - F) - (i + h)\,(D - F) \\ &= [p(1 + i) - h]\,(D - F) \end{aligned} \tag{6.19}$$

If income is charged interest at the preinflation rate *(i)* for the company's use of debt (relation 6.15), rather than the actual interest, another profit measure — inflationfree profit — will be obtained:

$$I_{\text{iff}} = (1 + p)(S - C - A/L) - i\,(1 + p)\,(D - F) \tag{6.20}$$

Total PLA profit will then be the sum of (6.20) and (6.17) or (6.19):

$$\begin{aligned} I_{\text{tot}} &= I_{\text{iff}} + \text{I.L.R.} \\ &= (1 + p)\,(S - C - A/L) + [p - (i + h)]\,(D - F) \end{aligned} \tag{6.21}$$

This, of course, is the same as (6.12).

6.5 Measuring Replacement-Cost Profit

In replacement-cost accounting, asset restatement is carried out by applying the specific asset price index, p_A, rather than a general price index p_G as in PLA accounting. Equity, on the other hand, is restated by means of a general price index in both accounting procedures. The resulting balance sheet is as follows:

$$(1 + p_A)(A - \Sigma A/L) + F = (1 + p_G)E + D + [p_A(A - \Sigma A/L) - p_G(E)] \qquad (6.22)$$

The last term in (6.22) represents the net restatement gains, which balance the balance sheet. The absolute level of these gains depends on the ratios A/E and p_A-p_G; the greater these ratios, the larger are the N.R.G.

The difference between the PLA balance sheet (equation 6.8) and the replacement-cost balance sheet (equation 6.22) is determined by the price index applied for restating the assets $[A - \Sigma A/L]$. In the former p-p_G has been used; in the latter, p_A. The difference between two price indices is called the "terms of trade" (Chapter 8).

If the general price index (p_G) is considered as "standard" (according to cost accounting terminology) and the specific index as "actual," the difference between the two balance sheets:

$$(p_A - p_G)(A - \Sigma A/L) \qquad (6.23)$$

is called the "terms of trade variance."

Replacement-cost operating profit is

$$I_{op_{rc}} = (1 + p_G)(S - C) - (1 + p_A)(A/L) - (i + h)(D - F) \qquad (6.24)$$

Adding net restatement gains, as calculated in (6.22), to this figure provides the total replacement-cost profit:

$$I_{tot_{rc}} = (1 + p_G)(S - C) - (1 + p_A)(A/L) - (i + h)(D - F) + [p_A(A - \Sigma A/L) - p_G(E)] \qquad (6.25)$$

Up to this point the discussion has assumed that sales and out-of-pocket costs rose at the same rate as the average price level. (Hence the original S and C variables increased in accordance with the general price index, p or p_G). In practice, however, specific price changes may affect these variables. When the actual specific price level changes (general p_G; assets, p_A; in sales, p_S; and in out-of-pocket costs, p_C) are taken into account, the adjusted total profit is

$$I_{\text{tot}_{\text{spec}}} = (1 + p_S)S - (1 + p_C)C - (1 + p_A)(A/L) - (i + h)(D - F) + [p_A(A - \Sigma A/L) - p_G(E)] \quad (6.26)$$

Relation (6.26) expresses, as a matter of fact, the replacement-cost profit because the variables $(1 + p_S)S$ and $(1 + p_C)C$ present actual sales and out-of-pocket costs, respectively. Relations (6.12) and (6.21), which express PLA total profit, can serve as a "standard" if $(1 + p)S$ and $(1 + p)C$ present not actual data, but rather expected data. Deducting the actual data from the standard data will provide the terms of trade variance of each item (Chapter 8).

Exhibit 6.1. Formal Presentation of Financial Statements

Type of Statement	Formula	Relation
Preinflation period		
Balance sheet	$(A - \Sigma A/L) + F = E + D$	6.1
Profit and loss	$I = S - C - A/L - i(D - F)$	6.2
Inflationary period		
Conventional accounting		
Profit and loss	$I_{con} = (1 + p)(S - C) - A/L - (i + h)(D - F)$	6.4
PLA accounting		
Balance sheet	$(1 + p)(A - \Sigma A/L) + F = (1 + p)E + D + p[(A - \Sigma A/L) - E]$	6.8
	or, $(1 + p)(A - \Sigma A/L) + F = (1 + p)E + D + p(D - F)$	
Profit and loss		
Operating	$I_{op} = (1 + p)(S - C) - (1 + p)(A/L) - (i + h)(D - F)$	6.5
Total	$I_{tot} = (1 + p)(S - C) - (1 + p)(A/L) - (i + h)(D - F)$ $+ p[(A - \Sigma A/L) - E]$	6.11
	or, $= (1 + p)(S - C) - (1 + p)(A/L) + [p - (i + h)](D - F)$	6.12
Inflationfree	$I_{iff} = (1 + p)(S - C) - (1 + p)(A/L) - i(1 + p)(D - F)$	6.20
Replacement-Cost Accounting		
Balance sheet	$(1 + p_A)(A - \Sigma A/L) + F = (1 + p_G)E + D + [p_A(A - \Sigma A/L) - p_G(E)]$	6.22
Profit and loss		
Operating	$I_{op_{rc}} = (1 + p_G)(S - C) - (1 + p_A)(A/L) - (i + h)(D - F)$	6.24
Total	$I_{tot_{rc}} = (1 + p_G)(S - C) - (1 + p_A)(A/L) - (1 + h)(D - F) + [p_A(A - \Sigma A/L) - p_G(E)]$	6.25

Part Three

Analysis for Decisions

Seven

Managerial Accounting Reports

During inflationary periods profit and loss statements report downward-biased costs and upward-biased profits; the bias is reversed during deflation. This bias is often more serious at the departmental level. Information on the company's segments (departments, products, resources, etc.) is used for decisions regarding resource allocation, product mix, prices, and control. Departmental profit and loss reports should be adjusted to price levels, parallel to company profit and loss statements. The economic costs of inputs, such as the implicit cost of capital and the replacement cost of assets, should be introduced into the reports.

The best procedure for estimating the service cost of assets is to determine their replacement cost by appraisal procedures. Control of performance is usually carried out on departmental profit. For appropriate control, inflationfree cost and profit figures should be used.

7.1 Distortions in Conventional Financial Reports

The distortion of profit and loss statements (costs and profit) and of balance sheets (assets and equity values) during a period of inflation is a function of several factors:

1. The rate and duration of price level change: The more rapid the change of price level (in one direction), the greater is the bias.
2. The shares of lagged costs (depreciation and materials drawn from

inventories, assuming the FIFO method) in total costs: The greater this share, the greater is the bias of cost and profit. In other words, the greater the asset intensity (which determines the amount of lagged costs), the more biased is the profit.

3. The time lag between acquisition of inputs and their realization through output: The more distant the acquisition date, the greater is the bias (assuming that inflation exists throughout the period).
4. The financial leverage: The greater the leverage, composed of nonlinked loans, the lower is the bias.
5. The rate of asset growth: The more rapid this growth, the "younger" is the average age of the relevant asset group, and the lower is the bias.
6. The method of inventory calculations: With the FIFO method, the bias of cost and profit is greater than with the LIFO method; the opposite holds for the bias of inventory value (Section 14.3).

Upward-biased reported profit during inflation tends to cause overspending and withdrawal of resources from the firm (through dividends, bonuses, wages, taxes, etc.) beyond its real profitability, causing the firm to be worse off than it was in the past. This situation may also engender liquidity problems, especially since the depreciation funds during a period of inflation fall short of covering the needs for plant and equipment renewal.

Downward-biased recorded asset values during inflation may cause insufficient investment in plant and equipment renewal. Downward-biased recorded equity value misrepresents the real financial mix, and shareholders may lose the benefit of utilizing the optimal financial leverage that could be at their disposal. The upward-biased reported profit and downward-biased recorded asset and equity values will show exaggerated returns on capital.

These dangers may be summarized by stating that upward-biased reported profit tends to cause capital erosion (Chapter 13). During a period of deflation most of the above conclusions would be reversed. The distortions in conventional accounting data during a period of price level changes also have implications for the national economy (Section 15.2).

Downward-biased cost and upward-biased profit may affect departmental reports much more than company statements because the share of lagged costs in total costs differs among departments. The greater the share of these costs in a department, the greater will be the bias. The distorted cost and profit figures may cause erroneous decisions in regard to expansion or contraction of the production levels of various departments. If prices are set on the basis of recorded costs, they will be biased downward during an inflationary period. Downward-biased recorded asset values during inflation may cause (1) insufficient investment in plant and equipment renewal, (2) erroneous decisions in regard to the replacement of individual assets, and (3) insufficient insurance coverage. Biased inventory value may cause erroneous decisions on inventory volume.

Distorted cost and profit figures make control difficult, since the budgeted standards are given in dollars of different purchasing power from those to which they are later compared. Interdepartment comparisons lose meaning because the share of lagged costs differs from one department to another. Time-series comparisons of costs, profit, returns on capital, and so on are also meaningless unless the data are restated and updated (Chapter 12). For example, a reduction in production efficiency during a period of inflation would not necessarily be discovered by conventional reports.

7.2 Appraisal of Asset Replacement Cost

Two terms have been used interchangeably in this book: (1) "price level adjusted" or "restated," and (2) "revalued." Actually they represent two different approaches. With the first, the acquisition cost (or net value) of an asset is inflated by a general price level index number. This method, in effect, restates historical costs in terms of dollars reflecting present purchasing power. It involves "price level adjustment" only; because of its foundation on historical "actual" cost, it is highly compatible with accounting procedures.

Another approach is to ascertain replacement cost. Replacement costing of fixed assets requires appraisal of each asset in terms, not of adjusting historical cost, but of estimating its alternative cost. Many assets will be revalued upward; others, redundant or obsolete, will be revalued downward.

There is an intermediate approach: inflating the historical costs of assets by a specific price index, as carried out in Section 3.5. This procedure provides an approximation of replacement cost. Revaluation with specific price indices assumes that no technological changes took place since the date of acquisition.[1] Furthermore, the new value is a function of asset age (restated acquisition cost minus accumulated restated depreciation), but the productive capacity of each individual asset is not necessarily directly connected to its age. There may be an "old" asset that provides better services than an equivalent "young" asset. Thus, if information on the productive capacity of each asset is required, the assets must be appraised.[2]

Appraisal of replacement cost requires inspection and examination of each asset and the collection of corresponding price data from the market. This is often carried out by an appraiser, aided by an engineer. For many assets there may not be a market price because of technological changes. Even when no technological changes have occurred, an asset similar in type to the one in question may be difficult to locate in the market.

The real value of an asset is influenced by its age, condition, and technology. The productive potential of the existing asset relative to a new one must be evaluated. Direct maintenance costs and indirect maintenance expenses due to interruptions in production need to be compared to those for a new asset. Also, different operational costs due to technological changes must be taken into account. If an active second-hand market for the asset exists, the appraisal is relatively easy. The market price "objectively" reflects the economics of all the factors mentioned above. When applying market prices to revaluation assessment, after-tax replacement cost should be recorded.[3]

Appraisal involves much greater complexity than mere price level adjustment and is usually a tedious job. On the other hand, it provides important information to management regarding operational and investment decisions. "Revaluation" includes price level adjustment since it is expressed in terms of present purchasing power dollars, but it is more comprehensive. It rests on alternative cost and not historical cost; for this reason it is more compatible with production engineering and economics.[4]

Revaluation of a company's assets by appraising their replacement costs provides data on the cost of setting up a company that exactly duplicates the existing production capacity. The difference between the sales value of the company as a whole and the aggregate appraised net value of the individual assets provides an estimate of the company's goodwill. Furthermore, the appraised value of assets provides data on the effective asset stock available for production. Price level adjustment, on the other hand, provides updated data on the historical investment in asset stock. Comparing the two provides an index of the company's efficiency regarding capital investment in productive assets.[5]

Stocks and raw material inventories are best revalued by appraising their current market prices. For these assets market prices are usually available, since they are traded actively on the market and no adjustment for age is usually required. The use of a specific price change index for each stock or type of raw material, rather than for a group of these, will provide the current market price.

In summary, there are several methods of asset revaluation. At one extreme, the historical costs of assets are restated to current money terms (the dollar's purchasing power) by using a general price index. At the other extreme, asset current values are appraised by relying on market replacement costs and checking the productive potentials of the assets. In between, the historical costs of assets are restated by using specific or group price indices.[6] These approaches are summarized in Exhibit 7.1.

Exhibit 7.1. Summary of Approaches to Asset Restatement and Revaluation

	Procedure	Use of Results
Restatement	Historical cost adjusted by general index	Company's financial statements
	Historical cost adjusted by specific indices	Company's segment analysis
Revaluation	Current cost–Appraised wear and tear	Company's segment analysis

7.3 Profit Measurement in Departments

Profit and cost at the departmental level are required for three purposes: (1) performance evaluation, (2) decision making (regarding expansion or contraction, making, leasing, or buying, etc.), and (3) price setting. To serve these purposes, departmental profit must be calculated after costs are adjusted and all cost items are charged to the appropriate departments, including cost of capital, overhead, and administration and selling expenses.

Advanced cost accounting procedures for calculating departmental profit charge the costs that the production process should cover in the long run, including cost of capital, to the various departments.[7] Conventional cost accounting procedures, on the other hand, charge actual interest expense rather than the implicit overall cost of capital. Therefore, since only a part of the company's capital (debt) carries an explicit cost (interest), financial accounting statements show lower capital costs than the total imputed cost of capital. When this practice is carried over into cost accounting, it causes a downward bias of costs charged to the various departments. The bias is significant in departments where the production process is capital intensive and, of course, causes an upward bias of the profit figure in such cases.

Consider the Manufacturing Leverage Company (illustrated in Exhibits 4.4, 4.5, and Appendix C). Suppose that the company, which is housed in a rented building, is organized into two departments. Each department produces a specific product; Department A utilizes labor and materials, while Department B utilizes labor, materials, and the two machines in its production process. As before, it is assumed that production equals sales. Further data are provided in Exhibit 7.2.

Determining PLA departmental profit requires: (1) charging interim depreciation expenses, which are inflated by creeping price rise indices rather than by the year-end price index (as explained in Section 5.1)[8], and (2) applying specific price change indices for asset revaluation, rather than using the general price level index (as suggested in Section 3.5). However, for the sake of simplified presentation, both procedures are not practiced here.

In accordance with the suggested procedure, imputed interest is charged on the revalued assets. On the assumption that the long-run inflationfree cost of capital is 15%, this rate is used in preparing the PLA departmental profit and loss statement, as illustrated in Exhibits 7.2 and 7.3.

Thus, in 19X1, imputed interest is $11.25 (15% on $75 assets) and, in 19X2, $12.38 (15% on $82.50).

This procedure implies that capital should earn at least 15% income in addition to preserving its real value during inflation. Profit earned by the departments over and above costs, which include the cost of capital at its long-run rate, provides returns to entrepreneurship and risk and should be considered as true operating returns.

The PLA departmental profits are comparable among departments since they are computed after full costs have been charged.

Thus the PLA profit of Department B (which uses all the company's machines) is comparable to that of Department A. Under conventional procedures, on the other hand, Department B's profit is upward biased since only $2.40 actual interest is charged rather than the $11.25 imputed cost of capital.[9]

The PLA departmental profits are also comparable over time since they are computed after price level adjustment has been made.

Thus, in 19X2, when prices rose by 10% but physical production was equal to that in 19X1, the PLA profits of the departments are also higher by 10% ($5.50 and $4.12 in 19X2, compared to $5 and $3.75 in 19X1).

The illustrated procedures require two control accounts in addition to the usual departmental accounts: (1) an interest account, to which charges of imputed interest to departments are credited and actual interest payments are debited; and (2) a capital account, to which asset restatement gains are credited and equity maintenance adjustment is debited. The profit figures in these accounts ($8.85 in 19X1, $11.18 in 19X2) represent returns to equity under conditions of 40% debt financing and 15% cost of capital.[10] The company's profit (Exhibit 7.4) has been decomposed into departmental profit (which represents returns to entrepreneurship and risk) and equity returns (which represent returns under a given financial situation).

In summary, the departmental costs, as calculated here, are real full costs: full, since all cost items (including implicit inflationfree cost of capital) are included; real, since they are price level adjusted. Hence, both the cost figures and the profit figures are suitable for decision making and performance evaluation.[11]

7.4 Inflationfree Profit

The PLA profit measures that are calculated for a company as a whole (operating and total profit) are not necessarily suitable for performance evaluation. Both PLA operating and total profit figures include inflationary leverage returns that are due to institutional restrictions on the rate of interest, if the company employs financial leverage. The profit measure to be developed for performance evaluation during a period of price level changes should represent the results of operations only, neutralizing external effects.

Very probably interest rates on loans will rise as inflation sets in (or increases in rate). This represents compensation for the loss of purchasing power of the original loan principal and interest; it also reduces the inflationary leverage benefit to equity holders.

To arrive at a long-run profit figure, neutralized from inflationary leverage returns, both effects—those of restatement gains and those of higher interest payments—must be considered. Inflationary leverage returns can then be reported separately.

Exhibit 7.2. Manufacturing Leverage Company
Departmental Profit and Loss Analysis for the Year 19X1
(No Inflation, 100% Fixed Assets, 60% Equity, 15% Cost of Capital)

	Conventional			PLA			
	Total	Dept. A	Dept. B	Total	Dept. A	Dept. B	Interest Account
Income							
Sales (production)	$200.00	$80.00	$120.00	$200.00	$80.00	$120.00	—
Interest (imputed cost of capital)	—	—	—	11.25	—	—	$11.25
Total income	200.00	80.00	120.00	211.25	80.00	120.00	11.25
Expenses							
Materials	60.00	24.00	36.00	60.00	24.00	36.00	—
Labor	60.00	50.00	10.00	60.00	50.00	10.00	—
Rent, insurance, etc.	10.00	1.00	9.00	10.00	1.00	9.00	—
Interest (actual)	2.40	—	2.40	2.40	—	—	2.40
Total out-of-pocket costs	132.40	75.00	57.40	132.40	75.00	55.00	2.40
Interest (imputed)	—	—	—	11.25	—	11.25	—
Depreciation	50.00	—	50.00	50.00	—	50.00	—
Total expenses	182.40	75.00	107.40	193.65	75.00	116.25	2.40
Profit	17.60	5.00	12.60	17.60	5.00	3.75	8.85*

*This figure indicates equity returns.

Exhibit 7.3. Manufacturing Leverage Company
Departmental Profit and Loss Analysis for the Year 19X2
(10% Inflation, 100% Fixed Assets, 60% Equity, 15% Cost of Capital)

	Conventional			PLA				
	Total	Dept. A	Dept. B	Total	Dept. A	Dept. B	Interest Account	Capital Account
Income								
Sales (production)	$220.00	$88.00	$132.00	$220.00	$88.00	$132.00	—	—
Interest (imputed cost of capital)	—	—	—	12.38	—	—	$12.38	—
Asset restatement gains	—	—	—	7.50	—	—	—	$7.50
Total income	220.00	88.00	132.00	239.88	88.00	132.00	12.38	7.50
Expenses								
Materials	66.00	26.40	39.60	66.00	26.40	39.60	—	—
Labor	66.00	55.00	11.00	66.00	55.00	11.00	—	—
Rent, insurance, etc.	11.00	1.10	9.90	11.00	1.10	9.90	—	—
Interest (actual)	4.20	—	4.20	4.20	—	—	4.20	—
Total out-of-pocket costs	147.20	82.50	64.70	147.20	82.50	60.50	4.20	—
Interest (imputed)	—	—	—	12.38	—	12.38	—	—
Depreciation	50.00	—	50.00	55.00	—	55.00	—	—
Equity maintenance adjustment	—	—	—	4.50	—	—	—	4.50
Total expenses	197.20	82.50	114.70	219.08	82.50	127.88	4.20	4.50
Profit	22.80	5.50	17.30	20.80	5.50	4.12	8.18	3.00

Exhibit 7.4. Manufacturing Leverage Company
PLA Profit and Loss Statement for the Year 19X2
Decomposition into Departmental Profit and Equity Returns

Departmental Operations Statement

Sales			$220.00
Out-of-pocket costs		$143.00	
Imputed interest on assets (cost of capital 15%)		12.38	
Depreciation		55.00	
			210.38
Departmental profit			9.62

Equity Returns Statement

Asset restatement gains	$7.50		
Less equity maintenance adjustment	(4.50)		
		3.00	
Imputed cost of capital	12.38		
Less actual interest	(4.20)		
		8.18	
Equity returns			11.18
PLA total profit			20.80

Source: Data from Exhibits 4.5 and 7.3.

Detailed calculations of inflationary leverage returns were carried out in Section 4.5; a different procedure is followed here to obtain the same result. Instead of charging operations with actual interest paid, interest at a long-run inflationfree rate on restated debt is imputed to operations.

The inflationfree interest rate on debt is not necessarily the same for all companies; it is influenced by such factors as financial leverage, past performance, and industry risk.[12] If the financial leverage is to be at all effective, this rate must obviously be lower than the rate that represents the company's long-run (inflationfree) cost of capital.

Restated debt is that which will maintain the equity–debt ratio as it was before the asset restatement adjustment. The procedure calculates, for outstanding loans (as for equity), the price level adjustment required to maintain real value. By imputing inflationfree interest to the "adjusted" loans, income compensation for both the recorded value and the restated adjustment of debt capital is computed.

Again consider the Manufacturing Leverage Company. The preinflation rate of interest of 8% is considered to be the inflationfree rate. Debt capital is restated from \$30 to \$33. Inflationfree profit, which summarizes the "Operations Statement" in Exhibit 7.5, consists of returns to equity, excluding inflationary leverage returns. It does, however, include regular leverage returns (Section 4.3).

Inflationary leverage returns are computed separately. The procedure involves balance sheet as well as profit and loss accounts since total indemnification for price level changes is split between these two classifications of accounts. The equity maintenance adjustment is deducted from the asset restatement gains (both are balance sheet accounts), leaving a balance that is a profit and loss (income) account. This balance, \$3 in Exhibit 7.5, represents debt capital's "share" in the asset restatement gains. A portion of this "share" has been paid to the lenders through increased interest charges (the interest rate rose from 8% to 14%). The difference of \$1.56 between actual interest expense and imputed inflationfree interest charges constitutes the price level compensation paid to the lenders. This sum is deducted from the net restatement gain (the leverage "share" in restatement gains), leaving \$1.44 inflationary leverage returns (see relation 6.20). A graphical illustration of these computations is presented in Exhibit 7.6.

The total yearly PLA profit (\$20.80) has been decomposed into two components. The first, inflationfree profit, represents the results of operations in real terms, not including short-run inflationary leverage returns. Thus the

Exhibit 7.5. Manufacturing Leverage Company
PLA Profit and Loss Statements for the Year 19X2
Decomposition into "Inflationfree" and "Inflationary Returns"

Operations Statement		
Sales		\$220.00
Out-of-pocket costs	\$143.00	
Imputed inflationfree interest	2.64	
Depreciation	55.00	
		200.64
Inflationfree profit		19.36
Inflationary Leverage Returns Statement		
Asset restatement gains	\$ 7.50	
Less equity maintenance adjustment	(4.50)	
Net restatement (leverage) gains		3.00
Imputed interest	2.64	
Less actual interest	(4.20)	
Leverage gains paid to lenders		(1.56)
Inflationary leverage returns		1.44
PLA total profit		20.80

Source: Data from Exhibits 4.5 and 7.3.

profit for 19X2 ($19.36) equals in real terms the preinflation profit for 19X1 ($17.60 + 10% PLA). The second component, inflationary leverage returns, represents the results of short-run institutional restrictions on the interest rate ($1.44), as explained in Section 4.5.

7.5 Company and Department Profit for Performance Evaluation

Price level adjusted department profit may be used for performance evaluation since it is comparable to other departmental figures. This is so because it is not distorted by differences in the intensity of capital in the various departments. Furthermore, it may serve for time-series comparisons, that is, comparisons of periodic profit figures over time, because it is not distorted by changes in capital intensity or in the price level.[13]

Inflationfree profit is designed for performance evaluation of the company as a whole. It may serve for time-series comparisons because it is not affected by external changes in the rate of interest resulting from the existence of inflation.

Since performance evaluation is made at both company and departmental levels, two types of PLA profit figures should be measured and reported for this purpose: (1) inflationfree profit for the company as a whole, and (2) departmental profit for each department. In both

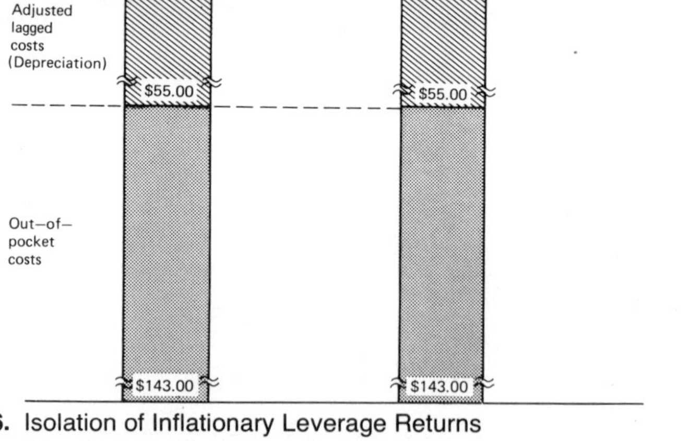

Exhibit 7.6. Isolation of Inflationary Leverage Returns Manufacturing Leverage Company

cases PLA profit is decomposed into two components, based on restatement of balance sheet items and on the imputed inflationfree cost of capital (or cost of debt) that is charged on restated sums. The two procedures are compared in Exhibit 7.7 by means of a summary and in Exhibit 7.8 by a schematic review of the main procedures and relevant computations regarding the Manufacturing Leverage Company.

Exhibit 7.7. Summary of PLA procedures for Measuring Company's and Departments' Profits

Procedure or Measure	Company	Department
Measured profit	1. Inflationfree profit 2. Inflationary leverage returns	1. Departmental profit 2. Equity returns
Asset restatement by:	General price index	Appraisal or specific price index or general price index
Equity maintenance adjustment by:	General price index	General price index
Debt restatement by:	General price index	
Imputed cost of capital on:	Restated debt	Revalued assets
Rate of cost of	Inflationfree cost of debt	Inflationfree cost of capital

The diagram in Exhibit 7.8 shows the parallelism of the procedures of PLA profit measurement for company and departmental reports.

1. In both computations asset restatement (revaluation) affects cost measurement through adjusted depreciation expenses and adjusted costs of goods drawn from inventory. In this manner asset restatement corrects distortions due to time lag.

2. In both computations capital restatement affects cost measurement through adjusted financial costs. For company reports financial costs are computed on the basis of restated debt capital, which bears the long-run, inflationfree cost of debt; for departmental reports, financial costs are computed on the basis of restated total capital, which bears the long-run, inflationfree cost of capital. In this manner capital restatement corrects distortions due to leverage.

Exhibit 7.8. Diagram of Company and Departmental Reports for a Stable Leverage Company Manufacturing Leverage Company's Financial Statements for the Year 19X2*

Balance Sheet Accounts (Exhibit 4.5)

Assets	
PLA net assets, end of year†	$82.50
– PLA recorded net assets, beginning of year	(75.00)
– Asset restatement gains	7.50
– Equity maintenance adjustment	(4.50)
= Net restatement (leverage) gains	3.00

Equity and Liabilities	
PLA equity, end of year†	$49.50
– PLA recorded equity, beginning of year	(45.00)
= Equity maintenance adjustment	4.50
+ PLA loans, end of year	33.00
– PLA recorded loans, beginning of year	(30.00)
= Equity and liabilities adjustment	7.50
(= Asset restatement gains)	

Profit and Loss Account for Company Reports (Exhibit 7.5)

Sales	$220.00	
– Actual interest	(4.20)	
– Conventional depreciation	(50.00)	
– Other costs	(143.00)	
= Conventional profit	22.80	
+ Conventional depreciation	50.00	
– PLA depreciation	(55.00)	
= PLA operating profit	17.80	
+ Actual interest	4.20	
– Imputed cost of debt	(2.64)	
= Inflationfree profit		19.36
Net restatement (leverage) gains	3.00	
– Leverage gains paid to lenders	(1.56)	
Inflationary leverage returns		1.44
		20.80

Profit and Loss Account for Departmental Reports (Exhibit 7.3)

Conventional profit	$22.80	
+ Conventional depreciation	50.00	
– PLA depreciation	(55.00)	
+ Actual interest	4.20	
– Imputed cost of capital	(12.38)	
= Departmental profit		9.62
Net restatement gains	3.00	
+ Imputed cost of capital	12.38	
	(4.20)	
= Equity returns		11.18
		20.80

8% 15%

*—→Direct transfer; - -→Basis for calculation.

†Restatement of PLA recorded figures, beginning of year.

3. In both computations the equity maintenance adjustment is charged to income, maintaining the real value of equity in the firm.

These adjustments result in profit figures that are comparable over time (comparison of reports from various periods) and also among segments (comparison of reports from various departments). The adjustment of accounting procedures to the reality of price level changes result in financial statements that better serve the various demands of decision makers.

Notes

1. It is plausible to assume that, on the average, the inflated historical cost of a given asset will be higher than its actual current replacement cost. This is so because new technology is usually acquired only if it assures lower cost per unit of output, except when it carries additional, nonpecuniary benefits such as prestige or convenience. Although, theoretically, price indices should take this factor into account, the task is difficult. We are indebted to Dr. L. Shashua for indicating this point.
2. For a recent review of this subject see Backer (1973, Chapter 8). See also, for example, American Institute of Real Estate Appraisers (1967) and Babcock (1968).
3. See Goldschmidt and Smidt (1969, pp. 323-324).
4. For two replacement-cost models see Edwards and Bell (1961) and Chambers (1966), and for the application of these see McKeown (1973), and Gray (1975). See also Beidleman (1973).
5. See Shashua et al. (1973).
6. The results of applying the three revaluation approaches are not necessarily correlated to each other. An interesting example of applying these approaches (replacement cost, restatement by specific price indices, restatement by a general price index) is provided by Stickney and Green (1974, p. 27) in regard to the cost of electricity utility plants in the United States:

Year	Average Cost per Kilowatt of New Plant Equipment	Specific Price Index	GNP Price Deflator
1955	$135.45	82.5	90.86
1960	124.47	100.0	103.29
1965	102.73	82.6	110.86
1970	123.95	82.5	135.23

7. Let us quote four sources on this subject:

> The interest cost of capital assets used in the manufacturing process should be included as an element of product cost. This cost should be assigned to products in the same way as depreciation on plant and equipment (Anthony 1973, p. 93).
>
> We argue that the cost of using equity capital funds is also a cost of holding assets even though the cost of acquiring the services of equity capital does not meet the criteria of an accountable cost (Staubus 1971, p. 35).
>
> The cost of capital (implicit interest) is charged to the users of capital. This procedure is contrary to accepted accounting principles. The costs related to the holding of capital assets are composed of implicit costs, such as interest and change in the asset's value (depreciation and obsolescence), and explicit costs, such as maintenance, insurance, and taxes. These costs are charged to the users of the asset's services (Goldschmidt 1970, p. 12).
>
> Interest based on "productive" capital, such as plant and machinery,...is an element of cost just the same as are materials or wages (Carter and Carter 1942, pp. 828, 829).

8. For practical purposes it may be advisable to compute depreciation expenses according to year end asset values. This procedure causes a downward bias in reported annual PLA profit, an effect in line with the accounting principle of conservatism.
9. This bias is often augmented by the convention of allocating administrative, selling, and finance expenses to departments via an overhead charge based on actual labor cost.
10. The returns to equity for both years may be computed as follows:

	19X1	19X2
Net restatement gains (leverage gains)	—	$ 3.00
Plus imputed cost of capital (15%)	$11.25	12.38
Less actual interest	(2.40)	(4.20)
Equity returns	8.85	11.18

11. These cost and profit figures should be used for decision making. The decision maker, should, however, take into consideration additional factors such as risk, special finance (e.g., special loans that increase the optimal leverage), and special customers and suppliers.
12. See Reisman (1971, Chapter 13) and Reisman and Rao (1973, Chapter 7) on this subject.
13. Note that time-series comparisons of the PLA data in Exhibit 4.5 required the deduction of the inflationary leverage returns ($1.44) from total profit. Here this item is absorbed by the interest account, and departmental profits are comparable without further adjustment.

References

American Institute of Real Estate Appraisers, *The Appraisal of Real Estate,* Chicago, 1967.

Anthony, R. N., "Accounting for the Cost of Equity," *Harvard Business Review,* November–December 1973, pp. 88-102.

Babcock, H. A., *Appraisal Principles and Procedures,* Irwin, Homewood, Ill., 1968.

Backer, M., *Current Value Accounting,* Financial Executive Research Foundation, New York, 1973.

Beidleman, C. R., *Valuation of Used Capital Assets,* Studies in Accounting Research No. 7, American Accounting Association, Sarasota, Fla., 1973.

Carter, R. N. and W. R. Carter, *Advanced Accounts,* Pitman, London, 1942.

Chambers, R. J., *Accounting, Evaluation and Economic Behavior,* Prentice-Hall, Englewood Cliffs, N.J., 1966.

Edwards, E. O. and P. W. Bell, *The Theory and Measurement of Business Income,* University of California Press, Berkeley and Los Angeles, 1961.

Goldschmidt, Y., *Information for Management Decisions—A System for Economic Analysis and Accounting Procedures,* Cornell University Press, Ithaca and London, 1970.

Goldschmidt, Y. and S. Smidt, "Valuing the Firm's Durable Assets for Managerial Information," *Accounting Review,* April 1969, pp. 317-329.

Gray, S. J., "Price Changes and Company Profits in the Securities Market," *Abacus,* June 1975, pp. 71-85.

McKeown, J. C., "Comparative Application of Market and Cost Based Accounting Models," *Journal of Accounting Research,* Spring 1973, pp. 62-99.

Reisman, A., *Managerial and Engineering Economics,* Allyn & Bacon, Boston, 1971.

Reisman, A., and A. K. Rao, *Discounted Cash Flow Analysis: Stochastic Extensions,* Monograph Series No. 1, American Institute of Industrial Engineers, Norcross, Ga., 1973.

Shashua, L., Y. Goldschmidt, and G. Levkovitz, "*Revaluation of the Productive Assets in the Kibbutz Sector*" Working Paper 67/73, Heshev, Tel Aviv, 1973. In Hebrew.

Staubus, G. J., *Activity Costing and Input–Output Accounting,* Irwin, Homewood, Ill., 1971.

Stickney, C. P. and D. O. Green, "No Price Level Adjusted Statements, Please (Pleas)," *CPA Journal,* January 1974, pp. 25–31.

Eight

Terms of Trade and Speculation

The analyses and illustrations in this book have assumed, for the sake of simplicity, that prices of all items change simultaneously at the same rate at the same time, except for one item—interest (and equipment, in the illustration in Section 3.5). In practice, however, the forces of supply and demand affect price changes in individual commodities in different directions and at different rates. This phenomenon is noticeable during both periods of price level changes and periods when the general price level is stable; it is not related to the purchasing power of money.

Specific price change differentials cause changes in the terms of trade and are the reason for speculation. This chapter indicates how to measure the terms of trade effect and speculative gains; it incorporates these measurements into profit measurement of the firm and of its departments.

8.1 Isolating the Effect of Terms of Trade[1]

Differentials in specific price changes are called "changes in the terms of trade." For example, if the price of a given commodity remains stable while the inputs used in producing it rise, it is said that the terms of trade of this commodity have worsened. The plastics industry in the United States illustrates such a situation. As shown at the end of Section 1.1, the index of plastics prices declined by 16% from 1960 to 1970 while the wholesale price index rose by 16%.

The change in terms of trade is measured by the difference between the specific price change and the general price level change.

In cost accounting terminology, when the general price level is stable, the base period price is considered to be the "standard price"; the difference between the actual price and the standard is termed the "price variance." During an inflationary period, price variance can be divided into two components: (1) the change in the general price level, and (2) the change in specific prices. Under these conditions, the standard price has to be determined by restating base period prices in accordance with the change in the general price index.

Consider the Manufacturing Leverage Company. As in former illustrations, the general price level rose in 19X2 by 10% and the interest rate by 75% (from 8% to 14%). In addition, suppose that the following specific price increases took place during 19X2: sales, 10%; out-of-pocket costs, 12%; equipment, 7%. The relevant PLA financial statements are presented in Exhibit 8.1. These statements are a consolidation of Exhibits 4.5 and 3.5 with the addition of changes in the out-of-pocket costs.

The terms of trade effect on total profit is isolated in Exhibit 8.2, which illustrates the adaptation of cost accounting "price variance analysis" to terms of trade changes. Since inflation exists, the standards are determined by inflating the sales and cost items for 19X1 by 10% (when standards are prepared in advance, the expected inflation rate should be used for this purpose). The differences between the actual data and the standard figures are called "variances".[2]

The change in terms of trade caused the following variances: unfavorable variances in out-of-pocket costs ($2.60) and in net restatement gains ($2.25); a favorable variance of $1.50 in depreciation. A graphical illustration of the isolation of these variances is presented in Exhibit 8.3.[3] The variance analysis of interest differs from the other items. The standard interest ($2.64) results from inflating the loans by 10%, on which inflationfree interest (8%) is charged. The result is inflationfree profit. After deducting the actual price level compensation that has been paid to the creditors ($1.56), the PLA operating profit can be calculated.

The expected PLA total profit for 19X2, assuming no change in physical production and sales, as well as 10% inflation, was $20.80. Changes in the terms of trade caused the profit to be only $17.45. The terms of trade worsened the company's situation. The total unfavorable variance ($3.35) represents the pure effect that the change in terms of trade had on the company's profit.

8.2 Terms of Trade Effect on Departmental Profit

Since the specific price indices change at different rates and even in different directions (i.e., the price level of one commodity increases, that of another decreases, as illustrated in Section 1.3), aggregation of items in financial statements may cushion or even cancel extreme terms of trade effects. For example, the 10% increase in the sales price level in the illustration of Section 8.1 is an aggregate figure. It might be that the price of one product rose by more than 10%, and that of another by less. Or two departments may use different types of inputs; the price changes in these inputs may diverge considerably. Therefore analysis of the terms of trade effect on segments of a company (departments, products) provides more information than analysis on the company as a whole.

Consider again the Manufacturing Leverage Company. Consolidating the data in Exhibits 8.1 and 8.2 and the departmental profit analysis in Exhibits 7.2 and 7.3 makes it possible to calculate a detailed terms of trade variance analysis. First, the standards should be determined, as shown in Exhibit 8.4. The 19X1 departmental data are inflated by 10% because of the general price level increase. The figures in the capital account result from inflating the asset and equity values by 10%.

Isolation of the terms of trade effect on departmental profit, that is, terms of trade variance analysis, is carried out in Exhibit 8.5. Total variance here ($3.35) equals, of course, that computed for the company as a whole in Exhibit 8.2. The total variances of the individual items (sales, out-of-pocket costs, etc.,) are equal as well.

The importance of the variance analysis illustrated lies in the information it provides on variances in the individual departments. Whereas in Department A there is an unfavorable variance ($1.50), in Department B the variance ($0.54) is favorable. Mainly because of a smaller percentage increase in asset values than in the general price level, an unfavorable capital income variance (interest and capital accounts) of $2.39 developed. In summary, the relevant variances are as follows:

	Variance	Standard Profit	Variance in Relation to Profit
Department A	$(1.50)	$ 5.50	–27%
Department B	0.54	4.12	+13%
Capital income	(2.39)	11.18	–21%
Whole company	(3.35)	20.80	–16%

Exhibit 8.1. Manufacturing Leverage Company
PLA Financial Statements for the Year 19X2
(10% Inflation, 100% Fixed Assets, 60% Equity)
Integration of Specific and General Price Indices
(Sales 10%, Out-of-pocket 12%, Equipment 7%,
Interest Rate 75%)

Balance Sheet as of

12.31.19X1	Assets	12.31.19X2*
$50.00	Machine 2	—
50.00	Machine 3	$53.50r
—	Machine 4	53.50
100.00	Assets, at cost	107.00
(25.00)	Accum. depr.	(26.75)
—	Investment	1.35
75.00		81.60

Profit and Loss Statement

19X1	
$200.00	Sales
(130.00)	Out-of-pocket costs
(50.00)	Depreciation
(2.40)	Interest
182.40	
17.60	PLA operating profit
—	Asset restatement gains
—	Less equity maint. adjustment
—	Net restatement gains
17.60	Profit = tax and dividend

Sources and Uses Statement

19X1	Sources	19X2
$50.00	Depreciation	$53.50
17.60	Profit	17.45
20.00	Loans	22.10
—	Equity maint.	4.50
87.60		97.55

*The letter *r* indicates restated figure.

December 31, 19X2

12.31.19X1	Liabilities and Equity	12.31.19X2
$10.00	Loan 2	—
20.00	Loan 3	$10.70
—	Loan 4	21.40
30.00		32.10
45.00	Equity	45.00
—	Equity maint. reserve	4.50
75.00		81.60

for the Year 19X2

	$220.00
$145.60	
53.50	
4.20	
	203.30
	16.70
5.25	
(4.50)	
	0.75
	17.45

for the Year 19X2

19X1	Uses	19X2
$50.00	Machine 4	$53.50
17.60	Tax and dividend	17.45
20.00	Loans repayment	20.00
—	Asset restatement	5.25
—	New investment	1.35
87.60		97.55

Exhibit 8.2. Manufacturing Leverage Company
PLA Profit and Loss Statement for the Year 19X2
Isolation of Terms of Trade Variance

19X1		Actual*		Standard†		Variance‡	
$200.00	Sales		$220.00		$220.00		—
(130.00)	Out-of-pocket costs	$145.60		$143.00		$(2.60)	
(50.00)	Depreciation	53.50		55.00		1.50	
(2.40)	Interest	4.20		2.64		(1.56)	
						(2.66)	
182.40			203.30		200.64		
17.60	Inflationfree profit		—		19.36		
	Leverage gains paid§		—		(1.56)	1.56	
17.60	PLA operating profit		16.70		17.80		$(1.10)
—	Assets restatement gains[11]	5.25		7.50		(2.25)	
—	Less equity maintenance adjustment	4.50		4.50		—	
—	Net restatement gains		0.75		3.00		(2.25)
17.60	PLA total profit		17.45		20.80		(3.35)

*As a result of specific price level increases: Sales, 10%; Out-of-pocket-costs, 12% Equipment, 7%; Interest rate, 75%.

†Base period figures (19X1) inflated by 10% general price level increase.

‡Actual figures less standard figures.

§Paid to creditors; see Exhibit 7.5.

[11] 7% and 10% on $75 net assets, respectively.

Exhibit 8.3. Isolation of Terms of Trade Variance
Manufacturing Leverage Company

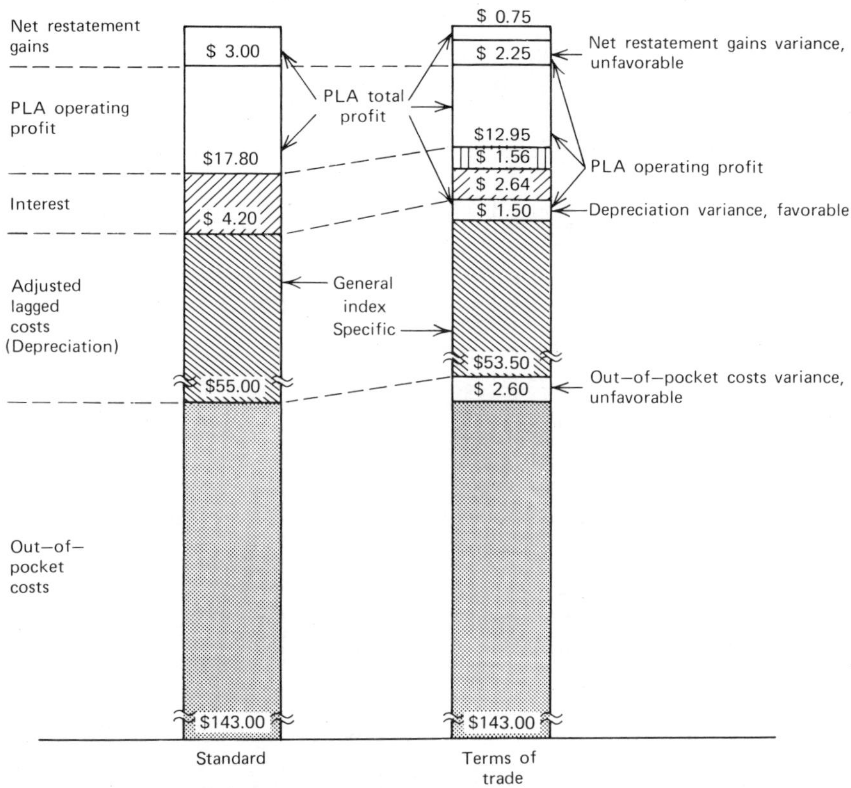

Source: Data from Exhibits 4.5 and 8.2.

8.3 Measuring Speculation Gains

Speculation is the economic activity of dealing in commodities in order to profit from expected price differentials.[4] Speculative gains accrue to the speculator by virtue of his correct decision (or good fortune) regarding future price changes. Speculative gains accrue either from premature purchase of replacement items (speculation for a rise in prices) or from postponing replacement (speculation for a fall in prices).

During a period of stable price levels, speculative gains accrue when the price of the specific commodity that serves for speculation changes. During periods of price level changes, on the other hand,

Exhibit 8.4. Manufacturing Leverage Company
Departmental PLA Profit and Loss Analysis
Standard Setting for the Year 19X2
(19X1's Figures Inflated by 10% General Index)

	19X1				19X2 Standard				
	Total	Dept. A	Dept. B	Interest Account	Total	Dept. A	Dept. B	Interest Account	Capital Account
Income									
Sales (production)	$200.00	$80.00	$120.00	—	$220.00	$88.00	$132.00	—	—
Imputed interest	11.25	—	—	$11.25	12.38	—	—	$12.38	—
Asset Restatement					7.50	—	—	—	$7.50
Total Income	211.25	80.00	120.00	11.25	239.88	88.00	132.00	12.38	7.50
Expenses									
Materials	60.00	24.00	36.00	—	66.00	26.40	39.60	—	—
Labor	60.00	50.00	10.00	—	66.00	55.00	11.00	—	—
Rent, insurance, etc.	10.00	1.00	9.00	—	11.00	1.10	9.90	—	—
Interest	2.40	—	—	2.40	2.64	—	—	2.64	—
Leverage gains paid*					1.56			1.56	
Total out-of-pocket costs	132.40	75.00	55.00	2.40	147.20	82.50	60.50	4.20	—
Imputed interest	11.25	—	11.25	—	12.38	—	12.38	—	—
Depreciation	50.00	—	50.00	—	55.00	—	55.00	—	—
Equity restatement	—	—	—	—	4.50	—	—	—	4.50
Total Expenses	193.65	75.00	116.25	2.40	219.08	82.50	127.88	4.20	4.50
Profit	17.60	5.00	3.75	8.85	20.80	5.50	4.12	8.18	3.00

*Paid to creditors; see Exhibits 7.5 and 8.2.

speculative gains accrue only when the rate of specific price change of the commodity that serves for speculation differs from the general price level change.

In other words, speculation is based on expected changes in the terms of trade. For example, suppose that the management of the Manufacturing Company bought, in addition to the machine required for replacement, another machine to be installed the following year because it speculated on increasing prices. The gains of holding this machine are the "output" of the speculative activity; they are measured like the terms of trade effect. The speculative activity involves specific costs that should also be matched to its output.

Profit from speculative activity is measured by the excess of holding gains over holding costs that are related to the speculative activity. The "output" of a speculative activity is the net sales value of the commodity that is held for speculative purposes. The inputs of this activity consist of (1) the acquisition cost of the commodity; (2) the actual holding cost, such as storage, maintenance, and spoilage; (3) the cost of capital (actual interest of debt capital if used, implicit interest when equity funds are used); and (4) the sum required for preserving the real value of equity capital, that is, equity maintenance adjustment.

The last item of cost, equity maintenance adjustment, will be positive during a period of inflation, negative during a period of deflation, and zero when the general price level is stable. For example, during a period of deflation a speculator will prefer to invest in a commodity the price of which is expected to decrease by less than the decline in the general price level. As a result, his equity will shrink less.

Consider a speculator who expects that the price of a given commodity will rise during the coming year by 20%, and that the general price level will rise by only 10%. Suppose that he considers purchasing $100 worth of this commodity for speculative purposes. The expected pure speculative effect on profit should be measured in the same manner as the terms of trade effect has been measured. The difference between the specific price level change (20%) and the general one (10%) provides the pure speculative effect; it is calculated as follows:

$$\$100(0.2 - 0.1) = \$10$$

The expected net profit resulting from the speculative activity illustrated is calculated after charging all cost items to income. On the assumption that storage will cost $1, three financing schemes are analyzed: (1) 100% debt, (2) 100% equity, and (3) 60% equity and 40% debt. The respective profitability analyses are presented in Exhibit 8.6.

Exhibit 8.5. Manufacturing Leverage Company
Departmental PLA Profit and Loss Analysis for the Year 19X2
Terms of Trade Variance

	Actual				
	Total	Dept.A	Dept.B	Interest Account	Capital Account
Income					
Sales (production)	$220.00	$88.00	$132.00	—	—
Imputed interest	12.24	—	—	$12.24	—
Asset restatement	5.25	—	—	—	$5.25
Total Income	237.49	88.00	132.00	12.24	5.25
Expenses					
Materials	67.20	26.88	40.32	—	—
Labor	67.20	56.00	11.20	—	—
Rent, insurance, etc.	11.20	1.12	10.08	—	—
Interest	4.20	—	—	4.20	—
Leverage gains paid	—	—	—	—	—
Total out-of-pocket costs	149.80	84.00	61.60	4.20	—
Imputed interest	12.24	—	12.24	—	—
Depreciation	53.50	—	53.50	—	—
Equity restatement	4.50	—	—	—	4.50
Total Expenses	220.04	84.00	127.34	4.20	4.50
Profit	17.45	4.00	4.66	8.04	0.75

Standard					Variance				
Total	Dept.A	Dept.B	Interest Account	Capital Account	Total	Dept.A	Dept.B	Interest Account	Capital Account
$220.00	$88.00	$132.00	—	—	—	—	—	—	—
12.38	—	—	$12.38	—	$(0.14)	—	—	$(0.14)	—
7.50	—	—	—	$7.50	(2.25)	—	—	—	$(2.25)
239.88	88.00	132.00	12.38	7.50	(2.39)	—	—	(0.14)	(2.25)
66.00	26.40	39.60	—	—	(1.20)	$(0.48)	$(0.72)	—	—
66.00	55.00	11.00	—	—	(1.20)	(1.00)	(0.20)	—	—
11.00	1.10	9.90	—	—	(0.20)	(0.02)	(0.18)	—	—
2.64	—	—	2.64	—	(1.56)	—	—	(1.56)	—
1.56	—	—	1.56	—	1.56	—	—	1.56	—
147.20	82.50	60.50	4.20	—	(2.60)	(1.50)	(1.10)	—	—
12.38	—	12.38		—	0.14	—	0.14	—	—
55.00	—	55.00	—	—	1.50	—	1.50	—	—
4.50	—	—	—	4.50	—	—	—	—	—
219.08	82.50	127.88	4.20	4.50	(0.96)	(1.50)	0.54	—	—
20.80	5.50	4.12	8.18	3.00	(3.35)	(1.50)	0.54	(0.14)	(2.25)

Exhibit 8.6. Profit Analysis of a Speculative Activity under Three Financing Schemes

	Zero Equity	100% Equity		60% Equity	
	Conventional and PLA	Conventional	PLA	Conventional	PLA
Sales	$120.00	$120.00	$120.00	$120.00	$120.00
Acquisition cost	(100.00)	(100.00)	(100.00)	(100.00)	(100.00)
Storage	(1.00)	(1.00)	(1.00)	(1.00)	(1.00)
Interest (8%)	(8.00)	—	—	(3.20)	(3.20)
Equity maintenance adjustment	—	—	(10.00)	—	(6.00)
Profit	11.00	19.00	9.00	15.80	9.80

Under the first scheme, investment is financed by a loan to be repaid after 1 year upon the sales of the commodity (using the commodity as collateral). Since the cost of capital (interest) of the loan is considered as expense in conventional accounting and no extra compensation for price level change is required, conventional profit and PLA profit are equal; $11 is the economic (Hicksian) profit from speculation.

In the case of 100% equity, the conventional profit figure indicates the return on equity capital, which is 19% ($19:$100). This sum should serve as a contingency for uncertainties, including the uncertainty of a decline in the value of equity capital caused by inflation. If expected inflation can be estimated, PLA procedures provide a profit figure that should be considered as the return to equity capital net of inflationary effects.

Under leverage conditions conventional profit is lower than in the 100% equity case, but the rate of return is higher: 26.3% ($15.80:$60) compared to 19.0%.

It should be noted that the profit figures, as computed in Exhibit 8.6, are holding gains (total gains for the conventional profit, net gains for the PLA profit). These are not restatement gains, as computed under PLA accounting procedures in all the illustrations in this book. *Ex post* analysis (of the type illustrated in Exhibit 8.6) carried out for a commodity that is still in stock will show restatement gains; the same analysis carried out for a commodity that has been sold will show holding gains.

In summary, speculation aims to profit from price changes in individual commodities. Measurement of the pure speculative effect is carried out in the same manner as measurement of the terms of trade effect. Among the cost items involved in speculation is the full cost of the capital invested in this activity; speculation is, in fact, a specific form of investment.

Notes

1. This section and the next one are based on our article: "Measuring Terms of Trade During Price Level Changes", published in *Abacus,* June 1977.

2. In terms of the formal presentation in Chapter 6, the "standard" figures are expressed by (6.11) minus (6.18), and adding and subtracting (6.15); while the "actual" data are expressed by (6.26). The terms of trade variance is computed by deducting the standard from the actual values, as follows:

$$
\begin{array}{lllll}
 & (1+p_S)\,S - & (1+p_C)\,C - & (1+p_A)\,A/L - & (i+h)\,(D-F) + \\
- & (1+p_G)\,S - & (1+p_G)\,C - & (1+p_G)\,A/L - & i(1+p_G)\,(D-F) - \\
\hline
= & (p_S-p_G)\,S - & (p_C-p_G)\,C - & (p_A-p_G)\,A/L - & (h-ip_G)\,(D-F) + \\
 & \$0 & \$(2.60) & \$1.50 & \$(1.56)
\end{array}
$$

$$
\begin{array}{ll}
 & + \left[p_A(A-\Sigma A/L) - p_G(E)\right] \\
- \left[(i+h)\,(D-F) - i(1+p_G)\,(D-F)\right] & + \left[p_G(A-\Sigma A/L) - p_G(E)\right] \\
\hline
= + \left[(i+h)\,(D-F) - i(1+p_G)\,(D-F)\right] & + (p_A-p_G)\,(A-\Sigma A/L) \\
\quad \$1.56 & \quad \$(2.25)
\end{array}
$$

3. For comparison, see Exhibits 4.6 and 7.6.

4. Money may also be considered as a commodity with respect to speculation.

Nine

Investment Analysis under Inflationary Conditions

The discussion up to this point has centered on *ex post* analysis of financial statements, in which historical data are price level adjusted or revalued. *Ex ante* analysis of projected data must also take expected price level changes into consideration. Projections should be based on both nominal-price-level and constant-price-level data; income tax and leverage considerations require the use of nominal data. Investment analysis should include projected financial statements that indicate the effect of a proposed investment on the company as a whole.

9.1 Nominal Versus Inflationfree Projected Data

Ex post analysis of financial statements during a period of price level changes requires price level adjustment (or restatement) of nominal data. Restatement is needed when the financial statements for a given year are analyzed, as well as when a series of annual financial statements is being analyzed. Time-series analysis (Section 12.2) requires two stages of adjustment: (1) the data of each financial statement are adjusted to the price level of the year in question, thereby stating all data for that year in dollars of equal value; and (2) the

PLA annual statements are updated ("rolled forward," inflated) to the price level of a base year, so that the data for all years are provided in a currency of constant purchasing power.

Ex ante investment analysis, under conditions of expected price level changes, raises the question of what value currency to use in presenting the projected data. Whereas in *ex post* analysis the actual data, which are "nominal," must be adjusted, in *ex ante* analysis the data could be presented directly in PLA form.

Two methods of treating price level changes in the projections are possible: (1) constant-price-level projection, in which all expected cash flow data are presented in terms of constant purchasing power currency; and (2) nominal-price-level projection, in which the expected data are presented in terms of nominal currency, that is, in current prices, and the resulting cash flow is then deflated to a base-year currency (the figures are "rolled backward"). With both methods the resulting cash flow should be discounted by the inflationfree cost of capital.[1]

These methods are illustrated by calculating the profitability of a projected investment. First (in this section), an artificial taxless situation is assumed, in which the investment is financed by 100% equity funds. Next (in Section 9.2), income tax considerations are introduced. Finally (in Section 9.3), the analysis is applied to a financial leverage situation.

Suppose that a firm is considering investing $50 in a machine that has a useful life of 2 years; its salvage value is zero. The machine can produce 50 units of a commodity per year with net sales value of $2 each. Out-of-pocket costs to produce one unit are $1.30. To simplify, it is assumed that all transactions take place at the end of the respective year, and that uncertainty does not exist. The pretax cost of capital is 15% per annum.

Consider first a situation in which there is no change in the price level (no inflation). The operating cash flow expected to be generated by the proposed investment is presented in the upper section of Exhibit 9.1. To make the cash flow figures additive, the net present value is calculated in the lower section of Exhibit 9.1.

Consider now the same investment proposal but under inflationary conditions. It is expected that a 10% increase in the price level of all items will occur on January 1 of Year 2. The corresponding operating cash flow is presented in the upper section of Exhibit 9.2. The dollars earned at the end of Year 2 do not have the same purchasing power as those earned in Year 1. To make the figures additive, this difference must be taken into account.

The first alternative is to apply the constant-price-level method, that is, to provide all data in terms of currency having constant

Exhibit 9.1. Taxless Equity Investment
Constant-Price-Level Projection
(No Inflation, No Tax, 100% Equity,
15% Cost of Capital)

	Year 0	Year 1	Year 2
	Operating Cash Flow		
Sales		$100.00	$100.00
Out-of-pocket costs		65.00	65.00
Operating cash flow		35.00	35.00
	Discounted Cash Flow		
Investment	$(50.00)		
Operating cash flow	—	35.00	35.00
Net cash flow	(50.00)	35.00	35.00
Discounting factor (15%)	1.0000	0.8696	0.7561
Present value	(50.00)	30.44	26.46
Net present value	6.90		

purchasing power, say, the purchasing power of the base year. The numerical result for Year 2 (when inflation exists) is obviously equal to that for Year 1 (before the price level changed). The resulting constant-price-level cash flow data are equivalent to those presented in the upper section of Exhibit 9.1; discounted data are given in the lower section of the exhibit.

The second method of treating price level changes in projections is first to present the nominal cash flow data and next to transform them to the base year price level, as illustrated in the lower section of Exhibit 9.2. The net present values, computed by both methods (Exhibits 9.1 and 9.2), are, of course, equal ($6.90).[2] Although the results are equal, the second method has an advantage since it presents the projected data in figures that are expected to prevail in the future. Comparison of actual results with projected (budgeted) data in the future can be carried out directly if the nominal price projection method is used.

In summary, both methods of treating price level changes in projections have advantages. The first, using constant-price-level data, excludes the inflationary effects from the projected data, which are therefore more comprehensible and manageable. Moreover, the effects

Exhibit 9.2. Taxless Equity Investment
Nominal-Price-Level Projection
(10% Inflation in Year 2, No Tax, 100% Equity,
15% Cost of Capital)

	Year 0	Year 1	Year 2
	Operating Cash Flow		
Sales		$100.00	$110.00
Out-of-pocket costs		65.00	71.50
Operating cash flow		35.00	38.50
	Discounted Cash Flow		
Investment	$(50.00)		
Operating cash flow	—	35.00	38.50
Net cash flow	(50.00)	35.00	38.50
Deflating factor (10%)	1.000	1.000	0.909
Deflated cash flow	(50.00)	35.00	35.00
Discounting factor (15%)	1.0000	0.8696	0.7561
Present value	(50.00)	30.44	26.46
Net present value	6.90		

of other factors, such as growth and terms of trade, on the projected results can be seen more clearly. The second method, using nominal-price-level data, presents the projection in figures that will be comparable to actual results in the future. Income tax considerations are another reason why nominal-price-level data are useful.

9.2 Investment Analysis, Inflation and Income Tax

To introduce income tax into the projections, profit and loss projections must first be prepared. Tax payments must be taken into consideration in the calculation of both profit (as an expense) and cash flow (as an outlay).

The tax rate in the illustration we are considering is 50%; the after-tax cost of capital used for discounting is 7.5% per annum [15% × (1—0.5)]. First, the constant-price-level method is illustrated in Exhibit 9.3. This method implies PLA depreciation, since all of the data for Year 2 are stated in terms of dollars of equal purchasing power. But since the tax law does not ordinarily

Exhibit 9.3. Equity Investment
Constant-Price-Level Projection
(10% Inflation in Year 2, 50% Tax, 100% Equity, 15% Cost of Capital)

	Year 0		Year 1		Year 2
Profit and Loss Statement					
Sales			$100.00		$100.00
Out-of-pocket costs		$65.00		$65.00	
Depreciation		25.00		25.00	
Total expenses			90.00		90.00
Profit, pretax			10.00		10.00
Income tax			(5.00)		(5.00)
Profit, after-tax			5.00		5.00
Discounted Cash Flow					
Investment	$(50.00)				
Depreciation	—		25.00		25.00
Profit, after-tax	—		5.00		5.00
Net cash flow	(50.00)		30.00		30.00
Discounting factor (7.5%)	1.0000		0.9302		0.8654
Present value	(50.00)		27.91		25.96
Net present value	3.87				

recognize price level adjustment of depreciation, the constant-price-level method has a serious limitation in analyzing projected data.

Conventional profit and loss projections must be prepared because income tax is levied on conventional accounting profit. These will show nominal data, as presented in the upper section of Exhibit 9.4. The nominal cash flow data must then be transformed to the base year price level, as illustrated in the lower section of Exhibit 9.4.

Whereas in the taxless example both methods of treating price level changes yield the same result (Exhibits 9.1 and 9.2), when tax exists the results obtained by the two methods differ (Exhibits 9.3 and 9.4). The divergence is due to the fact that income tax is levied on nominal profit (Exhibit 9.4). Part of the profit in Year 2, as computed under the nominal-price-level projection, is required for replacement funds to renew the asset, which now costs more nominally than the existing

Exhibit 9.4. Equity Investment
Nominal-Price-Level Projection
(10% Inflation in Year 2, 50% Tax, 100% Equity, 15% Cost of Capital)

	Year 0		Year 1		Year 2
Profit and Loss Statement					
Sales			$100.00		$110.00
Out-of-pocket costs		$65.00		$71.50	
Depreciation		25.00		25.00	
Total expenses			90.00		96.50
Profit, pretax			10.00		13.50
Income tax			(5.00)		(6.75)
Profit, after-tax			5.00		6.75
Discounted Cash Flow					
Investment	$(50.00)				
Depreciation	—		25.00		25.00
Profit, after-tax	—		5.00		6.75
Net cash flow	(50.00)		30.00		31.75
Deflating factor (10%)	1.000		1.000		0.909
Deflated cash flow	(50.00)		30.00		28.86
Discounting factor (7.5%)	1.0000		0.9302		0.8654
Present value	(50.00)		27.91		24.98
Net present value	2.89				

assets. But income tax is levied on this portion of profit, as well as on real (economic) profit. As a result the net value computed by this method is lower than that obtained by the incorrect constant-price-level method ($2.89 compared to $3.87).

In Exhibit 9.4 only the nominal cash flow has been deflated. The original profit and loss data are presented in nominal figures. As mentioned earlier, to make the projection more comprehensible deflation of all the data is recommended, so that they are presented in constant-price-level figures. The projection should therefore be prepared in two stages: (1) nominal-price-level data should be projected for computing after-tax profit and as a future basis for comparison with actual results, and (2) these data should be transformed into constant-price-level figures to facilitate comprehension of the projected data.

In real-life applications it is simpler to proceed by iteration: (1) preparing constant-price-level data regarding sales and costs, as presented in Exhibit 9.3; (2) adjusting for projected price level changes and preparing nominal-price-level data, as presented in Exhibit 9.4; and (3) after adding the income tax data (and interest charges, in the case of financial leverage), reverting to constant-price-level data, as illustrated in Exhibit 9.5.

Income tax payments, as calculated on conventional accounting profit in Exhibit 9.4, are deflated and recorded as expenses in Exhibit 9.5. The net cash flow in Exhibit 9.5 is, of course, deflated (−$50, $30, $28.86); therefore it equals that in Exhibit 9.4. Net present values in the two exhibits are identical as well.

Exhibit 9.5. Equity Investment
Constant-Price-Level Projection,
Nominal-Price-Level Adjusted Income Tax From Exhibit 9.4
(10% Inflation in Year 2, 50% Tax, 100% Equity,
15% Cost of Capital)

	Year 0	Year 1		Year 2	
		Profit and Loss Statement			
Sales			$100.00		$100.00
Out-of-pocket costs		$65.00		$65.00	
Depreciation		25.00		25.00	
Total expenses			90.00		90.00
Profit, pretax			10.00		10.00
Income tax (from Exhibit 9.4, deflated)			(5.00)		(6.14)
Profit, after-tax			5.00		3.86
		Discounted Cash Flow			
Investment	$(50.00)				
Depreciation	—		25.00		25.00
Profit, after-tax			5.00		3.86
Net cash flow	(50.00)		30.00		28.86
Discounting factor (7.5%)	1.0000		0.9302		0.8654
Present value	(50.00)		27.91		24.98
Net present value	2.89				

9.3 Investment Analysis with Financial Leverage

Consider a more realistic case in which a company uses financial leverage. The investment is financed partly by equity and partly by loan. Suppose that the optimal financial mix is 60% equity capital and 40% debt. Thus a $20 loan is obtained, with 50% of the principal to be repaid at the end of Year 1 and 50% at the end of Year 2. Interest, 8% per annum, is paid in yearly installments on the outstanding balance. To simplify the comparison with previous illustrations, the pretax cost of capital is still 15% per annum.

Calculations of investment profitability are similar to those carried out above for the case of 100% equity (Exhibit 9.4). The difference is that, with leverage financing, interest payments on debt are taken into consideration in the calculations of both profit (as an expense) and cash flow (as an outlay). Repayment of principal (and linkage appreciation of principal in the case of a price level linked loan[3]) is cash outlay but not expense. To save space, only the nominal-price-level method of treating price level changes in projections is presented.

The corresponding profit and loss statements and discounted data are presented in Exhibit 9.6. The net present value is higher under leverage conditions than under 100% equity ($4.66 in Exhibit 9.6, compared to $2.89 in Exhibit 9.4) for two reasons: (1) with leverage, equity earns extra "rent" for assuming the risks that are involved in undertaking the investment (see Section 4.3), and (2) the debt capital does not receive full compensation for price level changes (interest rate is 8% in both Year 1 and Year 2, despite the fact that the price level in Year 2 rose).[4]

In summary, because of the nonrecognition of price level adjustment of depreciation for tax calculations, investment analysis during a period of inflation must begin with projection of the nominal-price-level data. The nominal after-tax cash flow should be deflated to constant currency data before applying any of the methods of investment evaluation—net present value, internal rate of return, or payback period. For calculating net present value, the inflationfree cost of capital should be used for discounting purposes. When financial leverage exists, the pertinent payments—interest and principal—must be included in the nominal-price-level data calculations. The nominal-price-level projections will facilitate future comparisons of actual results (as recorded in the financial statements) with projected data. Furthermore, nominal-price-level projected financial statements provide relevant data for various analyses that are applied in practice on conventional financial statements. The optimal financial leverage is an example of such an analysis.

Exhibit 9.6. Leverage Investment
Nominal-Price-Level Projection,
Nonlinked Loan
(10% Inflation in Year 2, 50% Tax, 60% Equity,
15% Cost of Capital)

	Year 0	Year 1		Year 2	
Profit and Loss Statement					
Sales			$100.00		$110.00
Out-of-pocket costs		$65.00		$71.50	
Depreciation		25.00		25.00	
Interest (8%)		1.60		0.80	
Total expenses			91.60		97.30
Profit, pretax			8.40		12.70
Income tax			(4.20)		(6.35)
Profit, after-tax			4.20		6.35
Discounted Cash Flow					
Investment	$(50.00)				
Depreciation	—		25.00		25.00
Profit, after-tax	—		4.20		6.35
Loan	20.00		(10.00)		(10.00)
Net cash flow	(30.00)		19.20		21.35
Deflating factor (10%)	1.000		1.000		0.909
Deflated cash flow	(30.00)		19.20		19.41
Discounting factor (7.5%)	1.0000		0.9302		0.8654
Present value	(30.00)		17.86		16.80
Net present value	4.66				

9.4 Projected Financial Statements

The previous conclusion that *ex ante* analysis of projected data should apply the same techniques as *ex post* analysis of historical data is related to the fact that expectations are, to a great extent, based on history. Projections, in turn, should be presented in the form of "future history," so as to permit valid comparison when the future has become the past.

One reason for preparing projected financial statements is to evaluate the end result of a long-range program that consists of a variety of

Exhibit 9.7. Mini Manufacturing Equity Company
Nominal-Price-Level Projections
(10% Inflation in Year 2, 50% Tax, 100% Equity)

	New Investment			Existing Operation*		Combined			Marginal Result†		
	Year 0	Year 1	Year 2	19X1	19X2	19X0	19X1	19X2	19X0	19X1	19X2
				Profit and Loss Statements							
Sales		$100.00	$110.00	$100.00	110.00		$200.00	$220.00		$100.00	$110.00
Out-of-pocket costs		65.00	71.50	85.00	93.50		150.00	165.00		65.00	71.50
Depreciation		25.00	25.00	25.00	25.00		50.00	50.00		25.00	25.00
Profit, pretax		10.00	13.50	(10.00)	(8.50)		—	5.00		10.00	13.50
Income tax		5.00	6.75	—	—		—	2.50		—	2.50
Profit, after-tax		5.00	6.75	(10.00)	(8.50)		—	2.50		10.00	11.00
				Cash Flow							
Depreciation		25.00	25.00	25.00	25.00		50.00	50.00		25.00	25.00
Profit, after-tax		5.00	6.75	(10.00)	(8.50)		—	2.50		10.00	11.00
Net Cash flow	$(50.00)	30.00	31.75	15.00	16.50	$(50.00)	50.00	52.50	$(50.00)	35.00	36.00

*One machine with greater overhead.
†Marginal Result = Combined − Existing operation.
Source: Data from Exhibit 9.4

investments. The expected profitability of each investment is analyzed separately with the tools illustrated above. But the effect that proposed investments have on a company's economic situation is not a simple arithmetical summation of the individual investments. The interaction of cash flows, varying profitabilities, and their effects on the total tax liability of the firm make company financial projections a required procedure of investment analysis. Investment analysis provides information on the profitability of a given (isolated) project—this is microanalysis. The marginal profitability of the investment to the company is analyzed by financial statement projections. These provide information on the expected effect of the program on company net worth—this is macroanalysis.[5]

Consider a company similar to the Manufacturing Equity Company but employing only one machine; thus sales are one-half of the original company's level. Because of the smaller scale, out-of-pocket costs are not proportionate to those of the original company ($85 compared to $65 in 19X1). The management of this minicompany examines the effect of undertaking the investment proposal illustrated in Exhibit 9.4. Relevant projected profit and loss statements of the proposed investment, the existing operations before the investment is undertaken, and the combined operations are presented in Exhibit 9.7.

The data in Exhibit 9.7 illustrate the importance of the projected profit and loss statements for the company as a whole (the combined statements in Exhibit 9.7). The marginal cash flow generated by the new investment within the company is −$50, $35 and $36 for the respective years, compared to the cash flow generated directly by the investment itself: −$50, $30, and $31.75.

Because of income tax considerations the combined cash flow is not an arithmetical aggregation of the cash flows of the two components.

Notes

1. Alternatively, the nominal cash flow may be evaluated by using the inflation-compensated cost of capital for discounting purposes. The inflation-compensated cost of capital is the inflationfree cost inflated by the rate of price level change, that is,

$$1 + r = (1 + i)(1 + p)$$

where r is the inflation-compensated (nominal) rate of interest,
i is the inflationfree rate of interest, and
p is the inflation rate.

For a discussion on the rate of interest to be used in discounting cash flows during inflation see, for example, Mundell (1963), Grinyer (1974), Fleischer and Reisman (1967).

2. The same result would be achieved by using the inflation-compensated cost of capital for discounting the nominal cash flow as follows. The inflation-compensated cost of capital for Year 2 is (see Note 1)

$$r = (1 + 0.15)(1 + 0.10) - 1 = 0.265$$

Discounting \$38.50 (cash flow of Year 2 in Exhibit 9.2) by the discounting factor for 26.5% (0.7905) yields \$30.43 for Year 1. Discounting this sum plus \$35 (cash flow of Year 1) by the discounting factor for 15% (0.8696) yields \$56.90, and the net present value is again \$6.90. This procedure is inferior because of the tedious computations required when the rate of inflation fluctuates over time.

3. In some countries (e.g., in Israel since July 1975) linkage payments are considered as expenses for income tax purposes.
4. When both principal and interest are linked to changes in the price level index (Section 4.2), the net present value is \$3.84.
5. The discussion in the preceding sections analyzed the profitability of an investment in a machine. Suppose that a company is considering investing \$100 in two machines rather than \$50 in one machine. If 100% equity is assumed, the corresponding profit and loss statements under the nominal-price-level projection method will be as follows (based on Exhibit 9.4):

	Year 1		Year 2	
Sales		\$200.00		\$220.00
Out-of-pocket costs	\$130.00		\$143.00	
Depreciation	50.00		50.00	
		180.00		193.00
Pretax profit		20.00		27.00

These projections are identical to the respective 19X1 and 19X2 conventional profit and loss statements of the Manufacturing Equity Company (Exhibit 2.2) because the data for the investment illustration match those of the Manufacturing Company's assets. If the projected balance sheets were prepared, they would match those presented in Exhibit 2.2.

References

Fleischer, G. A. and A. Reisman, "Investment Decisions under Conditions of Inflation," *International Journal of Production Research,* Vol. 1, No. 2, 1967, pp. 87-95.

Grinyer, J. R., "Inflation and Capital Budgeting Decisions: A Comment," *Journal of Business Finance and Accounting,* Spring 1974, pp. 149-155.

Mundell, R., "Inflation and Real Interest," *Journal of Political Economy,* Vol. 71, 1963, pp. 280-283.

Part Four

Financial Statement Adjustment

Ten

Coefficients for Restating Aggregate Data [1]

Most of the deficiencies that inflation causes in conventional financial statements can be remedied by restating the company's assets in current monetary terms. Assets restatement, although tedious, can be carried out by the firm's management. However, the required data are not included in conventional financial statements and therefore are not available to external parties. This means that, as long as management does not publish the restatement, the usefulness of financial statements to external parties is rather limited during a period of inflation.

This chapter presents a new and simple method for price level adjustment of assets, making use of the aggregate data reported in conventional financial statements. The method provides two sets of restatement coefficients that are the ratios of current values to historical values. Both sets are used for (1) restating fixed assets (before and after depreciation), and (2) adjusting the costs of goods sold (depreciation and materials drawn from inventory).

10.1 Coefficients for Restatement of Gross Fixed Assets

The acquisition cost of a given asset is restated by multiplying its historical acquisition cost by an appropriate price index. The greater the rate of inflation and the greater the age of the asset, the larger the appropriate index number will be, and the more inflated the restated acquisition cost. However, the balance sheet reports only aggregate data on the total acquisition costs of all fixed assets. Since the company's assets have been acquired at different dates and therefore with dollars of differing "values," the problem is how to restate these aggregate data in terms of dollars reflecting current price levels.

Consider the set of assets (two machines, each productive for 2 years) of the Manufacturing Company. Assume that machines are bought and replaced at the beginning of each year (on January 1) rather than at the end of the year (on December 31) as assumed in all the preceding illustrations. Assume further that prices either jumped up by 10% on January 2 (rather than on January 1, as assumed in the illustrations above) or crept up by 10% during each year. Hence the acquisition costs, as recorded on the December 31, 19X3, balance sheet, are $50 for Machine 4 and $55 for Machine 5 (compared to $55 and $60.50, respectively, as recorded in Appendix C). Price level adjustment of the acquisition costs (gross values) as recorded on December 31, 19X3, is as follows:

	Acquisition		Inflating	PLA Value
	Date	Cost	Factor	on 12.31.19X3
Machine 4	1.1.19X2	$50.00	1.21	$60.50
Machine 5	1.1.19X3	55.00	1.10	60.50
		105.00		121.00

The ratio of the total PLA (aggregate restated) value ($121) to the total recorded historical value ($105) is 1.15238.

This is a weighted restatement coefficient. It is suitable for restating the gross value of a "mature" set of assets in which each unit has an economic life of 2 years, and under conditions of 10% annual inflation rate.

The above computations can be carried out by using a mathematical formula, assuming that (1) the aggregate data relate to a set of fixed assets of a given type, the age of which is evenly distributed, (2) the straight-line depreciation method is used, (3) a constant inflation rate has existed since the date of acquisition of the oldest unit in the set, and (4) the set of assets is constant in size that is, the company has remained stable in terms of productive assets. The formula that suits these assumptions, derived from the mathematical development in Shashua and Goldschmidt (1976), is

$$R_{gross} = \frac{(1 + p)^n \, n(p)}{(1 + p)^n - 1}$$

where R is the restatement coefficient,
p is the inflation rate, and
n is the average life span of assets.

Inserting the variables of the numerical illustration above ($n = 2$, $p = 0.10$) into this formula, we get a restatement coefficient of 1.15238.

Using the mathematical formula, we may compute coefficients for various inflation rates and asset life spans, as presented in Exhibit 10.1. (For a more detailed presentation see Appendix E.) As expected, greater inflation rates and longer asset lives require greater restatement coefficients. The coefficients in Exhibit 10.1 are useful for practical purposes, however, as will be shown in later sections and in the next chapter.

Coefficients at a given level, say 7.5, can be computed with the mathematical formula for various sets of inflation rates and average life spans of assets. The resulting data are presented graphically by isocoefficient lines in Exhibit 10.2.

10.2 Coefficients for Restatement of Net Fixed Assets

Restatement of the acquisition cost (gross value) of a single asset provides the data required for computing annual depreciation and net value (acquisition less accumulated depreciation). For example, the current gross value of Machine 4 on December 31, 19X3, is $60.50, the annual depreciation is $30.25, and the net value is $30.25. How-

Exhibit 10.1. Restatement Coefficients for Fixed Asset Gross Value and Depreciation (R_{gross})*,†

Life Span (periods)	Inflation Rate (% per period) 2	6	10	15	20
2	1.030	1.091	1.152	1.230	1.309
5	1.061	1.187	1.319	1.492	1.672
10	1.113	1.359	1.627	1.993	2.385
16	1.178	1.583	2.045	2.687	3.383
20	1.223	1.744	2.349	3.195	4.107
30	1.340	2.179	3.182	4.569	6.025

*Assuming zero rate of growth.

†Detailed tables are presented in Appendix E.

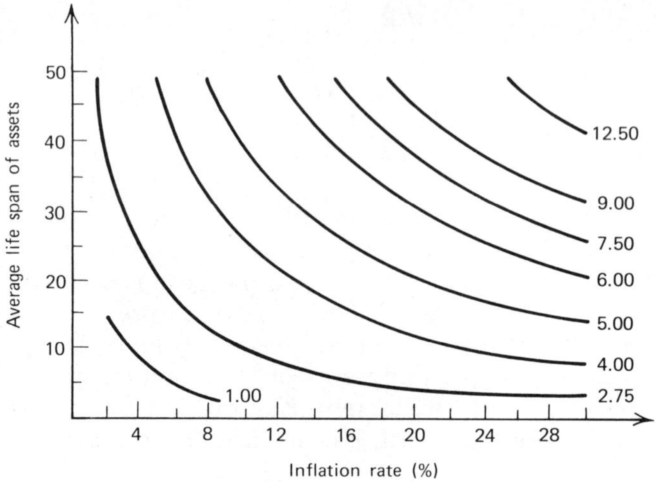

Exhibit 10.2. Coefficient Map for Various Inflation Rates and Asset Life Spans (for Restating Gross Value)

Source: Based on data from Appendix E.

ever, when the value of a set of assets is restated, different coefficients are required for restating the gross value (acquisition cost) and the net value.

Consider again the Manufacturing Company's set of two machines. Price level adjustment of their net historical values on December 31, 19X3, is as follows:

	Historical Net Value	Inflating Factor	PLA Net Value on 12.31.19X3
Machine 4	$25.00	1.21	$30.25
Machine 5	55.00	1.10	60.50
	80.00		90.75

The ratio of the total PLA (restated) net value ($90.75) to the recorded value ($80) is 1.13437 (compared to 1.15238 for the gross value).

This weighted coefficient is suitable for restating the net value of a "mature" set of assets, under the assumptions outlined above. The corresponding formula, assuming zero growth rate, is derived from the mathematical development in Shashua and Goldschmidt (1976):

$$R_{net} = \frac{(1 + p)^n \; n \; (p^2)/ \; (n + 1)/2}{[(1 + p)^n - 1] \; (np - 1) + n \; (p)}$$

where R is the restatement coefficient,
p is the inflation rate, and
n is the average life span.
Inserting the variables of the numerical illustration ($n = 2, p = 0.10$) into this formula, we get a restatement coefficient of 1.13437.

Again, by using this formula, coefficients for various rates of inflation and asset life spans may be computed, as presented in Exhibit 10.1. As expected, the restatement coefficients for the net values (Exhibit 10.3) are lower than those for the gross values (Exhibit 10.1).[2]

Exhibit 10.3. Restatement Coefficients for Fixed Asset Net Value (R_{net})*,†

Life Span (periods)	Inflation Rate (% per period)				
	2	6	10	15	20
2	1.026	1.080	1.134	1.202	1.271
5	1.046	1.143	1.240	1.365	1.493
10	1.081	1.250	1.427	1.656	1.894
16	1.123	1.384	1.663	2.031	2.413
20	1.151	1.477	1.828	2.292	2.776
30	1.223	1.718	2.260	2.976	3.717

*Assuming zero rate of growth.
†Detailed tables are presented in Appendix E.

In summary, the suggested method is suitable for price level adjustment of aggregate data such as the total value of a set of fixed assets; it is not suitable for restating individual asset values. Although it provides approximations, these are much closer to the current asset values than the random mixture of historical values that conventional accounting statements present.[3] The accuracy of the results, as compared with item by item calculation, depends on how closely actual conditions correspond to the conditions assumed while developing the formula. It should be remembered that conventional accounting procedures, even without price level changes, also provide only approximations of asset values.

10.3 Coefficients for Restatement of Inventory

Restatement of a given type of inventory is equivalent to restatement of a given type of fixed asset. Detailed restatement of a company's inventories is usually tedious since the number of inventory items to be restated (types, by dates of acquisition) is usually larger than that of fixed assets. Inventory restatement requires, of course, a lower adjustment index since the life span of inventory items is usually shorter than that of fixed assets.

Suppose that a company holds stock equal to 5 months' usage of a given type of inventory that is replenished monthly by new acquisitions. During a period of inflation, at the end of each month there are five batches of inventory in stock that have been acquired at different dates by dollars having different "values." The problem here, as in the case of fixed assets, is that the balance sheet reports only aggregate data on total acquisition costs. These data may be restated in a way similar to that used for restating fixed assets. The aggregate acquisition cost of a given type of inventory that is used and replenished currently, at a constant rate, may be regarded similarly to the aggregate acquisition cost of a set of a given type of fixed assets the ages of which are evenly distributed.

Consider the Manufacturing Company's set of two machines with an average life span of 2 years. Every year one machine (the older) is disposed of and a new machine is acquired. Consider now the Commercial Company's inventory (Section 5.3), which holds 75 units of a commodity. The company sells 15 units each month (recording the transactions by the FIFO method) and buys 15 units to replenish the inventory. Thus the inventory is held in stock for 5 months (75:15). In both cases, the oldest machine or batch (of 15 units of commodity) is taken off the premises and the remaining units are reported at their acquisition cost. Just as the aggregate acquisition cost (gross value) of the machines can be restated by means of the gross value restatement coefficient, so the aggregate inventory value can be restated (assuming that the FIFO method is used).

To compute an aggregate restatement coefficient for the Commercial Company's inventory, monthly inventory calculations under both conventional and PLA accounting procedures are carried out in Exhibit 10.4. The illustration in Exhibit 10-4 assumes that acquisitions take place at the beginning of the period (month, here) rather than at the end of the period (quarter, there) as assumed in Exhibit 5.3. During the year 19X2 prices crept up by 0.797% monthly (compared to quarterly price increments in Exhibit 5.3). The monthly price increment occurred after acquisition took place. Since inflation started on January 19X2 and inventory is held for 5 months, the first five interim inventory records (January 31 to May 31, 19X2) are transitory; only from June on may inventory be considered as being in equilibrium— that is, batches of equal size exist and enter inventory under conditions of a constantly increasing price level. (The calculations for the months August to November have been omitted in Exhibit 10.4 to save space.) On June 30, 19X2, the ratio between the PLA closing value ($78.66) and the conventional closing value ($76.81) is 1.02408. This is a weighted restatement coefficient for inventory that is composed of five batches of commodities that were acquired with dollars having different "values." The same ratio (except for minor differences due to rounding errors) prevails for the rest of the months.

Exhibit 10.4. Commercial Company
Interim Inventory Calculations for the Year 19X2
(10% Creeping Inflation, FIFO Method)

12.31.X1	Date:	1.31.X2	2.28.X2	3.31.X2	4.30.X2	5.31X2	6.30.X2	7.31.X2	12.31.X2
100.00	Price index:	100.80	101.60	102.41	103.23	104.05	104.88	105.71	110.00
				Conventional Accounting					
$75.00	Opening	$75.00	$75.00	$75.12	$75.36	$75.72	$76.20	$76.81	$79.92
15.00	Use	15.00	15.00	15.00	15.00	15.00	15.00	15.12	15.73
60.00	Balance	60.00	60.00	60.12	60.36	60.72	61.20	61.69	64.19
15.00	Buy*	15.00	15.12	15.24	15.36	15.48	15.61	15.73	16.37
75.00	Closing	75.00	75.12	75.36	75.72	76.20	76.81	77.42	80.56
				PLA Accounting					
75.00	Opening	75.00	75.60	76.20	76.81	77.42	78.04	78.66	81.84
15.00	Buy*	15.00	15.12	15.24	15.36	15.48	15.61	15.73	16.37
—	Restatement	0.72	0.72	0.73	0.73	0.75	0.74	0.76	0.79
90.00	Balance	90.72	91.44	92.17	92.90	93.65	94.39	95.15	99.00
15.00	Use	15.12	15.24	15.36	15.48	15.61	15.73	15.86	16.50
75.00	Closing	75.60	76.20	76.81	77.42	78.04	78.66	79.29	82.50

*Before price level rose.

The weighted restatement coefficient, as computed above, can be derived from the same mathematical formula that was used for restating the aggregate gross value of fixed assets. Inserting the variables of the numerical illustration ($n = 5, p = 0.0797$) into this formula, we get a restatement coefficient of 1.02403.[4] Using this formula, we can compute coefficients for various periodical inflation rates and inventory periods, as presented in Exhibit 10.5.

Exhibit 10.5. Restatement Coefficients for Inventories and for Materials Used When the FIFO Method is Practiced (R_{gross})*,†

Average Holding Time (periods)	Inflation Rate, (% per period)				
	0.1	0.5	1.0	1.5	2.0
1	1.001	1.005	1.010	1.015	1.020
3	1.002	1.010	1.020	1.030	1.040
5	1.003	1.015	1.030	1.045	1.061
7	1.004	1.020	1.040	1.061	1.082
9	1.005	1.025	1.051	1.076	1.103
12	1.007	1.033	1.066	1.100	1.135

*Assuming zero rate of growth.
†Detailed tables are presented in Appendix E.

The coefficients presented here are suitable for restating inventory when the FIFO method is practiced. When the average method is practiced, the restatement coefficients should be lower for the same set of inflation rates and inventory holding periods (as shown below). When the LIFO method is practiced, restatement of recorded values cannot be carried out with the aid of coefficients.[5]

10.4 Approximating Price Level Adjusted Profit

The major purpose of price level adjustments of conventional balance sheet data is to enable calculation of a company's economic profit during a period of inflation. This profit, as defined by Hicks (Section 2.1), is measured by the annual PLA operating profit (Section 15.6). The PLA operating profit may be estimated by applying the appropriate restatement coefficients to aggregate data from official financial statements regarding lagged costs, such as depreciation and materials used (drawn from inventory).[6]

Yearly historical depreciation charges may be adjusted by applying the gross value restatement coefficients, assuming straight-line depreciation, because depreciation charges are based on acquisition cost (gross value).

For example, the Manufacturing Company's depreciation expense in 19X3, as recorded in the conventional profit and loss statement, is $52.50.[7] The corresponding restatement coefficient (for $n = 2, p = 0.10$) is 1.15238 (Section 10.1), and the PLA depreciation is $60.50 ($52.50 × 1.15238).

The historical costs of materials used may also be adjusted by applying the restatement coefficients. The gross value coefficients are suitable for restating the historical costs of materials when the FIFO method is practiced; the net value coefficients are suitable when the average method is used. To illustrate this procedure on interim material inventory figures would require processing extensive data.[8] Instead, the Manufacturing Company's yearly data are used for illustration purposes, by considering the value of the machines as inventory that is held in stock for two periods (years).

Consider a Commercial Company holding on January 1, 19X3, two batches in inventory:

	Units in Batch	Acquisition Date	Acquisition Cost	Inflating Factor	PLA Cost on 12.31.19X3
Batch 1	25	1.1.19X2	$25.00	1.21	$30.25
Batch 2	50	1.1.19X3	55.00	1.10	60.50
			80.00		90.75

During the year 19X3, 50 units are drawn from inventory and sold. Under the FIFO method 25 units of Batch 1 and 25 units of Batch 2 are drawn from inventory. Under conventional accounting the resulting cost of goods sold is therefore as follows:

25 units of Batch 1	$25.00
25 units of Batch 2	27.50
	52.50

Applying to this figure the appropriate gross value restatement coefficient for $n = 2, p = 0.10$ (Section 10.1), we get

$$\$52.50 \times 1.15238 = \$60.50$$

The resulting restated figure corresponds to the PLA value ($30.25 plus one-half of $60.50).

Under the average method, on the other hand, two-thirds (50 units out of 75) of the total inventory of $80 are drawn as cost of goods sold, that is, $53.33. Applying to this figure the appropriate net value restatement coefficient (Section 10.2), we get

$$\$53.3333 \times 1.13437 = \$60.50$$

which also corresponds to the figure computed by PLA procedures.

Using the formula for the net value, we can compute restatement coefficients for inventory (under the average method) as presented in Exhibit 10.6.

Exhibit 10.6. Restatement Coefficients for Materials Used When the Average Method Is Practiced (R_{net})*,†

Average Holding Time (periods)	Inflation Rate (% per period)				
	0.1	0.5	1.0	1.5	2.0
1	1.001	1.005	1.010	1.015	1.020
3	1.002	1.008	1.017	1.025	1.033
5	1.002	1.012	1.023	1.035	1.047
7	1.003	1.015	1.030	1.045	1.061
9	1.004	1.018	1.037	1.056	1.074
12	1.005	1.023	1.047	1.071	1.095

*Assuming zero rate of growth.
† Detailed tables are presented in Appendix E.

In summary, PLA operating profit may be approximated by applying restatement coefficients to the lagged cost of goods sold: the gross value coefficient (R_{gross}) should be applied to the aggregate depreciation charges (Exhibit 10.1) and cost of materials used when the FIFO method is practiced (Exhibit 10.5); the net value coefficient (R_{net}), to the aggregate cost of materials used when the average method is practiced (Exhibit 10.6). With the LIFO method, the cost of materials used should not be restated.

10.5 Restrictions on the Applicability of the Coefficients

The mathematical formulas are affected by three variables: (1) inflation rate, (2) asset life span, and (3) asset rate of growth.[9] The construction of the formulas is based on some simplifying assumptions regarding the behavior of these variables. These assumptions, as listed in Section 10.1, restrict the applicability of the coefficients. The restrictive effect of these assumptions is checked below.

The assumption of a constant inflation rate over time may be quite restrictive for restating fixed asset values. This restriction usually affects the restatement of inventories to a lesser degree, because shorter periods are considered. When the inflation rate fluctuates over time, the average rate for the period under analysis may be used.

The assumption of one type of assets whose ages are evenly distributed may not be restrictive for many companies, especially those that hold a diversified set of assets acquired gradually over the years. The average life span of the assets held by such a company provides, in this case, a good approximation to be used in choosing the restatement coefficient. The use of restatement coefficients is not suitable, however, for a company that invested large sums in given years in the past.[10] The assumption of even age distribution suits most cases of inventories, assuming that the FIFO or average method is practiced, because materials are ordinarily used and bought on a current basis.

The assumption of even age distribution does not hold when a firm is growing. The greater the growth, the larger is the share of "young" assets in the set, and the lower is the restatement coefficient. The mathematical model takes this variable into consideration. However, since the effect of this variable is less significant than that of the inflation rate and asset life span (as shown in Section 11.2), it is ignored in this book.

Notes

1. This chapter is based on ideas and techniques that were developed together with Dr. Leon Shashua. It relies heavily on Shashua and Goldschmidt (1976).
2. When net asset value is considered, the net value of newer assets is closer to their acquisition cost than that of older assets; they have been depreciated over fewer years. As a result, their relative weight in total net value is greater than their relative weight in total gross value. Since their acquisition was more recent, the inflating factor is smaller for newer than for older assets. Their greater weight in total net value requires a lower restatement coefficient for net asset value than for gross asset value.
3. The use of these coefficients is especially suitable for the restatement of aggregate data related to an industry or the economy as a whole.
4. This is a relatively accurate figure. The ratio that has been computed on empirical data from Exhibit 10.4 (1.02408) is inaccurate because of rounding errors.

5. See Note 7, Chapter 5.
6. Goldsmith (1955, Vol. II, p. 544) applied a similar approach: he computed a ratio from empirical data, with which he corrected the reported depreciation allowances on a national scale. Stickney and Green (1974, p. 26) claim that restated information can be obtained by transforming data from conventional financial statements.
7. Detailed calculations of depreciation expense for December 31, 19X3, are as follows:

Acquisition		Conventional	Inflating	PLA
Date	Cost	Depreciation	Factor	Depreciation
1.1.19X2	$50.00	$25.00	1.21	$30.25
1.1.19X3	55.00	27.50	1.10	30.25
		52.50		60.50

8. It would require the preparation of (1) interim cost calculations under conventional and PLA procedures, as carried out in Exhibit 10.4, for a nontransitional year (say 19X3, since the first 5 months in Exhibit 10.4 are transitional), and (2) the year's profit and loss statement (in a form similar to that in Exhibit 5.4). These must be prepared for both the FIFO and the average methods.
9. Taking into account the rate of growth, the corresponding formulas (Shashua and Goldschmidt, 1976) are as follows:

$$R_{\text{gross}} = \frac{(1+p)^n S_{\overline{n}|k}}{S_{\overline{n}|(k+p)}}$$

$$R_{\text{net}} = \left(\frac{k+p}{k}\right) \frac{(1+p)^n \left[S_{\overline{n}|k}\,(n\mathrm{k}-1)+n\right]}{S_{\overline{n}|(k+p)}\,(nk+np-1)+n}$$

where

R is the restatement coefficient,
p is the inflation rate,
n is the average life span of assets,
k is the average annual real rate of growth of investments, and
$S_{\overline{n}|\alpha}$ is the accumulated sum of an ordinary annuity, growing periodically at the rate of α for n periods.

10. When the major investments have been carried out in a few given years, these sums can be restated by applying the appropriate index number directly.

References

Goldsmith, R. W., *A Study of Saving in the United States,* Princeton University Press, Princeton, N.J., 1955.

Shashua, L. and Y. Goldschmidt, "A Tool for Inflation Adjustment of Financial Statements," *Journal of Business Finance and Accounting,* Spring 1976, pp. 33–42.

Stickney, C. P. and D. O. Green, "No Price Level Adjusted Statements, Please (Pleas)," *CPA Journal,* January 1974, pp. 25–31.

Eleven

Tools for Adjusting Financial Statements

The practicality of the concepts developed in this book depends, in part, on simple procedures of application. The objective of this chapter is to provide tools for the outlines of such procedures for various levels of accuracy, each determined by the time and effort expended. Thus, depending on the aim or the user, the appropriate method of adjustment can be chosen.

11.1 Transforming Price Index into Restatement Factor

Detailed restatement of a company's set of assets is carried out by applying the appropriate price index to the historical acquisition-cost figure of each asset or a group of assets in the following way:

$$\frac{\text{Index number at restatement date}}{\text{Index number at acquisition date}} \times \text{Historical cost}$$

In this manner the restatement factor (the ratio of indices) is computed that measures the price change between acquisition date and restatement date. For example, suppose that the price index at the present time is 115.5 and that on the acquisition date it was 110; then the factor to be used for restatement purposes is 1.05 (115.5:110).

To make restatement work simple, the relevant series of price index numbers should be transformed by the above method. A series of restatement factors emerges, the base year of which is the restatement date. These factor numbers can be used as direct multiplicants for restating historical costs. This is illustrated in Exhibit 11.1 on a "linked" series. The dates of acquisition of some of the assets to be restated are often earlier than the base date of the appropriate price index series. In this case the former series must be "linked" to the last series. This procedure is also illustrated in Exhibit 11.1. Transformed linked series make restatement work simple: suppose that an asset was acquired in 1968 for $1,000; then its restated value for 1975 is $1310 ($1000 × 1.31, a factor from Exhibit 11.1).

Exhibit 11.1 Illustration of Linking and Transforming a Hypothetical Price Index Series

Year	Original Price Index		Linked Series*	Transformed Series† (Inflating factor)
	1960=100	1971=100		
1967	114.1		87.6	1.32
1968	115.2		88.4	1.31
1969	125.0		95.9	1.20
1970	127.1		97.5	1.18
1971	130.3	100.0	100.0	1.16
1972		105.8	105.8	1.09
1973		110.0	110.0	1.05
1974		112.3	112.3	1.03
1975		115.5	115.5	1.00

*The relevant original index number divided by that of 1971 (the later base), multiplied by 100, and rounded.
†The index number of 1975 (the current price level) divided by the relevant linked number, and rounded.

11.2 Estimating the Life Span and Growth of Assets

The average life span of fixed assets can be estimated from data reported by conventional financial statements if the straight-line depreciation method is used. By dividing the total acquisition cost (gross value taken from the balance sheet) by the annual depreciation charge (data from the profit and loss statement) the average life span can be approximated. The corresponding computations on data from conventional financial statements of the Manufacturing Company for 19X2

(Appendix C) are as follows: \$105:\$50 = 2.1 years. This is approximately the weighted average life span of the assets held by the company (the exact figure is 2 years).[1]

The length of time that inventory is held in stock can also be estimated from conventional financial statement data. Multiplying the average value of inventory (i.e., one-half of the value of both opening and closing figures) by 12 and dividing this sum by the yearly usage of materials gives the number of months that inventory is held.

The corresponding computations on data from conventional financial statements of the Commercial Company for 19X2 (Exhibit 5.4) are as follows:

$$\frac{\left[(\$75 + \$81.72) / 2\right] \times 12 \text{ months}}{\$184} = 5.1 \text{ months}$$

This is approximately the time that inventory is held in stock by the company (the exact figure is 5 months).

The real rate of asset growth (either fixed assets or inventories) can be estimated by deducting the inflation rate (average per period for the series of periods under analysis) from the average nominal rate of asset growth.[2] The nominal rate of asset growth is computed by dividing the recorded value of assets at the date of analysis (say, at present) by that at the beginning of the series of periods under analysis. The resulting figure is the compound amount of growth for the series of periods; the per period rate of growth can be derived from the relevant tables.[3]

Suppose that a company's recorded fixed asset value in 1960 is \$1 million and, in 1975, \$2 million; then the average annual growth rate is 5% (derived from compound interest tables for 15 years). Suppose further that the average annual inflation rate over this period was 3.5%; then the real rate of growth is approximately 1.5% (5.0% – 3.5%).[4]

11.3 Rules of Thumb for Estimating Restatement Coefficients[5]

As mentioned in Section 10.5, the mathematical formulas for restating aggregate data are affected by three variables: (1) inflation rate, (2) asset life span, and (3) asset rate of growth. The computed coefficients, for various levels of the three pertinent variables, have been explained by regression analysis (Shashua and Goldschmidt 1976).

The resulting relationships indicate that the effect of asset rate of growth is negligible for moderate rates of inflation and growth.

The resulting relationships (between the estimated coefficients and the affecting variables) provide very good estimates of these coefficients. By rounding the regression figures the following formulas are derived:

$$R_{\text{gross}} = 1 + (n \times p \times 0.6),$$
$$R_{\text{net}} = 1 + (n \times p \times 0.4)$$

where R is the restatement coefficient,
n is the asset life span (average), and
p is the inflation rate per period (average for the n periods).

These formulas, which are easy to remember, may serve as rules of thumb for restating aggregate data. For example, suppose that the average fixed asset life span is 16 years ($n = 16$), and the inflation rate during the last 16 years was 2% per annum ($p = 0.02$). Then the restatement coefficients will be approximately as follows: for gross value and depreciation, $1 + (16 \times 0.02 \times 0.6) = 1.19$ (the corresponding value in Exhibit 10.1 is 1.178); for net value, $1 + (16 \times 0.02 \times 0.4) = 1.13$ (the exact value in Exhibit 10.3 is 1.123). As can be seen, the approximating formulas usually provide very good estimates of the actual coefficients. Applying the formulas to extreme cases (regarding the level of n and p) provides less reliable estimates.

A simpler rule of thumb, which provides rougher estimates of current fixed asset values, may be calculated on national average data. Such a rule for the United States, assuming the average life span of fixed assets to be 15 years and the average inflation rate (1959 – 1974) to be 3.5% per annum, is as follows[6] (using either the rule of thumb formulas or the data in Appendix E):

$$R_{\text{gross}} = 1.3$$
$$R_{\text{net}} = 1.2$$

These restatement coefficients are simple to remember and practical, providing rough estimates of the restated aggregate value of fixed assets in the United States.[7]

11.4 Outlines for Adjusting Profit and Loss Statements

In this section and the next one, outlines for PLA procedures are provided. Several procedures are suggested for various levels of accuracy. These outlines are not necessarily in accord with the directions that have been published lately by accounting institutions in many countries.[8]

The main adjustment is, of course, that of the reported profit figure. For this purpose two lagged cost items must be adjusted: depreciation and materials used (drawn from inventory). It is interesting to note that on a national scale the absolute size of the adjustment for depreciation is considerably smaller than that for inventory.[9] Furthermore, the dollar amount of inventory adjustment fluctuates considerably over time because of the relatively short replacement cycle of inventory items.[10] Adjusting the two lagged cost items will provide an approximation of the PLA operating profit figure. This figure should be used instead of the conventional profit figure in order to avoid capital erosion during a period of inflation.

Adjusted depreciation may be derived from detailed restated fixed asset values. Alternatively, adjusted aggregate depreciation expense may be approximated by applying (1) the appropriate restatement coefficient, (2) the rule of thumb formula, or (3) the general coefficient (Section 11.2). Adjustment of the cost of materials used may also be derived from detailed restated inventory values, or approximated by applying the appropriate restatement coefficient. In addition, adjustment of the cost of materials used may be approximated by another method, that is, by adding the restatement gains on the opening value of inventory as cost to the materials used. This method provides, of course, a rougher estimate than that arrived at by applying the restatement coefficient.

Price level adjustment of materials used means that the realized portion of the restatement gains on inventory value is deducted from conventional accounting profit (i.e., added to costs of materials used). The division between realized and nonrealized restatement gains depends on the time that inventory is held in stock. (See Exhibit 14.3.) Since this time is relatively short, the nonrealized restatement gains are relatively small. The shorter the period that inventory is held in stock, the smaller the nonrealized restatement gains; in turn, the more accurate will be the results obtained by the suggested approximation method.

To determine PLA total profit, net restatement gains must first be calculated and added to PLA operating profit. For this purpose, assets and equity must be restated at the beginning and at the end of the year.[11]

Alternatively, if only the profit and loss statement is to be adjusted, the net restatement gains can be calculated without adjusting all recorded balance sheet data. The formal presentation in Chapter 6 shows that the net restatement gains equal to price level gains on net debt (relation 6.10). The latter is computed by applying the price level change for the year to the difference between recorded debt and recorded financial assets (which are not price level linked).[12]

11.5 Outlines for Adjusting Balance Sheets

Company assets may be classified into the following categories:

1. Nondepreciable fixed assets (land).
2. Depreciable fixed assets (plant and equipment).
3. Inventories (materials, goods).
4. Investments in ordinary shares.
5. Investments in bonds.
6. Money assets (cash and debtors).

Categories 1 to 4 are usually price level linked and therefore require restatement; categories 5 and 6, on the other hand, are usually not price level linked, and hence the recorded value does not change as a result of price level change. Liabilities, similarly to categories 5 and 6, are usually not price level linked, and again, therefore, the recorded values are not affected by price level change.

Depreciable fixed assets may be restated by various methods, as listed here in decreasing order of complexity, reliability, and accuracy:

1. Detailed restatement of each asset or group.
2. Restatement of aggregate data by applying coefficients to:
   a. Starting point data (Section 12.4).
   b. Current period data, using:
      (i) Coefficients from table.
      (ii) Coefficients approximated by formula.
      (iii) General coefficient.

Inventories may be restated by inflating the acquisition cost (of individual types or groups) by a general price index. Alternatively, restated aggregate inventory value may be approximated by applying the appropriate restatement coefficient. Better information on inventory value can be obtained by appraising the current market value.

Nondepreciable assets and investments in ordinary shares are best revalued by appraising their current market values.

If detailed restatement or revaluation is carried out, some balance sheet items are kept at their face values (left-hand column in Exhibit 11.2). The others are either restated (for PLA accounting) or revalued according to their market values or replacement costs (for replacement-cost accounting). The details are listed in Exhibit 11.2.

After restatement and revaluation has once been carried out, yearly updating is a relatively simple activity, especially when it is computerized.

11.6 Adjusting Financial Statements with Restatement Coefficients

The discussion in Chapter 10 indicated that the restatement coefficients are practical tools. Two types of coefficients are available: for gross value (R_{gross}) and for net value (R_{net}). These coefficients may also be approximated by a simple formula (Section 11.3) and then applied as rules of thumb in adjusting financial statements. The various uses of these coefficients (or formulas) are summarized in Exhibit 11.3.

As a summary of this chapter and Chapter 10, the following outline is presented. It lists the procedures required for adjusting the aggregate data of conventional financial statements by using the restatement coefficients. The procedures outlined below are applicable only when the fixed assets and inventories are composed of a relatively large number of units with more or less even age distribution.

1. Compute the average asset life span from the data of conventional financial statements (Section 11.2).
2. Find the average rate of inflation for the analyzed period.
3. Find the inventory accounting method.
4. Compute the PLA lagged costs by applying restatement coefficients to depreciation charges and materials used.
5. Compute the PLA operating profit.
6. Restate the balance sheet by applying the restatement coefficients to fixed asset and inventory values at the beginning and the end of the year.
7. Compute the net restatement gains.
8. Compute the PLA total profit.
9. Restate the balance sheet of an earlier year.
10. Compute the accumulation of real assets and equity over the years between the dates of the two balance sheets. (Sections 12.4 and 13.4).

Exhibit 11.2. Method of Detailed Valuation of Balance Sheet Items

Item	Face Value	Restatement for PLA Accounting	Replacement-Cost Accounting	
			Market Value	Adjusted Current Replacement Cost
Cash, time deposits	X			
Accounts receivable, notes receivable, allowance for bad debts	X			
Short-term marketable securities		X	X	
Inventories				
Marketable		X	X	
Others		X		X
Investment in stock of other firms (unquoted)		X		X
Equipment and buildings		X		X
Land under buildings		X		X
Natural resources		X	X	
Intangible assets		X		X
Accounts payable, accrued expenses payable, notes payable	X			
Bonds payable	X			
Deferred income	X			
Paid in capital	X			
Retained earnings	X			
Capital maintenance reserve		X		X
Minority interest		X		X

Exhibit 11.3. Types of Restatement Coefficients and List of Applications

Type of Coefficient	Approximating Formula	Application for Adjustment	Exhibit Showing Sample of Coefficient
Gross value (R_{gross})	$1 + (n \times p \times 0.6)$	Fixed asset gross value	10.1
		Fixed asset depreciation charge	10.1
		Inventory value under FIFO	10.5
		Materials used under FIFO	10.5
Net value (R_{net})	$1 + (n \times p \times 0.4)$	Fixed asset net value	10.3
		Materials used under average method	10.6

It should be noted that every method of asset restatement will provide a different asset value. But the limited objectivity in regard to asset values applies also to conventional accounting statements.[13]

Notes

1. This figure is inaccurate since the numerical illustration assumes acquisition in the preceding year, before prices changed. If this assumption is changed, the results are accurate, as calculated for December 31, 19X3:

Acquisition		
Date	Cost	Depreciation
1.1.19X2	$50.00	$25.00
1.1.19X3	55.00	27.50
	105.00	52.50

$105.00 : $52.50 = 2 years

2. Stated formally, the nominal growth over a given period is as follows:

$$(1 + q) = (1 + k)(1 + p)$$

Hence $$1 + k = \frac{1 + q}{1 + p}$$

$$k = \frac{1 + q}{1 + p} - 1 = \frac{q - p}{1 + p}$$

where q is the nominal growth rate,
$1 + q$ is the measured nominal growth,
k is the real growth rate, and
p is the inflation rate.

If p is relatively small, the denominator, $1 + p$, is close to 1, and $k \cong q - p$.

3. Stated formally, the compound amount of growth over a series of periods is as follows:

$$x = (1 + q)^n$$

Hence
$$q = \sqrt[n]{x} - 1$$

where x is the compound amount factor,
q is the per period growth rate, and
n is the number of periods.

4. More accurately, $k = \dfrac{q - p}{1 + p} = \dfrac{0.015}{1.035} = 0.0145,$

that is, 1.45%.

5. This section is based on Dr. Leon Shashua's development as published in Shashua and Goldschmidt (1976).
6. The GNP implicit price deflator (U.S.) was 144.7 in 1974 and 86.4 in 1959 (Note 8, Chapter 1). This is a total increase of 67.5% (144.7:86.4 = 1.675), equivalent to a compound annual growth of 3.5% (derived from compound interest tables, or from the formula in Note 3 above).
7. It is interesting to compare the coefficients above to empirical ratios. Goldsmith (1955, Vol. I, p. 955), provides the following depreciation data on transportation and public utilities in the United States:

Year	Original Cost	Current Cost	Ratio
1945	\$3977	\$5003	1.26
1946	4199	5729	1.36
1947	5220	7897	1.51
1948	6150	9418	1.53
1949	6750	9768	1.45

It should be noted that the computed ratio is "gross" and that n is larger than the value assumed in the text.

Shashua et al. (1977), found in an empirical study of the kibbutz sector in Israel for the years 1958 to 1968, when the average inflation rate was 4.8% (annual rates of 0 to 10.4%) and the average life span of assets was $n = 16.7$ years, that the average ratio of depreciation was 1.38 (range: 1.27 to 1.55), and the average ratio for net asset value was 1.24 (range: 1.08 to 1.37).

8. For example, Institute of Chartered Accountants in England and Wales (1974), Financial Accounting Standards Board (1974), Institute of Chartered Accountants in Australia, (1974), National Council of Chartered Accountants in South Africa (1975), and Canadian Institute of Chartered Accountants (1975). For a summary see Sandilands (1975, pp. 106-112), and for a summary of earlier statements see Gynther (1966, Chapter 5).

9. The effect that inventories have on profit can be seen from the following data (American Institute of Certified Public Accountants and other institutions, 1968, Paragraph 13):

	Canada	United Kingdom	United States
Sample size	116,000	1800	10,000
Type of company	All types	Industrial concerns	Manufacturing corporations
Year	1964	1966	1966
Percentage of total net assets that inventories comprise	25	29	24
Ratio of inventories to pretax profit	2.9	2.5	1.9

For a discussion on the importance of inventory and fixed asset values in profit measurement see Edwards and Bell (1961, pp. 137–139 and 163–171, respectively).

According to Goldsmith (1955, Vol, II, p. 543), "the average yearly adjustment...of depreciation...is about $600 million, disregarding sign, compared with an average inventory valuation adjustment of about $1000 million" in the U.S. economy. These findings were based on a series of data for 1897 to 1949.

10. See the data in Note 11, Chapter 1. For more recent data see *Business Week,* September 22, 1975, p. 105.

11. Only if PLA total profit is computed, can inflationfree profit be determined by applying inflationfree cost of debt to the restated loans (see Exhibit 7.8).

12. For a similar procedure see Davidson and Weil (1975).
13. In this connection let us mention a paper by H. Ross (1971): "Is It Better to Be Precisely Wrong Than Vaguely Right?"

References

American Institute of Certified Public Accountants and Institutes of Chartered Accountants of Canada, England and Wales, Scotland, and Ireland, *Accounting and Auditing Approaches to Inventories in Three Nations,* 1968.

Canadian Institute of Chartered Accountants, *Accounting for Changes in the General Purchasing Power of Money,* July 1975.

Davidson, S. and R. L. Weil, "Inflation Accounting," *Financial Analyst Journal,* January–February 1975, pp. 27–31, 70–84.

Edwards, E. O. and P. W. Bell, *The Theory and Measurement of Business Income,* University of California Press, Berkeley and Los Angeles, 1961.

Financial Accounting Standards Board, *Financial Reporting in Units of General Purchasing Power,* Exposure Draft, Stamford, Conn., December 1974.

Goldsmith, R. W., *A Study of Saving in the United States,* Princeton University Press, Princeton, N.J., 1955.

Gynther, R. S., *Accounting for Price Level Changes–Theory and Procedures,* Pergamon Press, Oxford, 1966.

Institute of Chartered Accountants in Australia, *A Method of Accounting for Changes in the Purchasing Power of Money,* Preliminary Exposure Draft, December 1974.

Institute of Chartered Accountants in England and Wales, *Accounting for Changes in the Purchasing Power of Money,* Provisional Statement of Standard Accounting Practice No. 7, May 1974.

National Council of Chartered Accountants in South Africa, *Accounting for Inflation and Other Changes in Price Level,* Discussion Paper, May 1975.

Ross, H., "Is It Better to Be Precisely Wrong Than Vaguely Right?" *Financial Executive,* June 1971, pp. 8-12.

Sandilands, F. E. P., *Inflation Accounting,* Report of the Inflation Accounting Committee, Her Majesty's Stationery Office, London, 1975.

Shashua, L. and Y. Goldschmidt, "A Tool for Inflation Adjustment of Financial Statements," *Journal of Business Finance and Accounting,* Spring 1976, pp. 33–42.

Shashua, L., Y. Goldschmidt, and G. Levkovitz, "Alternative Methods of Estimating the Capital Stock of the Kibbutz" forthcoming in *Issues in the Economy of Israel,* Maurice Falk Institute for Economic Research in Israel, 1977. In Hebrew; forthcoming in English.

Twelve

Financial Statement Adjustment

As this book stresses, distortions in conventional financial statements during a period of inflation can be avoided by following PLA accounting procedures. Since, however, these procedures are not used by most companies, conventional financial statements must be adjusted if the price level distortions are to be corrected.

Balance sheet adjustment requires restatement of most assets and of equity. Profit and loss statement adjustment requires restatement of lagged costs (depreciation and materials used). As a result, reported profit shrinks (during inflation) to provide PLA operating profit. The adjusted figures, in absolute or ratio form, can be used for both time-series (over the years) and cross-section (among firms) comparisons.

12.1 Inflation Distortions of Financial Ratios

Financial ratios are used extensively in analyzing the financial and economic situations of firms. These ratios are computed from conventional financial statements data. The fact that a ratio is independent of the scale in which the original measurements (the numerator and denominator) were carried out may cause the impression that financial ratios are unaffected by price level changes. This impression is false when the dollars in the numerator of the ratio differ from those in the denominator. Just as different currency scales should not be added in the financial statement, they should not be divided one by another when preparing ratios. Since the unadjusted dollar values in each year's balance sheet and profit and loss statement represent a conglomeration of different purchasing power units, the use of these values as ratios is misleading.

During a period of price level changes the data distortions in the financial statements affect the ratios that are derived from such data. The direction of bias in some of the more important financial ratios is shown in Exhibit 12.1. The extent of bias is dependent on the rate of price level changes during the relevant past and on the other factors listed in Section 7.1.

As can be seen, most of the ratios listed in Exhibit 12.1 are affected by inflation. The expected direction of bias in most ratios is upward. A more important conclusion from the analysis in Exhibit 12.1 is that, of 12 ratios, 8 show bias toward an optimistic picture of the analyzed company.[1]

The strongest effect of the bias is on the profitability ratios: the bias during a period of inflation is, of course, toward unjustified optimism. The reverse would hold during a period of deflation.

The distortions in these ratios are illustrated for the Manufacturing Leverage Company, as shown in Exhibit 12.2. The resulting biases in the ratios are determined mainly by the rate of price level change in the past. For example, the price increase in the relevant past (19X1 to 19X3) affects the first ratio by 21%. The other two ratios are biased by 25% since numerator and denominator are affected in opposite directions.

In summary, during an extended period of price level changes time-series comparisons of financial ratios that are computed from conventional financial statement data will produce a distorted picture. Cross-section comparisons among firms in a given year will also provide a distorted picture unless asset intensity, asset age, and financial leverage are equal in all the analyzed firms. Adjustment of the relevant data before financial ratios are computed is therefore of importance.

12.2 Updating for Time-Series Comparisons

The discussion in this book shows how the conventional financial statements for a given year should be price level adjusted during a period of price level changes. The adjustments are relevant for the

Exhibit 12.1. Effect of Inflation on Financial Ratios

Ratio	Formula for Calculation	Bias of Variables During Inflation	Direction of Bias	Effect of Bias
Liquidity				
1. Current	Current assets / Current liabilities	Conventional < PLA / Conventional = PLA	Downward	Pessimistic
2. Quick, or acid test	Current assets − inventory / Current liabilities	Conventional = PLA / Conventional = PLA	None	None
Leverage				
3. Debt to total assets	Total debt / Total assets	Conventional = PLA / Conventional < PLA	Upward	Pessimistic
4. Times interest earned	Profit before interest charges / Interest charges	Conventional > PLA / Conventional = PLA	Upward	Optimistic
5. Fixed charge coverage	Income available for meeting fixed charges / Fixed charges	Conventional > PLA / Conventional = PLA	Upward	Optimistic
Activity				
6. Turnover of inventory	Sales / Inventory	Conventional = PLA / Conventional < PLA	Upward	Optimistic
7. Average collection period	Receivables / Sales per day	Conventional = PLA / Conventional = PLA	None	None
8. Turnover of fixed assets	Sales / Fixed assets	Conventional = PLA / Conventional < PLA	Upward	Optimistic
9. Turnover of total assets	Sales / Total assets	Conventional = PLA / Conventional < PLA	Upward	Optimistic

Ratio	Formula	Comparison	Direction	Outlook
Profitability				
10. Profit margin on sales	$\frac{\text{Net profit}}{\text{Sales}}$	$\frac{\text{Conventional} > \text{PLA}}{\text{Conventional} = \text{PLA}}$	Upward	Optimistic
11. Return on total assets	$\frac{\text{Net profit}}{\text{Total assets}}$	$\frac{\text{Conventional} > \text{PLA}}{\text{Conventional} < \text{PLA}}$	Strongly Upward	Optimistic
12. Return on net worth	$\frac{\text{Net profit}}{\text{Net worth}}$	$\frac{\text{Conventional} > \text{PLA}}{\text{Conventional} < \text{PLA}}$	Upward	Optimistic

Source: The list of ratios and the corresponding formulas for calculation are taken from Weston and Brigham 1969, Table 3-3.

Exhibit 12.2. Manufacturing Leverage Company
Profitability Financial Ratio Analysis
PLA and Conventional Pretax Data, 19X3, 19X5

Ratio	Conventional Accounting Data	PLA Accounting Data	Conventional in Relation to PLA
Period of Inflation (19X3)			
Profit margin on sales	0.115	0.095	1.21
Returns on total assets	0.315	0.252	1.25
Returns on net worth	0.525	0.420	1.25
Period of Deflation (19X5)			
Profit margin on sales	0.048	0.072	0.66
Returns on total assets	0.123	0.191	0.64
Returns on net worth	0.205	0.319	0.64

Source: Data from Appendix C.

given year—that for which the statements have been made. The items that are adjusted for a given year cannot be compared with equivalent items (nonadjusted or adjusted) of different years because different "value" (purchasing power) dollars are involved.

Comparing time-series financial data requires the updating of reported data to currency of a given date. Usually, updating is done in terms of the most recent dollars. This makes the data meaningful to the user. Updating or "rolling forward" is carried out by applying a general price index to the recorded historical data.[2] Even if PLA accounting is practiced, the PLA items must be updated for time-series comparisons.

Consider the Manufacturing Leverage Company's financial statements for the years 19X1 to 19X3. Neither the original data of conventional nor the data of PLA statements are comparable unless they are first updated, as illustrated in Exhibits 12.3 and 12.4.

Consider first the balance sheet data, as shown in Exhibit 12.3. The updated asset values (indicated by *u*) equal those recorded in the PLA balance sheet as of December 31, 19X3 (see Appendix C). On the other hand, the real value of debt, as shown by the updated figures, decreased in 19X2. This decrease is balanced by a restatement gains reserve. It should be noted that conventional balance sheet data are updated only after restatement of each asset (as under PLA accounting procedures). If PLA accounting is practiced, the recorded total figures should be updated directly by applying the appropriate inflating factor.

Consider now the profit and loss data in Exhibit 12.4. Each item in both the conventional and PLA statements is updated directly (indicated by *u*), except the conventional depreciation charges. The latter (as well as other lagged cost items) are derived from updated balance sheet data.[3]

Exhibit 12.3. Manufacturing Leverage Company
Comparison of Balance Sheets, December 31, 19X1–19X3
(Updated Data to 19X3 Dollars)

	Reported			Updated		
Year:	19X1	19X2	19X3	19X1*	19X2*	19X3*
Price index:	100.0	110.0	121.0			
Inflating factor:				1.21	1.10	1.00
Conventional Accounting						
Assets						
Machine	$\$50.00$	$\$50.00$	$\$55.00$	$\$60.50^u$	$\$60.50^u$	$\$60.50^u$
Machine	50.00	55.00	60.50	60.50^u	60.50^u	60.50^u
Assets, at cost	100.00	105.00	115.50	121.00	121.00	121.00
Accum. depr.	(25.00)	(25.00)	(27.50)	(30.25)	(30.25)	(30.25)
	75.00	80.00	88.00	90.75	90.75	90.75
Liabilities and Equity						
Loan	10.00	10.00	11.00	12.10^u	11.00^u	11.00
Loan	20.00	22.00	24.20	24.20^u	24.20^u	24.20
Total loans	30.00	32.00	35.20	36.30	35.20	35.20
Equity	45.00	45.00	45.00	54.45^u	49.50^u	45.00
New equity	—	3.00	7.80	—	3.30^u	7.80
Restatement gains reserve†					2.75	2.75
	75.00	80.00	88.00	90.75	90.75	90.75
PLA Accounting						
Assets						
Machine	50.00	55.00	60.50	60.50^u	60.50^u	60.50
Machine	50.00	55.00	60.50	60.50^u	60.50^u	60.50
Assets, at cost	100.00	110.00	121.00	121.00	121.00	121.00
Accum. depr.	(25.00)	(27.50)	(30.25)	(30.25)	(30.25)	(30.25)
	75.00	82.50	90.75	90.75	90.75	90.75
Liabilities and Equity						
Loan	10.00	10.00	11.50	12.10^u	11.00^u	11.50
Loan	20.00	23.00	24.80	24.20^u	25.30^u	24.80
Total loans	30.00	33.00	36.30	36.30	36.30	36.30
Equity	45.00	45.00	45.00	54.45^u	49.50^u	45.00
Equity maint.	—	4.50	9.45	—	4.95^u	9.45
	75.00	82.50	90.75	90.75	90.75	90.75

*The letter *u* indicates an updated figure.
†Residual amount.
Source: Data from Appendix C.

Exhibit 12.4. Manufacturing Leverage Company
Comparison of Profit and Loss Statements, 19X1–19X3
(Updated Data to 19X3 Dollars)

	Reported			Updated		
Year	19X1	19X2	19X3	19X1*	19X2*	19X3
Price index:	100.0	110.0	121.0			
Inflating factor:				1.21	1.10	1.00
Conventional Accounting						
Sales	\$200.00	\$220.00	\$242.00	\$242.00^u	242.00^u	242.00
Out-of-pocket costs	(130.00)	(143.00)	(157.30)	(157.30)^u	(157.30)^u	(157.30)
Interest	(2.40)	(4.20)	(4.48)	(2.90)^u	(4.62)^u	(4.48)
Depreciation†	(50.00)	(50.00)	(52.50)	(60.50)	(60.50)	(60.50)
Profit, pretax	17.60	22.80	27.72	21.30	19.58	19.72
Tax (50%)	(8.80)	(11.40)	(13.86)	(10.65)^u	(12.54)^u	(13.86)
Profit, after-tax	8.80	11.40	13.86	10.65	7.04	5.86
Dividend	(8.80)	(11.40)	(13.86)	(10.65)^u	(12.54)^u	(13.86)
Distribution from equity	—	—	—	—	(5.50)	(8.00)
PLA Accounting						
Sales	200.00	220.00	242.00	242.00^u	242.00^u	242.00
Out-of-pocket costs	(130.00)	(143.00)	(157.30)	(157.30)^u	(157.30)^u	(157.30)
Interest	(2.40)	(4.20)	(4.62)‡	(2.90)^u	(4.62)^u	(4.62)
Depreciation	(50.00)	(55.00)	(60.50)	(60.50)^u	(60.50)^u	(60.50)
PLA operating profit	17.60	17.80	19.58	21.30	19.58	19.58
Net restatement gains	—	3.00	3.30	—	3.30	3.30
Profit, PLA total pretax	17.60	20.80	22.88	21.30	22.88	22.88
Tax (50% on conventional profit)	(8.80)	(11.40)	(13.86)	(10.65)^u	(12.54)^u	(13.86)
Profit, PLA total after-tax	8.80	9.40	9.02	10.65	10.34	9.02

*The letter *u* indicates an updated figure.
†The updated depreciation is calculated from updated balance sheet data.
‡This figure is lower than that under conventional accounting since an additional loan has been taken to keep 60% equity in the PLA statement.
Source: Data from Appendix C.

In summary, time-series comparison of financial statement data requires stating all data in terms of the present year's currency. This involves two steps: (1) applying PLA procedures to each of the conventional financial statements that are analyzed, and (2) updating ("rolling forward") the figures of the resulting PLA statements. In both steps data are restated (adjusted, inflated). In the first step PLA procedures are applied to state all the data of a given year's financial statements in that year's currency. Historical values, as recorded in the balance sheet (acquisition costs of assets that were purchased in the past), and lagged costs, as recorded in the profit and loss statement, are inflated. In the second step PLA financial statements are inflated so that all data are expressed in the present year's currency.

The first step in the illustrations in Exhibits 12.3 and 12.4 is based on the adjustment of each asset in the balance sheets. This means that such time-series comparisons can be carried out only by an analyst who has all the data at his disposal. An outsider may use the restatement coefficients instead, thereby obtaining a close estimate of asset restatement.

The updated figures in Exhibits 12.3 and 12.4 show the development trends of the Manufacturing Leverage Company, in terms of 19X3 currency. Because of the company's physical stability most updated items are constant during the 3 years under analysis and equal the 19X3 PLA accounting data. The exceptions are interest charges and tax payments, as well as profit (both pretax and after-tax). The updated conventional pretax profit for 19X2 is lower than that for 19X1 because all items are equal except the interest charges. These profit figures are very close to the PLA operating profit.[4]

The PLA total pretax profit for 19X2 is $22.88 as compared to $21.30 for 19X1; the excess of $1.58 (all sums in 19X3 currency) is the net inflationary leverage returns. Yet, since income tax is levied on conventional reported profit, income tax payments increased from 19X1 to 19X2 by $1.89 ($12.54–$10.65). The PLA total after-tax profit was reduced from $10.65 to $10.34; despite inflationary leverage gains, income tax reduced net profit by $0.31 ($1.89–$1.58). The situation is aggravated by the fact that conventional after-tax profit for 19X2, equivalent to $12.54, was distributed as dividends, whereas only $10.34 was available. The difference of $2.20 constitutes dividend distribution from equity.

12.3 Restating the Opening Balance Sheet

The illustrations in Chapters 2 to 9 assumed that inflation started at the beginning of the period (on January 1, 19X2). All items in the last conventional balance sheet (of December 31, 19X1) were stated in dollars of equal purchasing power; therefore they were able to serve as valid opening balances for the year's price level adjustment. Usually, however, such price level adjustment takes place after several years of inflation, and the opening balance sheet must be restated.

The magnitude of this opening adjustment is determined by several factors, such as (1) the rate of price level changes in the past, (2) the age of the real assets, and (3) the net financial leverage (nonlinked debt less nonlinked financial assets).

Theoretically, revaluation should be carried out by different methods in accordance with the item involved. For example, equity should be restated with a general price level index, while fixed asset revaluation is best related to specific price indices, and inventories can be adjusted by comparison to going market prices. In practice, however, it is simpler to carry out restatement by means of one set of index numbers.

Each side of the balance sheet is restated separately applying the concepts developed in Chapter 4. On the assumption that debt is not price level linked, only equity is restated in terms of current purchasing power; the restatement charges represent the required equity maintenance reserve. If new shares were issued during the period preceding the date of restatement, or if retained earnings were increased on this date, these are set off against the required equity maintenance reserve.

Assets are then restated, and thereby the asset restatement gain is derived. At this stage the balance sheet should be balanced. The balancing item represents under-(or over-) leverage, that is, the amount of loans that would maintain the previous equity–loan ratio.

Consider the Manufacturing Leverage Company (Exhibit 4.5), for which only conventional financial statements are available. Suppose that at the beginning of year 19X3 the company's management asks for PLA data. Equity is restated (Exhibit 12.5) with a required maintenance reserve of \$4.50, which was financed by \$3 of new shares issued at the end of 19X2. The balance of \$1.50 indicates equity erosion (see the next chapter). Total equity and liabilities are now \$81.50, leaving \$1 for the shrinkage of leverage (\$32 in loans instead of \$33, which could be taken to maintain 40% leverage).

If assets are restated without parallel restatement of equity, the result is illusory holding gains. Asset restatement gains are mechanically balanced by an addition to equity, without checking whether this addition is, in fact, sufficient to maintain equity at its original value. This erroneous procedure is presented in the right-hand column of Exhibit 12.5. The example shows an addition to equity of \$2.50, whereas in reality erosion of \$1.50 took place.

Exhibit 12.5. Manufacturing Leverage Company
Balance Sheet as of December 19X2
Adjustment of Official Balance Sheet

Assets				Liabilities and Equity				
12.31.19X1		12.31.19X2		12.31.19X1		12.31.19X2		
							Adjusted†	
Official*		Official*	Adjusted†,‡	Official*		Official*	Correctly	Erroneously
$50.00	Machine 2	—		$10.00	Loan 2	—		
50.00	Machine 3	$50.00	$55.00[r]	20.00	Loan 3	$10.00	$10.00	$10.00
—	Machine 4	55.00	55.00	—	Loan 4	22.00	22.00	22.00
100.00		105.00	110.00	30.00	Total liabilities	32.00	32.00	32.00
(25.00)	Accum. depr.	(25.00)	(27.50)	45.00	Equity	45.00	45.00	45.00
				—	New shares	3.00	3.00	3.00
					Net equity adjustment[11]	—	1.50	—
					Balance	—	—	2.50
				45.00	Total equity	48.00	49.50	50.50
					Liabilities and equity		81.50	
					Underleverage§		1.00	
75.00		80.00	82.50	75.00		80.00	82.50	82.50

*Source: Data from Exhibit 4.5.

†Adjustment of the official (conventional) balance sheet, not PLA accounting as illustrated in Exhibit 4.5 (where an additional loan, 3a, has been taken to keep 60% equity).

‡The letter *r* indicates restated figure.

[11]Required equity maintenance less new shares.

§To keep 40% out of $82.50.

12.4 Starting Point of Fixed Asset Restatement

Restatement of an opening balance sheet, as explained in Section 12.3, can be carried out by an analyst who has the required data on each asset at his disposal. If an external analyst wants to restate the financial statements of a given company, he may do so on the aggregate data reported in the statements. In this case, restatement of fixed assets should start on data of the earliest balance sheet available. From this point on, year to year price level adjustments should be carried out, up to the current period.[5]

Using restatement coefficients (Sections 10.1 and 10.2) simplifies this procedure. The appropriate restatement coefficient may be applied to the fixed asset value that was recorded in an earlier year. The resulting figure should be used as a starting point from which annual price level adjustment is carried out up to the current year.[6]

Application of the restatement coefficient may provide only a rough estimate of the true value of the fixed assets. This happens when the conditions in practice diverge from those assumed in developing the coefficients: even age distribution and constant inflation and growth rates (Sections 10.1 and 10.5). From the date of the starting point, the original restated value is depreciated and so declines, while the share of the more recently acquired assets (in the pool) increases.

It should be noted that the "starting point" method has a drawback when its output is used in time-series comparisons (Section 12.2). Under this method all existing assets are lumped into one "synthetic" asset whose life span is equal to the weighted average life span of the actual assets. For the starting point year, the yearly depreciation charge will be correct (under the assumption of even age distribution, as explained in Section 10.5). However, during the following years these charges will be biased upward. The bias will exist until the "synthetic" asset is completely depreciated. Later on, the assets with a long life span will continue to provide services, but depreciation is not charged. Thus, the depreciation charges would be biased downward. In other words, while the total depreciation charges over the whole life period will be correct, the yearly charge will be biased. When the starting point method is applied to each group of assets (for which the life span is identical), the biases will be reduced.

Consider Company X's fixed assets for the years 1970 to 1974. December 31, 1970, is the starting point for adjusting the fixed asset value; December 31, 1974, is the target date for analysis. Relevant data are presented in Exhibit 12.6, and the required computations are shown in Exhibit 12.7.

The calculations in Exhibit 12.7 are carried out in two stages. First, the net

Exhibit 12.6. Company X: Data on Fixed Assets 1970–1974 (million dollars)

Year:	1970	1971	1972	1973	1974	Total 1974
Price index:	115.00	120.75	123.85	131.73	144.90	
"Old" asset (existing in 1970) account						
Assets, at cost (gross value)*	20.00	18.00	16.00	14.00	12.00	
Accumulated depreciation	9.00	9.00	8.80	8.40	7.80	7.80
Net value	11.00	9.00	7.20	5.60	4.20	
"New" asset (1971-1974) account						
Annual investment		3.40	2.10	0.50	5.20	
Annual depreciation						
Of 1971 assets		—	0.30	0.30	0.30	0.90
Of 1972 assets		—	—	0.20	0.20	0.40
Of 1973 assets		—	—	—	0.10	0.10

*Asset life span is 10 years; hence annual depreciation of the original "mature" set is 2. The gross value declines over time since assets disposed of are not replaced.

value of each set of assets (related to a given year's investment) has been calculated in terms of acquisition year dollars. Second, the resulting net value figures have been updated to 1974 dollars. The "old" assets, as recorded on December 31, 1970, provide a unique set. During the years 1971 to 1974 the individual assets that exist in the set are not replaced by new ones (the new, replacing assets, are recorded separately). Restatement of this "old" set should take this into account.

The $11 million net asset aggregate value, as recorded on December 31, 1970, is reduced to $4.2 million on December 31, 1974 (Exhibit 12.6). To simplify the computations, the final net value of the "old" set of assets is restated in 1970 currency (Exhibit 12.7) by applying the appropriate restatement coefficient for December 31, 1970 (the average life span of fixed assets is 10 years; the average inflation rate during the period 1960 to 1970 is 2%). In other words, the final net value (for 1974) of the "old" set of assets is restated in 1970 terms. The resulting restated net value of this set ($4.54 million) is treated like the "new" sets of assets (resulting from the annual investments). Updating this sum to 1974 provides $5.72 million. Updating all the "annual sets" of net assets provides a total of $16.35 million.

Because of depreciation and reinvestment over the years, the assets restated on December 31, 1974, are mainly "young" assets. The "old" assets

Exhibit 12.7. Company X: Restatement of Fixed Assets December 31, 1974 (million dollars)

Year:	1970	1971	1972	1973	1974	Total 1974
Price index:	115.00	120.75	123.85	131.73	144.90	
Inflating factor:	1.26	1.20	1.17	1.10	1.00	
Old asset gross value	11.00					
Add annual investment		3.40	2.10	0.50	5.20	
Less accumulated depreciation on year's investment	7.80	0.90	0.40	0.10	—	
1974 net asset value (of year's set)	4.20	2.50	1.70	0.40	5.20	14.00
Restated old asset net value, 1970	4.54*					
Net asset value, updated to 1974	5.72	3.00	1.99	0.44	5.20	16.35

*4.20 multiplied by 1.08 restatement coefficient (R_{net})from Exhibit 10.3 ($n = 10, p = 0.02$).
Source: Data from Exhibit 12.6.

that were recorded on December 31, 1970, compose only 35% of total net value ($5.72 million out of $16.35 million in Exhibit 12.7). Even if restatement at the starting point is inaccurate, the inaccuracy will have little effect on current total restated value.

At the starting point (1970) the company's recorded asset value was $11 million. Restatement of this sum by the appropriate coefficient ($n = 10, p = 0.02, R_{net} = 1.08$) results in a net asset value of $11.88 million in 1970 currency. Updating this sum to 1974 dollars by the factor 1.26 gives $14.96 million. The nominal change of $3.08 million is the inflationary increase in the original asset prices, as shown in Exhibit 12.8. Actual assets on December 31, 1974, after restatement, were $16.35 million. The difference between this actual sum and the updated sum ($14.96 million), $1.39 million, is the real increase in assets over the 4-year period.

The analysis shows that the company experienced real growth during this period, although much less than reported by the conventional balance sheet ($1.39 million versus $3 million). Further questions are to what extent it was able to maintain the shareholders' equity value, and whether it continued to utilize its appropriate financial leverage. These problems are analyzed in Section 13.4.

Exhibit 12.8. Company X: Asset Restatement Analysis December 31, 1974 (million dollars)

Restated net value, 1970	11.88*	
Net value updated to 1974	14.96†	
Net asset value required for stability		3.08
Actual restated net value, 1974	16.35‡	
Original net value, updated to 1974	14.96	
Real asset growth		1.39
Nominal growth during period		4.47

*11 from Exhibit 12.6 times 1.08 restatement coefficient.
†11.88 x 1.26 inflating factor.
‡From Exhibit 12.7.

Notes

1. For empirical research on a related subject see Petersen (1975).
2. For a detailed discussion of this subject see, for example, Financial Accounting Standards Board (1974).
3. Applying the appropriate index number directly to conventional depreciation data will provide erroneous results: the resulting "restated" depreciation will be $50 for 19X1, $55 for 19X2, and $52.50 for 19X3.
4. They differ from the PLA operating profit as calculated in the lower section of Exhibit 12.4 because under PLA accounting loans were taken so as to maintain 60% equity.
5. Stating this method formally, we have as the current net value of fixed assets:

$$K_t = (K_{t-1})p_t + I_t - D_t$$

where K is the PLA net value (depreciated) of assets,
t denotes a given year,
p is the inflation rate,
I is the gross investment, and
D is the yearly adjusted depreciation.

For a detailed analysis of this method, called "perpetual inventory of capital," see Goldsmith (1962, pp. 8–22). This method is often used for restating an industry's or a nation's stock of capital. Applying the starting point approach simplifies the restatement procedure.

6. The starting point technique was suggested and has been tested empirically by Shashua et al. (1977).

References

Financial Accounting Standards Board, *Financial Reporting in Units of General Purchasing Power,* Exposure Draft, Stamford, Conn., December 1974.

Goldsmith, R. W., *The National Wealth of the United States in the Postwar Period,* National Bureau of Economic Research, New York, 1962.

Petersen, R. J., "A Portfolio Analysis of General Price Level Restatement," *Accounting Review,* July 1975, pp. 525–532.

Shashua, L., Y. Goldschmidt and G. Levkovitz, "Alternative Methods of Estimating the Capital Stock of the Kibbutz," forthcoming in *Issues in the Economy of Israel,* Maurice Falk Institute for Economic Research in Israel, 1977. In Hebrew; forthcoming in English.

Weston, J. F. and E. F. Brigham, *Managerial Finance,* Holt, Rinehart & Winston, New York, 1969.

Thirteen

Measuring Capital Erosion

The process of withdrawing resources from a company at a higher rate than is warranted by economic profit causes the company's or investor's capital position to decline during a given period; this process is called "capital erosion."[1] Capital erosion takes place when a sum that is larger than the PLA profit is paid out as tax, dividend, or other profit-sharing payment. The cause of such erosion is understatement of assets, equity, and lagged costs during a period of inflation. Since income tax is levied on profit that is upward biased, the company and, in the final stage, the equity investor suffers from a loss that is here called "investor's capital erosion."

> In the days after the First World War, a German nail merchant lived near his country's frontier. It was a time of runaway inflation.
>
> The nail merchant had 10,000 marks which he took across the frontier to buy a ton of nails. He took his purchase home and sold the nails at retail for a total of 20,000 marks. An excellent profit—or so he thought until he went again across the frontier to find that the 20,000 marks would now buy only half a ton of nails. With some misgivings, he bought half a ton and returned home with them—to discover to his considerable delight that the retail price of nails had risen substantially in his absence. He was pleased to sell his half-ton for 40,000 marks. His mood changed to dismay, however, when on his next journey across the frontier, he learned that that sum would purchase only a quarter of a ton of nails.

> The nail merchant's journeys continued until one day he carried an extraordinarily large quantity of marks across the frontier in a wheelbarrow and found he was able to buy only a single nail. He returned home once again, and, using a rope, a hammer...and the nail...he hanged himself.[2]

13.1 Asset Erosion

A company that aims at stability over time in both physical (production and sales) and financial terms should distribute its after-tax profit as dividends, assuming stability in the economy. If the price level is stable, annual depreciation charges set aside sufficient funds for asset renewal, as shown in Exhibit 2.1 for the Manufacturing Equity Company. Such a company will maintain its asset position as long as the price level is stable. During an inflationary period, however, investment at the level of conventional depreciation charges will not purchase the new assets required for maintaining stable production (Exhibit 2.2). If the preinflation dividend policy is continued, the company's asset position will deteriorate in real (productive) terms, although in money terms stability will be maintained.

Suppose that the Manufacturing Equity Company persists in its preinflation dividend policy of 100% payout without subscribing for additional shares. Before inflation started, this policy allowed for stability in both physical and financial terms. After inflation sets in, however, investment at the level of conventional depreciation charges (i.e., \$50 in 19X2) will purchase fewer assets than in the past (only \$50: 1.10 = \$45.45) because prices have risen (by 10%). As a result, physical deterioration begins. (The productive capacity of the machines at the end of 19X2 in terms of 19X1 prices is \$50 of the "old" machine and \$45.45 of the "new" machine.) The company would, however, be stable in nominal financial terms, as shown in Exhibit 13.1. This point must be further explained.

Suppose that each machine is composed of 5000 units priced at 1 cent each; the depreciation charges in 19X1 set aside funds to purchase (at the end of 19X1) 5000 units. In 19X2, when prices rose by 10%, these machines produced, as in 19X1, 100 sets of finished goods at a sales value of \$220 (\$200 in 19X1 plus 10% PLA). The \$50 depreciation charge in 19X2 set aside funds to purchase only 4545 units, because their price also rose by 10%. At the end of 19X2 there were therefore 9545 units (5000 "old" ones and 4545 "new" ones), recorded at \$100 gross value. Their real value, in 19X1 prices, was, however, \$95.45, that is, 0.9545 of the 19X1 price level (Exhibit 13.1).

Suppose now that in 19X3 the price level rises again by 10% (above the 19X2 level). The productive capacity in nominal terms of the 9545 units, in 19X3, is \$231 (\$200 in 19X1 prices, inflated by 1.21, times 0.9545 machine

Exhibit 13.1. Manufacturing Equity Company
Conventional Profit and Loss Statements for the Years 19X0–19X4
(Nominal Financial Stability, Asset Erosion)

Year:	19X0		19X1		19X2		19X3		19X4	
Price index:	1.000		1.000		1.100		1.210		1.331	
Profit and Loss Statement										
Sales		$200.00		$200.00		$220.00		$231.00		$231.00
Out-of-pocket costs	$130.00		$130.00		$143.00		$150.15		$150.15	
Depreciation	50.00		50.00		50.00		50.00		50.00	
Total costs		180.00		180.00		193.00		200.15		200.15
Profit = tax and dividend		20.00		20.00		27.00		30.85		30.85
Analysis										
Depreciation for reinvestment	$50.00		$50.00		$50.00		$50.00		$50.00	
Gross asset value, end of year (nominal)	100.00		100.00		100.00		100.00		100.00	
Productive value of assets, end of year, in 19X1 prices*	$50.00 +50.00		$50.00 +50.00		$50.00 +45.45		$45.45 +41.41		$41.32 +37.57	
Price index, following year	1.000		1.100		1.210		1.331		1.464	
Production capacity index, following year†	1.000		1.100		1.155		1.155		1.155	

*Assuming that machine's production ability is equal in first and second years.
†Price index of the following year times productive value of assets divided by gross asset value (nominal).

value). If the price level similarly rises by 10% in 19X4, productive capacity will again be $231.00 ($200 inflated by 1.331, times 0.8677). It should be noted that in 19X4 inflation is assumed (not deflation, as shown in Appendix C). Assuming that the price level increases by 10% annually, the nominal profit will be the same every year, as shown in Exhibit 13.1.

The profit and loss statements in Exhibit 13.1 show that after a transitionary year (19X2) the recorded monetary values of all items are equal over the years, and the company is stable in nominal monetary terms. Since the purchasing power of the dollar declines during the period under analysis, real profit and asset values also decline. (Gross asset values in 19X1 prices, as recorded in the lower section of Exhibit 13.1, are $100, $95.45, $86.77, and $78.89 for the years 19X1 to 19X4, respectively.)

If inflation continues at 10% annually for 7 years, the recorded $50 depreciation will buy only $25.66 worth of machinery in base year prices (at a 10% annual rate, prices almost double over 7 years). The money illusion maintains a steady stream of depreciation ($50) over time.

If deflation sets in, nominal stability will collapse with a crash. Suppose that the price level in 19X4 drops by 9.09% (to the 19X3 level, at a price index of 1.21). The company's productive capacity will be 0.955 (0.7889 × 1.21), instead of 1.155 in Exhibit 13.1 (where inflation is assumed). Then pretax profit will be $16.85, as calculated below:

Sales	$191.00
Out-of-pocket costs	(124.15)
Depreciation	(50.00)
Profit	16.85

In summary, disregarding the effects of inflation on profit as reported by conventional financial statements will cause capital erosion in a company. The erosion is caused by withdrawal of resources by various claimants to profit, mainly through income tax and perhaps also through increased employee remunerations.

13.2 Equity Erosion

A company may suffer erosion of both assets and equity, as shown in Section 13.1, or, more commonly, equity erosion only, as shown in this section. Equity erosion may take place even when a company's real value of assets increases. Equity erosion occurs when the company's real value (purchasing power) of equity declines over time. This happens when annual new equity that is added to the existing equity (retained earnings and new shares) is below the sum required for maintaining the equity value.

To a company financed by 100% equity, equity erosion is not harmful—it is merely a transfer of equity funds from the company to the investor (albeit the investor receives less than the company loses).

Consider the Manufacturing Equity Company's financial statements for the years 19X1 to 19X4 (Appendix C). Assume, however, that inflation at the rate of 10% continues in 19X4 (rather than 9.09% deflation, as assumed in Appendix C). The company maintains stability in assets, production, and sales over the analyzed period, as shown in Exhibit 13.2 (in contrast to the nominal stability assumed in Exhibit 13.1). Total after-tax profit is distributed as dividends.

Equity erosion of $2.50 took place when inflation started in 19X2. As a result of this erosion, the company's assets are recorded at a value that is too low and the corresponding real value of equity (which finances the assets) is below the preinflation level. Since inflation continued (in 19X3 and 19X4) at a constant rate and the company observed asset stability, no additional erosion took place. The original sum ($2.50) was carried on in real terms ($2.75 in 19X3, $3.03 in 19X4).

As can be seen, the very fact of equity erosion did not affect the Manufacturing Equity Company. However, when the company employs financial leverage, equity erosion may cause underleverage and consequent failure to reap the full benefits of financial leverage.

Consider the Manufacturing Leverage Company operating under the same conditions as the Equity Company, as shown in Exhibit 13.3. Instead of a $2.50 erosion in 19X2, the Leverage Company suffered equity erosion of $1.50 and underleverage of $1 (Section 12.3). Both equity erosion and underleverage continue over time at their respective real values.

Both illustrations indicate equity erosion. Equity may be accumulated, however, if the new equity exceeds the level required for equity maintenance. Suppose that the Manufacturing Leverage Company retained, in 19X2, $2 of its net earnings (rather than 100% payout), keeping the loans at the 19X1 level ($30). In this case the new equity is $5 ($3 in new shares, $2 in retained earnings), the required equity maintenance reserve is $4.50, and thus equity accumulation is $0.50.

13.3 Investor's Capital Erosion

Taxation of fictitious profit (the difference between conventional and PLA profit) causes withdrawal of capital from the company which, in the final stage, is a loss to the equity investor.

Exhibit 13.2. Manufacturing Equity Company
Conventional and PLA Balance Sheets as of December 31, 19X1–19X4
(Financial and Asset Stability, Equity Erosion)

Year:	19X1	19X2*	19X3*	19X4*
Price index:	100.00	110.0	121.0	131.1
Conventional Accounting				
Assets	$50.00	$50.00	$55.00	$60.50
	50.00	55.00	60.50	66.55
Gross asset value	100.00	105.00	115.50	127.05
Accumulated depreciation	(25.00)	(25.00)	(27.50)	(30.25)
Net asset value	75.00	80.00	88.00	96.80
Equity				
Opening equity	75.00	75.00	75.00	75.00
New shares	—	5.00	13.00	21.80
	75.00	80.00	88.00	96.80
PLA Accounting				
Assets	50.00	55.00r	60.50	66.55
	50.00	55.00	60.50	66.55
Gross asset value	100.00	110.00	121.00	133.10
Accumulated depreciation	(25.00)	(27.50)	(30.25)	(33.37)
Net asset value	75.00	82.50	90.75	99.83
Equity				
Opening equity	75.00	75.00	75.00	75.00
Equity maintenance	—	7.50	15.75	24.83
	75.00	82.50	90.75	99.83
Erosion in company, accumulated				
Required equity maintenance		7.50	15.75	24.83
New shares		5.00	13.00	21.80
Erosion		2.50	2.75	3.03

*The letter *r* indicates restated figure.

Consider the Manufacturing Equity Company's profit and loss statement for the year 19X2 (Exhibit 2.2). Conventional profit is overstated by $5. If 50% income tax is assumed, only $2.50 of this sum reached the investor. The company, on the other hand, subscribed for $5 in new shares to finance the purchase of the new machine. Thus the investor's net loss of cash flow was $2.50. This is the investor's capital erosion.

Exhibit 13.3. Manufacturing Leverage Company
Conventional and PLA Liabilities and Equity* as of December 31, 19X1–19X4
(Financial and Asset Stability, Equity Erosion)

Year:	19X1	19X2	19X3	19X4
Price index:	100.0	110.0	121.0	131.0
Conventional Accounting				
Loans	$30.00	$32.00	$35.20	$38.72
Opening equity	45.00	45.00	45.00	45.00
New shares	—	3.00	7.80	13.08
	75.00	80.00	88.00	96.80
PLA Accounting				
Loans	30.00	32.00	35.20	38.72
Opening equity	45.00	45.00	45.00	45.00
Equity maintenance	—	4.50	9.45	14.90
Total equity	45.00	49.50	54.45	59.90
	75.00	81.50	89.65	98.62
Underleverage†	—	1.00	1.10	1.21
	75.00	82.50	90.75	99.83
Equity erosion in company, accumulated				
Required equity maintenance		4.50	9.45	14.90
New shares		3.00	7.80	13.08
Erosion		1.50	1.65	1.82

*Assets as in Exhibit 13.2.
†To keep 40% of restated asset value.

Whereas equity erosion measures the transfer of money from the company to others (including the investor), investor's capital erosion measures the transfer of money from the company to external parties (government). From the investor's point of view it is a loss.

Capital erosion for the years 19X2 to 19X4 is calculated in Exhibit 13.4. Erosion stems from the fictitious profit which is the difference between PLA total profit and conventional profit. This difference is composed of the difference between depreciation expense (PLA added depreciation) and net restatement gains (asset restatement gains less equity maintenance adjustment). During the analyzed period, there was considerable investor's capital erosion: $11.43 million in the Equity Company and $7.80 million in the Leverage Company as illustrated in Exhibit 13.4.

Exhibit 13.4. Manufacturing Companies
Profit Analysis for the Years 19X2–19X4
(Financial and Asset Stability, Investor's Capital Erosion)

	Equity Company			Leverage Company		
Year:	19X2	19X3	19X4	19X2	19X3	19X4
Price index:	110.0	121.0	133.1	110.0	121.0	133.1
Inflating factor:	1.21	1.10	1.00	1.21	1.10	1.00
PLA added depreciation	$5.00	$8.00	$8.80	$5.00	8.00	$8.80
Less asset restatement gains	(7.50)	(8.25)	(9.08)	(7.50)	(8.25)	(9.08)
Equity maintenance adjustment	7.50	8.25	9.08	4.50	4.95	5.45
Fictitious profit	5.00	8.00	8.80	2.00	4.70	5.17
Tax on above, 50%	(2.50)	(4.00)	(4.40)	(1.00)	(2.35)	(2.58)
Investor's extra receipts	2.50	4.00	4.40	1.00	2.35	2.59
New shares	(5.00)	(8.00)	(8.80)	(3.00)	(4.80)	(5.28)
Investor's capital erosion, annual	2.50	4.00	4.40	2.00	2.45	2.69
Updated erosion to 19X4	3.03	4.40	4.00	2.42	2.69	2.69
Accumulated erosion			11.43			7.80

Investor's capital erosion takes place as long as there is a difference between conventional and PLA total profit. It is a negative cash flow to the investor. This cash flow has been used for extra tax payments in the 100% equity case. In the leverage case, on the other hand, the investor's cash flow has been used for both extra tax payments and the reduction of real leverage, causing underleverage.

Investor's capital erosion in the Manufacturing Leverage Company (Exhibits 13.3, 13.4) is as follows:

	19X2	19X3	19X4
Tax in fictitious profit	$1.00	$2.35	$2.58
Underleverage	1.00	0.10	0.11
Investor's capital erosion	2.00	2.45	2.69

If PLA procedures were practiced, or, alternatively, if income tax did not exist, investor's capital erosion would not take place. It should be mentioned that other profit-sharing payments or employee requirements that are based on reported profit (Section 2.3) also contribute to investor's capital erosion.

Erosion of both equity and investor's capital may take place even when the real value of a company's assets increases.

Suppose that the Manufacturing Leverage Company's net assets increased from 1.5 machines in 19X1 to 2.5 in 19X2 and to 3 in 19X3. The company raised new equity to cover both overpayment of profit (which causes equity erosion) and asset growth. To measure equity erosion, the new equity that was used for expansion should be isolated, as shown in Exhibit 13.5.

Real growth is measured (under PLA accounting) by subtracting the original value of net assets (in current terms) from the total net asset value. Thus the company's real growth in 19X2 was $55 (1 machine), and in 19X3 $30.25 (0.5 machine). The growth should have been financed by 60% equity and 40% loans (in 19X2 $33 and $22, respectively). When the required equity maintenance is computed, the underleverage appears.

The illustration in Exhibit 13.5 shows that, parallel to asset growth (at the end of 19X2), there was equity erosion. Furthermore, investor's capital was also eroded[3].

13.4 Measuring Equity Erosion in Practice

Erosion of equity capital is a common phenomenon during inflation because most of the reported profit is usually withdrawn from the companies. If the income tax rate is 50%, and cash dividends are 50% of after-tax profit[4] the company may accumulate not more than 25% of the upward-biased conventional profit.

The extent of equity erosion during a given series of years can be estimated by using the "starting point of restatement" technique (Section 12.4). This is illustrated on Company X's data. Relevant liabilities and equity data are presented in Exhibit 13.6. Carrying out several computations on the data in this exhibit, as well as on the asset data (Exhibit 12.6), provides the adjusted balance sheets, as presented in Exhibit 13.7.

At the starting point (1970) the recorded equity of $6.6 million was restated to $7.13 million by applying the same restatement coefficient ($n = 10$, $p = 0.02$) as was applied to the recorded net assets (Section 12.4). This procedure assumes that the real value of equity is linked to the real value of net assets. Updating this sum to December 31, 1974, yields $8.98 million. Adding the required equity for real growth provides the total restated equity for 1974. The underleverage is calculated in the same manner as in Exhibits 12.5 and 13.3.

Exhibit 13.5. Manufacturing Leverage Growth Company
Conventional and PLA Balance Sheets as of December 31, 19X1–19X3
(Financial and Asset Growth, Equity Erosion)

Year:	19X1	19X2*	19X3*
Price index:	100.0	110.0	121.0
Number of machines (net value):	1.5	2.5	3.0
	Conventional Accounting		
Assets	$ 50.00	$ 50.00	$110.00
	50.00	110.00	121.00
Gross asset value	100.00	160.00	231.00
Accumulated depreciation	(25.00)	(25.00)	(55.00)
Net asset value	75.00	135.00	176.00
Liabilities and Equity			
Loans†	30.00	54.00	70.40
Opening equity	45.00	45.00	45.00
New shares	—	36.00	60.60
	75.00	135.00	176.00
	PLA Accounting		
Assets			
Gross asset value	100.00	165.00r	242.00r
Accumulated depreciation	(25.00)	(27.50)	(60.50)
Net asset value	75.00	137.50	181.50
Former year's real assets	(75.00)	(82.50)	(151.25)
Real growth	—	55.00	30.25
Liabilities and Equity			
Loans	30.00	54.00	70.40
Equity			
1.5 machines	45.00	45.00	45.00
1.0 machines	—	33.00‡	33.00
0.5 machines	—	—	18.15‡
Required maintenance	—	4.50	12.75[11]
	45.00	82.50	108.90
Total liabilities and equity	75.00	136.50	179.30
Underleverage	—	1.00	2.20
	75.00	137.50	181.50
Equity erosion			
Required equity maintenance		4.50	12.75
New shares for maintenance§		3.00	9.45
Erosion		1.50	3.30

*The letter *r* indicated restated figure.
†In 19X2, $32 for old machines, $22 for 40% of new machine. In 19X3, $35.20 for first set, $23.10 for second, and $12.10 for third machine.
‡60% of real growth.
[11]$4.50 + 10% on $82.50
§New shares less required for growth: in 19X2, $36 – 33 = 3; in 19X3, $60.60 – 33 – 18.15 = 9.45.

Exhibit 13.6 Company X: Balance Sheet Data 1970–1974 (million dollars)

Year:	1970	1971	1972	1973	1974
Price index:	115.00	120.75	123.85	131.73	144.90
Inflating factor:	1.26	1.20	1.17	1.10	1.00
Assets					
Net Value of old asset (Exhibit 12.6)	11.00	9.00	7.20	5.60	4.20
Add cost of new assets		3.40	5.50	6.00	11.20
Less accumulated depreciation		—	(0.30)	(0.80)	(1.40)
Net asset value	11.00	12.40	12.40	10.80	14.00
Liabilities and equity					
Equity					
Original	6.60	6.60	6.60	6.60	6.60
New shares		0.80	0.80	0.80	0.80
Retained earnings		—	—	—	1.00
Loans	4.40	5.00	5.00	3.40	5.60
Liabilities and equity	11.00	12.40	12.40	10.80	14.00

Real asset growth during the period was $1.39 million (Exhibt 12.8). To finance this, $0.83 million equity was required to maintain the previous equity–debt ratio of 60–40. Analysis of the liabilities and equity is carried out in Exhibit 13.8. The required equity in 1974 is $9.81 million, as shown in Exhibit 13.7, while the restated equity in 1970 was $7.13 million. The difference, $2.68 million, is the required increase in equity during the analyzed period. In fact, only $1.96 million of new equity has been raised. The difference of $0.72 million represents equity erosion during the period. In addition to the process of equity erosion, underleverage in the sum of $0.59 million has developed during the period in question. In 1974 there was a total underleverage of $0.94 million ($0.35 in 1970 plus $0.59 during 1970 to 1974).

The data in Exhibit 13.7 indicate that the financial leverage, stated in 1974 dollars, is 34.4% ($5.60 million out of $16.35 million), rather than 40% as recorded in the conventional balance sheet ($5.60 million out of $14.00 million).

If management wishes to maintain the former mix, it could take additional loans ($0.94 million to finance the underleverage); the cash might be invested in assets to expand the company, or, if regulations permit, special dividends could be distributed. In any case, over time, the financial mix will tend to return to its optimal composition if management so desires. It can finance asset replacements so as to gradually absorb the excess equity; if the stock of assets is not only maintained but also increased, this process can, of course, be quicker.

Exhibit 13.7. Company X: Adjusted Balance Sheets
December 31, 1970, and 1974 (million dollars)

		Adjusted Balance Sheet as of December 31, 1970	
Restated net assets	11.88*	Original equity	6.60
		Equity restatement (balance)	0.53
		Restated required equity	7.13†
		Loans	4.40
			11.53
		Underleverage	0.35
	11.88		11.88
		Adjusted Balance Sheet as of December 31, 1974	
Restated net assets	16.35	Restated equity (old)	7.13
		Equity maintenance (balance)	1.85
		Restated equity	8.98‡
		Equity for real growth	0.83[11]
		Total restated equity	9.81
		Loans	5.60
			15.41
		Underleverage	0.94
	16.35		16.35

*11.00 from Exhibit 12.6 times 1.08 restatement coefficient.
†6.60 from Exhibit 13.6 times 1.08 restatement coefficient.
‡7.13 of 1970 times 1.26 inflating factor.
[11] 1.39 from Exhibit 12.8 times 0.60 share of equity.

13.5 Measuring Investor's Capital Erosion

The convention of levying income tax on the upward-biased reported profit causes an unjustified loss to the investor of equity capital. The extent of actual investor's capital erosion during a given series of years can be measured from the figures arrived at while using the "starting point of restatement" technique. The rate of income tax (and other claims to profit) relevant to the company under analysis must, of course, be known.

Consider Company X data for the years 1970 to 1974. Suppose that 60% of reported profit is withdrawn as tax and other kinds of levies. To measure the investor's capital erosion (as outlined in Exhibit 13.4), the difference between PLA total profit and conventional profit (the fictitious profit) must be calculated. Thus the following annual figures are computed: PLA added deprecia-

Exhibit 13.8. Company X: Equity and Loans Restatement Analysis, December 31, 1974 (million dollars)

Equity		
Restated equity, 1970	7.13	
Equity updated to 1974	8.98*	
Required maintenance adjustment		1.85
Required equity for real growth		0.83†
Total required equity		2.68
New shares, updated	0.96‡	
Retained earnings	1.00	
Total new equity		1.96
Equity erosion		0.72
Loans		
Existing loans, 1970	4.40	
Underleverage (Exhibit 13.7)	0.35	
Total leverage, 1970		4.75
Leverage updated to 1974		5.98[11]
Loans required for stability		1.23
Loans required for real growth		0.56§
Total required leverage		1.79
Existing loans		
In 1970	4.40	
In 1974	6.60	
		2.20
Underleverage during period		0.59

*7.13 x 1.26 inflating factor.
†1.39 from Exhibit 12.8 times 0.60 share of equity.
‡0.80 in 1971 (Exhibit 13.6) times 1.20 inflating factor.
[11]4.75 x 1.26.
§1.39 x 0.40.

tion (in Exhibit 13.9) and net restatement gains (asset restatement gains less equity maintenance adjustment) (in Exhibit 13.10).

The investor's capital erosion is calculated in Exhibit 13.11. The accumulated erosion during the period was $0.911 million, in 1974 currency. This erosion is a negative cash flow to the investor. It has been used for extra tax payments ($0.312 million, in nominal, not updated terms) and for reducing the leverage (underleverage of $0.591 million in nominal terms). It should be noted that the $0.591 underleverage, as computed here (Exhibit 13.11), equals the figure that is computed in Exhibit 13.8 ($0.59 million).

Several techniques that have been developed in this book are applied in this section and the preceding one: (1) restatement of

Exhibit 13.9. Company X: Annual Depreciation*
1971–1974 (million dollars)

Year:	1971		1972		1973		1974	
Price index:	120.75		123.85		131.73		144.90	
Inflating factor:	1.26		1.20		1.17		1.00	
	Conventional	PLA	Conventional	PLA	Conventional	PLA	Conventional	PLA
Old assets	2.000	2.268	1.800	2.094	1.600	1.979	1.400	1.905
1971 assets	—	—	0.300	0.308	0.300	0.327	0.300	0.360
1972 assets	—	—	—	—	0.200	0.213	0.200	0.234
1973 assets	—	—	—	—	—	—	0.100	0.110
	2.000	2.268	2.100	2.402	2.100	2.519	2.000	2.609
PLA added depreciation		0.268		0.302		0.419		0.609

*Conventional depreciation derived from Exhibit 12.6. PLA depreciation = conventional depreciation restated by 1.08 and updated by the appropriate inflating factor.

Exhibit 13.10. Company X: Annual Restated Value 1970–1974 (million dollars)

Year:	1970		1971		1972		1973		1974
Price index:	115.00		120.75		123.85		131.73		144.90
Annual price change:			1.050		1.026		1.064		1.100
Restated Net Assets									
Opening restated value*			12.474		13.960		14.532		13.764
Add annual investment (Exhibit 12.6)		3.400		2.100		0.500		5.200	
Less PLA depreciation (Exhibit 13.9)		2.268		2.402		2.519		2.609	
Real growth (decline)			1.132		(0.302)		(2.019)		2.591
Total restated net asset	11.880		13.606		13.658		12.513		16.355
Asset restatement gains†			0.594		0.354		0.874		1.251
Restated Equity									
Opening restated value*	7.128		7.484		8.375		8.911		9.802
Equity required for growth			0.679						0.010
Total restated equity	7.128		8.163		8.375		8.911		9.812
Equity maintenance adjustment†			0.356		0.212		0.536		0.891

*Former year's total times annual price change.

†Opening restated value less former year's total restated value.

Exhibit 13.11. Company X: Investor's Capital Erosion 1971–1974 (million dollars)

Year:	1971	1972	1973	1974	Total
Price index:	120.75	123.85	131.73	144.90	
Annual price change:	1.050	1.026	1.064	1.100	
Inflating factor:	1.20	1.17	1.10	1.00	
PLA added depreciation (Exhibit 13.9)	0.268	0.302	0.419	0.609	
Less asset restatement gains (Exhibit 13.10)	(0.594)	(0.354)	(0.874)	(1.251)	
Equity maintenance adjustment (Exhibit 13.10)	0.356	0.212	0.536	0.891	
Fictitious profit*	0.030	0.160	0.081	0.249	
Tax on above, 60%	0.018	0.096	0.049	0.149	0.312
Investor's extra receipts	0.012	0.064	0.032	0.100	
New shares	(0.800)			(1.000)	
Equity required for growth	0.679			0.010	
Investor's capital erosion, annual	(0.109)	0.064	0.032	(0.890)	(0.903)
Underleverage					(0.591)
Updated erosion to 1974	(0.131)	0.075	0.035	(0.890)	
Accumulated erosion				(0.911)	

*Difference between PLA total and conventional profit.

equity parallel to asset restatement Chapter 4), (2) the use of the restatement coefficient (Chapter 10) to a starting point (Chapter 12), and (3) updating adjusted data for measuring real developments in a company (Chapter 12).

The application of these techniques made it possible to measure the developments in Company X during the period from 1970 to 1974: (1) asset growth ($1.39 million, Exhibit 12.8), (2) equity erosion and underleverage ($0.72 million and $0.59 million, respectively, Exhibit 13.8), and (3) investor's capital erosion ($0.91 million, Exhibit 13.11).

Notes

1. We are indebted to Dr. Leon Shashua for suggesting a separate treatment of this subject.
2. An apochryphal tale, quoted from Arthur Young & Company (1975, p. 2).
3. In 19X3 investor's capital erosion was as follows:

PLA added depreciation	$10.72
Less asset restatement gains	(13.75)
Equity maintenance adjustment	8.25
Fictitious profit	5.22
Tax on above, 50%	(2.61)
Investor's extra receipts	2.61
New shares	(24.60)
Amount required for expansion	18.15
Investor's extra payments	(6.45)
Investor's capital erosion	3.84

4. Data for the United States indicate that during the 1950's corporate dividends were approximately 50% of after-tax profits (Ray 1960, p. 126).

References

Arthur Young & Company, *Measuring and Reporting the Impact of Inflation through Price-Level Accounting,* New York, 1975.

Ray D. D., *Accounting and Business Fluctuations,* University of Florida Press, Gainesville, 1960.

Part Five

Company–Economy Interaction

Fourteen

Income Tax Considerations during Inflation

Since income tax is levied as a percentage of profits as reported by conventional accounting, it is expected that during inflation company income taxes will be higher than those intended by the law. For example, the effective tax rate on true profits in the United States rose from about 43% in 1965 to 69% in 1974.[1] During a period of deflation, on the other hand, the reverse would be expected. Although this countercyclical characteristic of the effective tax rate has advantages from the macroeconomic point of view, it is not administered equitably.[2] Differences in financial leverage, production function, and asset structure among companies cause tax discrimination.[3]

Overtaxation (or undertaxation) is measured by the tax levied on the difference between the conventional reported profit and the PLA total profit (which represents the period's true economic profit).[4] In terms of the formal presentation in Chapter 6, the amount of overtaxation (O.T.) in a given period (year) is determined by the tax rate, t, that is applied to relation (6.14):

$$\text{O.T.} = t\,[p(A/L) - p\,(D - F)]$$

Overtaxation depends on the share of lagged costs (A/L), the net financial leverage $(D-F)$, and, of course, the inflation rate (p), which affects the first two variables in opposite directions. If normal financial leverage is assumed, there is overtaxation during a period of inflation and undertaxation during deflation.

14.1 Tax Discrimination Due to Financial Structure

One source of bias in conventional accounting stems from the fact that price level compensation, which is required for maintaining the real value of equity, is not recorded by conventional accounting procedures. Debt price level compensation (through increased interest charges), on the other hand, is recorded and therefore recognized for income tax purposes. Hence the portion of recorded profit that is generated by equity capital is overtaxed.

Again consider the Manufacturing Company. Suppose that income tax of 50% is levied on conventional accounting profit. This sum is considered as a cost item in the PLA profit and loss statement, as illustrated in Exhibit 14.1, in both the Equity Company and the Leverage Company. As can be seen, overtaxation of the 100% equity company is $2.50 (3.3% on equity), whereas for the 60% equity company it is only $1 (2.2% on equity).

Exhibit 14.1. Manufacturing Companies
PLA Profit Calculations for the Year 19X2
Effect of Financial Leverage on overtaxation

19X1		19X2		
PLA and Conventional		Conventional	PLA	Overtaxation
	*Equity Company (100% Equity)**			
$20.00	Profit, total pretax	$27.00	$22.00	
10.00	Tax, 50%	13.50	11.00	$2.50
	Leverage Company (60% Equity)†			
$17.60	Profit, total pretax	$22.80	$20.80	
8.80	Tax, 50%	11.40	10.40	$1.00

*Exhibit 2.2.
†Exhibit 4.5.

When companies employ financial leverage, the inequity of a flat rate income tax, levied on conventional accounting profit, is cushioned to some extent. The larger the financial leverage (i.e., the net debt–equity ratio), the smaller is the inequity caused by income tax. In addition, financial leverage during a period of inflation often generates inflationary leverage returns because of institutional restrictions on the rate of interest. These returns can be considered as short-run windfall income to the borrowing company; as such, they may be considered as 100% taxable. Thus the "inflated" tax on conventional profit is offset, to a greater or lesser extent, by the "inflated" leverage returns during inflation (see Section 4.3). It has, however, a serious drawback as it discriminates among companies with different financial structures.

14.2 Tax Discrimination Due to Production Function and Asset Structure

The upward bias in conventional profit during a period of inflation is affected by the proportion of net financial leverage (net of financial assets), as shown above, and by some asset characteristics. Three aspects that affect a company's profit, mainly through the production function, are discussed and illustrated: real asset "intensity," life span, and vintage. These aspects are illustrated by changing the assumptions regarding the Manufacturing Equity Company's set of assets.

The most significant bias in conventional profit results from the share of lagged costs in total costs; the greater this share, the greater is the bias of reported cost and profit and of levied income tax. The extreme case with no lagged costs occurs when no assets are involved in production.

Consider an extreme and artificial case in which a company does not hold assets. Suppose that the Manufacturing Company rents, rather than owns, assets. For the sake of identification, call it the Manufacturing Renting Company. The company maintains stability in physical production and sales. The yearly out-of-pocket costs (before inflation started) were $180. The corresponding conventional profit and loss statements are as follows:

	19X1	19X2
Sales, 100 units	$200	$220
Out-of-pocket costs	180	198
Profit = tax and dividend	20	22

Since no lagged costs are involved, conventional and PLA statements for 19X2 are identical. Income tax, levied on the nonbiased conventional profit, is equitable in this case.[5]

In the case of the Manufacturing Equity Company (Exhibit 2.2), on the other hand, lagged costs are involved in the profit and loss statement. Conventional profit for 19X2 ($27) is upward biased by $5 (PLA profit is $22). If income tax of 50% is levied on conventional profit, the Manufacturing Equity Company is overtaxed by $2.50. A comparison of the Manufacturing Company (with lagged costs) and the Renting Company (without lagged costs) is presented in Exhibit 14.2.

This exhibit illustrates how conventional accounting procedures cause tax discrimination among companies with different production functions.

The life span of assets also affects the bias in conventional profit. The longer the life of assets, the larger is the nonrealized portion of restatement gains, as depicted in Exhibit 14.3.

Exhibit 14.2. Manufacturing Companies
Conventional Profit and Loss Statements for the Year 19X2
Effect of Asset Ownership on After-Tax Profit

19X1		19X2 Equity Company ($75 Assets)*		19X2 Renting Company (No Assets)	
	Profit and Loss				
$200.00	Sales, 100 units		$220.00		$220.00
(130.00)	Out-of-pocket costs	$143.00		$198.00	
(50.00)	Depreciation	50.00		—	
			193.00		198.00
20.00	Profit, pretax		27.00		22.00
10.00	Tax, 50%		13.50		11.00
10.00	Profit, after-tax		13.50		11.00
	Cash Generation				
10.00	Profit		13.50		11.00
50.00	Depreciation		50.00		—
(50.00)	Replacement investment		(55.00)		—
10.00	Net cash generation		8.50		11.00

*Exhibit 2.2.

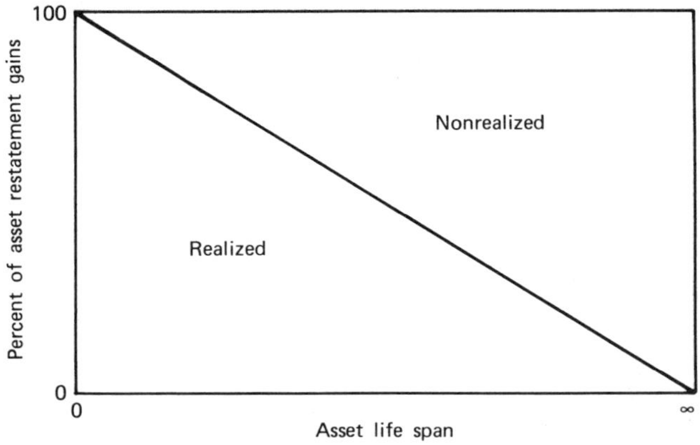

Exhibit 14.3. Division of Restatement Gains during a Period of Inflation

This is illustrated in Section 5.2, where out of $7.50 restatement gains the realized portion in the case of materials in inventory (which are held in stock for 3 months) is $6.72 compared to $5.00 in the case of fixed assets (whose life span is 2 years).

One of the biases in conventional accounting stems from the inclusion of realized restatement gains (which are not offset by corresponding equity maintenance adjustment). The longer the life span of assets, the larger is the nonrealized portion of restatement gains and, in turn, the smaller is the bias in conventional profit. Since income tax is levied on conventional profit, the bigger the share of short-lived assets (e.g., inventory items in relation to fixed assets) in total assets, the more overtaxed is the company.[6]

The effect of asset age on reported conventional profit is illustrated in Exhibit 14.4. The practice of levying income tax on conventional profit favors companies that bought assets in later periods at high prices. During an extended period of inflation, the older a set of assets the less equitable is the tax levied.

In summary, three aspects related to assets cause upward bias in conventional profit and, in turn, overtaxation of companies during a period of inflation. There is tax discrimination among companies since their asset structures are not identical. The tax levied is less equitable when (1) more assets are involved in production (since the more "capital intensive" the production process, the greater is the share of lagged costs), (2) the share of short-lived assets is larger (since the share of realized restatement gains is larger), and (3) the set of assets is older (since the difference between acquisition price and replacement cost is greater). The cause of tax inequitability is

Exhibit 14.4. Manufacturing Equity Companies
Conventional Financial Statements for the Year 19X2
Effect of Asset Age on After-Tax Profit

Balance Sheets as of December 31, 19X2

Older Assets Company				Younger Assets Company			
Machine 1 (1.1.X1)*	$50.00	Equity	$80.00	Machine 1 (7.1.X1)*	$55.00	Equity	$82.50
Machine 2 (12.31.X1)*	55.00			Machine 2 (7.1.X1)*	55.00		
Assets, at cost	105.00			Assets, at cost	110.00		
Accumulated depr.	25.00			Accumulated depr.	27.50		
	80.00		80.00		82.50		82.50

Profit and Loss Statements for the Year 19X2

	Older Assets Company		Younger Assets Company	
Sales		$220.00		$220.00
Out-of-pocket costs	$143.00		$143.00	
Depreciation	52.50		55.00	
		195.50		198.00
Profit, pretax		24.50		22.00
Tax, 50%		12.25		11.00
Profit, after-tax		12.25		11.00

Cash Generation

	Older Assets Company	Younger Assets Company
Profit	$12.25	$11.00
Depreciation	52.50	55.00
Total cash generation	64.75	66.00

*Acquisition dates.

that conventional profit includes realized gains stemming from asset restatement. These gains are, in part at least, not profit for current consumption, but should be allocated to equity maintenance.

14.3 Effect of Various Depreciation and Material Cost Calculations

The method by which the lagged costs of goods sold are calculated may affect the bias in conventional profit. In this book the straight-line depreciation and FIFO (first in, first out) methods are used throughout. However, tax concessions, especially during a period of inflation, are often provided by allowing accelerated depreciation of fixed assets and material cost determination by the LIFO (last in, first out) inventory method. The effects of these calculations on conventional profit during a period of inflation, as compared to straight-line depreciation and FIFO calculations, are illustrated below.

Introduction of an accelerated depreciation method during a period of price level stability causes profit to decrease at the beginning, when depreciation expenses increase suddenly. As the accelerated depreciation expense stabilizes, however, its effect on profit vanishes. This is illustrated below.

Consider the Manufacturing Company in a preinflation period. Assume that accelerated depreciation (75% of acquisition cost depreciated in the first year, 25% in the second) is introduced in 19X0. Profit for 3 years is as follows:

	19X9	19X0	19X1
Sales	$200.00	$200.00	$200.00
Out-of-pocket costs	(130.00)	(130.00)	(130.00)
Machine 0	(25.00)		
Machine 1	(25.00)	(25.00)	
Machine 2		(37.50)	(12.50)
Machine 3			(37.50)
Profit	20.00	7.50	20.00

Introduction of the accelerated depreciation method caused a one-time deduction of $12.50 from profit. If the company's set of assets is growing, such a "one-time amount" is recorded for each batch of additional assets.

During a period of inflation the method results in a further tax concession that continues as long as inflation persists. Its source is the continuous nominal increase in newly acquired assets and the concomitant rise in accelerated depreciation charges.

Suppose that accelerated depreciation is introduced in 19X2 (when inflation begins). As a result, recorded profit and tax payment decrease considerably, as shown in Exhibit 14.5. On the assumption that inflation continues (at a rate of 10% annually), depreciation charges are higher under the accelerated method than under the straight-line method (by 10% of the old machine's charge, i.e., $1.25 in 19X3, $1.38 in 19X4). Recorded profit is lower and tax payments decline as well. In turn, the resulting cash generation is higher.

Application of the LIFO method for inventory calculations during a period of inflation causes the cost of materials used to be closer to current market prices. Therefore conventional reported profit will be lower than if computed by the FIFO method. The relations between these methods are as follows:

Cost of material used	FIFO $<$ LIFO
Profit	FIFO $>$ LIFO
Inventory value	FIFO $>$ LIFO

The LIFO method provides concessions in both income tax (lower profit) and property taxes (lower inventory value).

Since the cost of materials used is close to their current market price when the LIFO method is practiced, the resulting conventional profit is expected to be relatively close to PLA profit. LIFO inventory value, on the other hand, is expected to be below the PLA value. The relations of the two methods to PLA figures are as follows:

Cost of materials used	FIFO $\leqslant$ PLA	LIFO $<$ PLA
Profit	FIFO $\geqslant$ PLA	LIFO $>$ PLA
Inventory value	FIFO $<$ PLA	LIFO $\leqslant$ PLA

where $\leqslant$ means strongly below and $\geqslant$ means strongly above.

Inventory calculations by the LIFO method for the Commercial Equity Company are illustrated in Exhibit 14.6. The resulting profit ($25.74) is between that arrived at by the FIFO method ($27.96) and the PLA profit ($21.24), as shown in Exhibit 14.7. With the LIFO method taxation is lower than with the FIFO method, but higher than with PLA calculations. Inventory value ($79.50), on the other hand, is below the figures arrived at with the FIFO method ($81.72) and also below the PLA value ($82.50), as shown in Exhibit 5.3.

14.4 Profit Measure for Income Tax

The foregoing illustrations have shown that employing conventional profit as a tax base discriminates among companies with different

Exhibit 14.5. Manufacturing Equity Company
Conventional Profit and Loss Statements for the Years 19X2–19X4
Effect of Depreciation Method on After-Tax Profit

Year:		19X2				19X3				19X4			
Price index:		110.0				121.0				133.1			
Depreciation Method:		Straight Line		Accelerated*		Straight Line		Accelerated*		Straight Line		Accelerated*	
Sales			$220.00		$220.00		$242.00		$242.00		$266.20		$266.20
Out-of-pocket costs		$143.00		$143.00		$157.30		$157.30		$173.03		$173.03	
Depreciation (Acquisition Cost)													
Machine 2	($50.00)	25.00		25.00		—		—		—		—	
Machine 3	($50.00)	25.00		37.50		25.00		12.50		—		—	
Machine 4	($55.00)	—		—		27.50		41.25		27.50		13.75	
Machine 5	($60.50)	—		—		—		—		30.25		45.38	
			193.00		205.50		209.80		211.05		230.78		232.16
Profit, pretax			27.00		14.50		32.20		30.95		35.42		34.04
Tax, 50%			13.50		7.25		16.10		15.48		17.71		17.02
Profit, after-tax			13.50		7.25		16.10		15.47		17.71		17.02
Cash Generation													
Profit			13.50		7.25		16.10		15.47		17.71		17.02
Depreciation			50.00		62.50		52.50		53.75		57.75		59.13
Replacement investment			(55.00)		(55.00)		(60.50)		(60.50)		(66.55)		(66.55)
Net cash generation			8.50		14.75		8.10		8.72		8.91		9.60

*First year: 75%, second year: 25%

Exhibit 14.6. Commercial Equity Company
Conventional Interim Profit and Loss Statements for the Year 19X2
(10% Creeping Inflation, 100% Raw Materials Inventory, LIFO Method)*

Date:	3.31.X2	6.30.X2	9.30.X2	12.31.X2	Total
			Profit Calculation		
Sales	$51.21	$52.44	$53.70	$55.00	$212.35
Cost of goods sold	45.00	46.08	47.20	48.33	186.61
Profit	6.21	6.36	6.50	6.67	25.74
			Inventory Cost Calculation		
Opening	$75.00	$76.08	$77.20	$78.33	
Use	45.00	46.08	47.20	48.33	$186.61
Balance	30.00	30.00	30.00	30.00	
Buy	46.08	47.20	48.33	49.50	191.11
Closing	76.08	77.20	78.33	79.50	

*Parallel to Exhibit 5.3.

Exhibit 14.7. Commercial Equity Company
Conventional Profit and Loss Statements for the Year 19X2
Effect of Inventory Method on After-Tax Profit

	PLA*	FIFO*	LIFO§
Sales, 100 units	$212.35	$212.35	$212.35
Cost of goods sold	191.11	184.39	186.61
Profit, pretax	21.24	27.96	25.74
Tax, 50%	10.62	13.98	12.87
Equitable tax	10.62	10.62	10.62
Overtaxation	—	3.36	2.25

**Source:* Data from Exhibit 5.4.
§*Source:* Data from Exhibit 14.6.

capital and asset structures, as summarized in Exhibit 14.8. Employing different cost calculation methods (depreciation, materials used) causes tax discrimination as well. Using PLA profit as a tax base should correct this discrimination.[7] The problem is which PLA profit measure to use.

For income tax to be really equitable, extra inflationary gains that originate from either leverage or a depressed interest rate should be taxed; extra deflationary losses should be tax deductible as well. This could be achieved by a 100% tax on inflationary leverage returns (this is a windfall income) and a tax on inflationfree profit at the regular rate (say, 50%).

Applying this approach to the Manufacturing Leverage Company (data from Exhibit 7.5) provides the following (equitable) tax and after-tax profit for 19X2:

	Taxable Income	Tax Rate	Tax	After-Tax Profit
Inflationfree profit	$19.36	50%	$9.68	$9.68
Inflationary leverage returns	1.44	100	1.44	—
			11.12	9.68

Is this an equitable after-tax profit? The answer will be positive if the sum equals, in real terms, that of 19X1 (before inflation started), given that production and sales did not change. The after-tax profit for 19X1 was as follows:

Pretax profit	$17.60
Tax at 50%	8.80
Profit after tax	8.80

Exhibit 14.8. Effect of Capital and Asset Structure on Equitable Taxation during Inflation

Factor	Overtaxation Resulting from Higher Share
Financial leverage	of equity
Asset intensity	of lagged costs (asset ownership)
Asset life span	of short-lived assets
Asset age	of older assets

In real terms of 19X2 it is $9.68 ($8.80 + 10% PLA). Since income tax is levied on conventional profit, actual income tax will be $11.40 (50% on $22.80 in Exhibit 14.1), that is, $0.28 too high ($11.40−$11.12).[8]

Using PLA total profit as a measure of taxable income is simpler than using the inflationfree measure. In this case, inflationary leverage returns are taxed at the same rate as is ordinary profit. The after-tax portion provides returns for the risk involved in financial leverage. During inflation, restatement gains due to undercompensation of debt capital would be taxable, just as restatement losses during deflation would be tax deductible. Company income taxes would be levied in a countercyclical manner, and this could have important macroeconomic implications. The disadvantage of basing income tax on PLA total profit is that this profit figure includes nonrealized restatement gains. Levying tax on nonrealized income may cause solvency problems in extreme cases.[9]

An alternative tax base could be PLA operating profit. It does not include restatement gains which are partially nonrealized and is therefore also easier to compute.[10] Since it is an advisable basis for dividend policy (Section 15.6), the advantage is that the same profit measure is applied. However, this measure involves two drawbacks: (1) it lacks a countercyclical effect, and (2) it is below the long-run preinflation profit level when financial leverage is employed (see Exhibit 15.10). The greater the financial leverage and the rate of inflation, the larger is the bias.

Since PLA operating profit is below the real economic profit (assuming that financial leverage exists), using this measure as tax base would result in undertaxation during a period of inflation.

For example, income tax for the Manufacturing Leverage Company for 19X2 would be $8.90 (50% tax on $17.80 PLA operating profit), compared to the equitable tax payment of $11.12 (as computed above). For comparison, the tax payment based on PLA total profit is $10.40 (50% tax on $20.80).

Using PLA operating profit as a tax base would cause tax payments that might be more inequitable than those with conventional profit as a tax base. The inequitability would depend on the proportion of financial leverage, the rate of inflation, and the adjustment of the rate of interest to the rate of inflation. In the case of the Manufacturing Leverage Company, for example, the tax on conventional profit is much more equitable than that on PLA operating profit.[11]

The relative advantages of the various profit measures as a practical tax base are summarized in Exhibit 14.9. Both inflationfree profit

Exhibit 14.9. Comparison of Profit Measures as Income Tax Bases, Listed in Decreasing Order of Advantages Regarding Equitability, Ease of Computation, and Countercyclical Effect

Equitability	Ease of Computation	Macroeconomic Stabilizing Effect over Trade Cycle
Inflationfree	Conventional	Conventional
PLA total	PLA operating	Inflationfree
PLA operating*	PLA total	PLA total
Conventional*	Inflationfree	PLA operating

*Assuming small financial leverage. If leverage is large, conventional profit may be more equitable.

and PLA operating profit have serious disadvantages; thus the only PLA profit measure that could in practice substitute for conventional profit as the tax base is PLA total profit.[12]

Notes

1. Source: W. E. Simon, U.S. Secretary of the Treasury, in testimony before the Joint Economic Committee, February 5, 1975 (reproduced from Jones 1975, p. 51).
2. For a review of this subject see Morley (1974, Chapter 3). It should be mentioned that inflation also causes inequitability in income tax between companies and individuals, as shown by Petrei (1974).
3. Field studies indicate that differences between PLA and conventional profit vary widely among companies and that some companies are affected dramatically by PLA procedures. See, for example, Rosenfield (1969, p.47), Cutler and Westwick (1973), Davidson and Weil (1975, pp. 43, 44), and Petersen (1975, p. 532).
4. The upward bias occurs with capital gains taxes also if restatement gains are realized when an asset is sold, and because of inflation its selling price is higher than its net book value. Usually the tax rate on capital gains is lower than that on income; therefore it seems that during a period of inflation it is worthwhile to sell assets that are salable and to buy new ones in their place. However, this activity also involves an indirect cost—the capital gains tax must be paid the year when the asset is sold,

whereas income tax savings, on differences in the depreciation expenses of the two assets, will be gained in several annual payments in the future. The difference in the timing of the taxes involves interest (cost of capital) charges which must be taken into account.

5. In terms of the formal presentation in the introduction to this chapter (and in Chapter 6), if $D = F$ (i.e., net debt does not exist) and that, $A/L = 0$ (i.e., no lagged costs) overtaxation is zero.
6. In terms of the formal presentation, $p(A/L)$ represents the realized restatement gains. The larger L (the asset life span), the smaller is A/L, thus the smaller are the realized restatement gains and, in turn, the overtaxation.
7. For tax purposes it would be best to calculate PLA profit, using a general price index for restatement rather than specific indices. See also Morley (1974, p. 108).
8. Given that inflationary leverage returns (I.L.R.) should be 100% taxed, overtaxation (O.T.) is measured as follows:

$$\text{O.T.} = t\,[\,p\,(A/L) - p\,(D - F)\,] - (1 - t)\,\text{I.L.R.}$$
$$= 0.50\,(5.00 - 3.00) - 0.50 \times 1.44 = 0.28$$

9. In some cases tax is levied on nonrealized income. For example, in Israel there are property taxes (e.g., on urban land) that are levied annually, but actual payments may be deferred until income is realized (e.g., sale of the property).
10. Adjustment of depreciation expense for income tax purposes is permitted or even compulsory in several countries (Section 1.5).
11. Tax payments when the different profit measures are used as a tax base for the Manufacturing Leverage Company for 19X2 are as follows:

Profit Measure	Taxable Income	Tax Rate	Tax Payment
1. Conventional profit	$22.80	50%	$11.40
2. Inflationfree profit	19.36	50	
Inflationary leverage returns	1.44	100	11.12
3. PLA total profit	20.80	50	10.40
4. PLA operating profit	17.80	50	8.90

12. For a study of the implications of using PLA accounting procedures for tax purposes see Morley (1974).

References

Cutler, R. S. and C. A. Westwick, "The Impact of Inflation Accounting on the Stock Market," *Accountancy,* March 1973, pp. 15–24.

Davidson, S. and R. L. Weil, "Impact of Inflation Accounting on 1974 Earnings," *Financial Analyst Journal,* September–October 1975, pp. 42–54.

Jones, R. H., "Why Business Must Seek Tax Reform," *Harvard Business Review,* September–October 1975, pp. 49–55.

Morley, M. F., *The Fiscal Implications of Inflation Accounting,* Institute for Fiscal Studies and Institute of Chartered Accountants in England and Wales, London, 1974.

Petersen, R. J., "A Portfolio Analysis of General Price Level Restatement," *Accounting Review,* July 1975, pp. 525–532.

Petrei, A. H., "Inflation and Personal Income Tax," *Finance and Development,* September 1974, pp. 38–41.

Rosenfield, P., "Accounting for Inflation—A Field Test," *Journal of Accountancy,* June 1969, pp. 45–51.

Fifteen

Inflation and Deflation Cycles

Inflation has been a constant phenomenon for several decades. Understandably, problems associated with deflation are not at present of public concern.[1] Yet, when analyzing price level changes, downward changes cannot be ignored. Deflation affects reported profit in the opposite direction to that of inflation: inflation causes upward-biased conventional profit; deflation, downward-biased. The bias over the whole trade cycle is not necessarily symmetric, especially when financial leverage is employed. Moreover, not only does the direction of price level changes affect reported profit, but the rate of change has its effect as well. These facts are of interest both to managers at the company level and to policy makers at the national level.

15.1 Effect of Deflation on Profit Measurement

The effects of deflation on conventional financial statements can be illustrated using the same example as before.

The year 19X4 opened with a drop of 9.09% in all prices on January 1. The 19X4 prices retreated to the level of 19X2 and stayed at that level for the rest of the year. Sales remained at 100 units, now priced at $2.20 each. Conventional depreciation expense was calculated as $27.50 for Machine 4, and 50% of the price of Machine 5, that is, $30.25. Relevant financial statements are presented in Exhibit 15.1. (Financial statements for 19X3 are given in Appendix C.)

Pretax profit, as computed by conventional accounting procedures in 19X4 ($19.25), is lower than in 19X2 ($27 in Exhibit 2.2), although in real terms there is no difference in the company activity level, and the price levels in the two years are the same.

Because of the fall in sales value, the shareholders had expected a drop in profit and dividends. Nevertheless, they were taken aback by the extent of the decline and to their surprise found, at the end of a "poor" year, that $2.75 of their shares was redeemed. (Excess cash that developed served for share redemption, to simplify the illustration.)

Under PLA procedures asset values are adjusted downward. Machines are restated according to the new price level, and thus their recorded value ($55 each) is consistent with that of 19X2; so is depreciation expense. The PLA pretax profit for 19X4 ($22) is equal to that of 19X2, as well as equal in real terms to the corresponding values of 19X1 and 19X3.

During a period of deflation, assets and equity are adjusted downward. The illustration indicates that restatement of the company's assets and equity corrected the representation of the conventional financial statements.

15.2 Implications of Biased Profit over the Trade Cycle

The effect of inflation and deflation on profit measurement is of interest to managers at the company level and policy makers at the national level.

Consider the Manufacturing Equity Company for the period of 19X1 to 19X7. Assume that in 19X5 the price level declined again by 9.09% to the 19X1 level, and in 19X6 to 19X7 the price level did not change. This depicts a symmetric trade cycle during which prices rose for 2 years (19X2 and 19X3) from a price index of 100 to 121, and then declined for 2 years (19X4 and 19X5) back to the price index of 100. Relevant financial statements are presented in Appendix C. Summary data on net asset values and profit under both conventional and PLA accounting procedures are presented in Exhibit 15.2.

The differences between the conventional and PLA figures, as calculated in Exhibit 15.2, indicate the bias caused by conventional accounting procedures. As can be seen, the positive and negative biases are balanced over the symmetric cycle. This is so because (1) the volume of physical assets remained stable, as did efficiency, during the cycle, (2) the life span of the assets in the example (2 years) is

Exhibit 15.1. Manufacturing Equity Company
Financial Statements for the Year 19X4
(9.09% Deflation, 100% Fixed Assets, 100% Equity)

Balance Sheet as of December 31, 19X4

Assets

12.31.19X3 Conventional	12.31.19X3 PLA		12.31.19X4 Conventional	12.31.19X4 PLA*
$55.00	$60.50	Machine 4	—	—
60.50	60.50	Machine 5	$60.50	$55.00^r
—	—	Machine 6	55.00	55.00
115.50	121.00	Assets, at cost	115.50	110.00
(27.50)	(30.25)	Accum. depr.	(30.25)	(27.50)
88.00	90.75		85.25	82.50

Liabilities and Equity

12.31.19X3 Conventional	12.31.19X3 PLA		12.31.19X4 Conventional	12.31.19X4 PLA
$75.00	$75.00	Equity	$75.00	$75.00
13.00	—	New shares	10.25	—
—	15.75	Equity maint. reserve	—	7.50
88.00	90.75		85.25	82.50

*The letter *r* indicates restated figure.

Exhibit 15.1. (continued)

Profit and Loss Statement for the Year 19X4

	Conventional		PLA	
Sales, 100 units		$220.00		$220.00
Out-of-pocket costs	$143.00		$143.00	
Depreciation	57.75		55.00	
		200.75		198.00
PLA operating profit		—		22.00
Asset restatement gains (losses)		—	(8.25)	
Plus equity maint. adjustment		—	8.25	
Net restatement gains		—		—
Profit = tax and dividend		19.25		22.00

Sources and Uses Statement for the Year 19X4

Sources	Conventional	PLA	Uses	Conventional	PLA
Depreciation	$57.75	$55.00	Machine 6	$55.00	$55.00
Profit	19.25	22.00	Tax and dividend	19.25	22.00
Asset restatement	—	8.25	Equity maint.	—	8.25
			Share redemption	2.75	—
	77.00	85.25		77.00	85.25

Exhibit 15.2. Manufacturing Equity Company
Summary of Value and Profit Figures over the Trade Cycle

Year:	19X1	19X2	19X3	19X4	19X5	19X6	19X7	Total
Price index:	100.0	110.0	121.0	110.0	100.0	100.0	100.0	Difference
			Bias in Balance Sheets					
Net asset value on 1.1								
1. Conventional	$75.00	$80.00	$88.00	$85.25	$77.50	$75.00	$75.00	
2. PLA	75.00	82.50	90.75	82.50	75.00	75.00	75.00	
3. Difference: (1) – (2)	—	(2.50)	(2.75)	2.75	2.50	—	—	—
			Bias in Profit and Loss Statements					
Profit								
4. Conventional	20.00	27.00	32.20	19.25	12.25	17.50	20.00	
5. PLA	20.00	22.00	24.20	22.00	20.00	20.00	20.00	
6. Difference (bias): (4) – (5)	—	5.00	8.00	(2.75)	(7.75)	(2.50)	—	—
7. Relative bias: (4)/(5)	1.00	1.23	1.33	0.88	0.61	0.88	1.00	

Source: Data from Appendix C.

short, compared to the cycle span (6 years), and (3) the illustration is based on 100% equity, and all profit is paid out in taxes and dividends. With financial leverage the results would of course be different, as shown in Section 15.4.

The bias in reported (conventional) profit exists not only during the period of price level change (19X2 to 19X5) but also after the price level stabilizes (19X6), because of the time lag between acquisition and realization. In the numerical illustration the lag is 1 year: the last machine bought at pre-stabilized price (Machine 6, acquired on December 31, 19X4, at $55) is still depreciated in 19X6 when prices are already stable.

Comparison of the profit figures for the series of the years in question (19X2 to 19X7) in both conventional and PLA statements, as illustrated in Exhibit 15.3, reveals two very important aspects of the bias caused by conventional accounting procedures. First, during a period of inflation the conventional statements report upward-biased profit, whereas during deflation the reported profit is downward biased.[2] Second, the effects of a change in price level persist even after the cause has disappeared.

The procycle bias, as shown by the broken lines in the lower sections of Exhibit 15.3, may have a cumulative effect on the national economy, through unjustified optimism and unnecessary pessimism, generated by conventional financial statements, during periods of inflation and deflation, respectively. It may promote overspending and overinvestment by management during inflationary years, and vice versa during deflation.[3] The upward-biased reported profit during inflation may cause the potential savings of companies to be distributed to shareholders, managers, and labor, as shown in Section 2.3. The recipients are unlikely to save all this extra income and thus will increase total consumption.

Income tax may, to some extent, cushion the procycle bias of reported profit. Since income tax is levied on profit reported on the basis of conventional accounting, it will be higher than intended by the spirit of the law during inflationary periods and lower during deflation. The extra tax during inflation may cause capital erosion in a company, as explained in Chapter 13.

If it is assumed that prices are set, to some extent, in accordance with cost, then some prices may be downward-biased during inflation and upward-biased during deflation. This, in turn, may also have some macroeconomic effects. When prices are regulated or controlled, such effects are stronger. Usually prices of public utilities, government contracts and purchasing, are based on cost data; in these cases

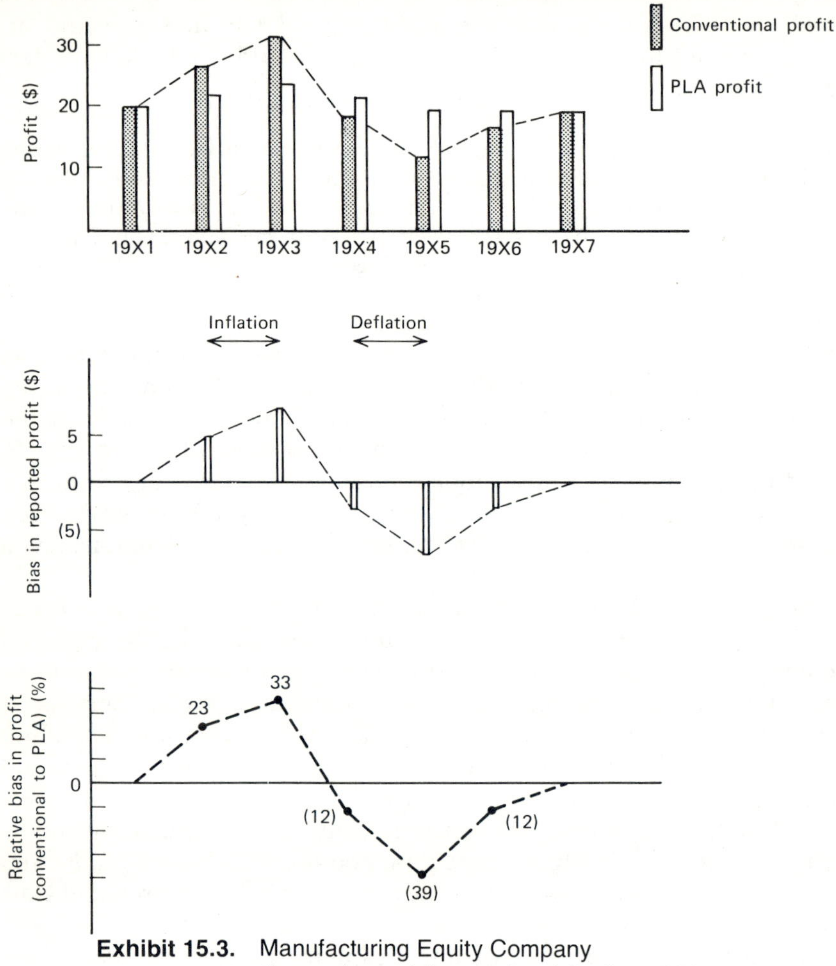

Exhibit 15.3. Manufacturing Equity Company Comparison of Conventional Profit and PLA Profit over the Trade Cycle

Source: Data from Exhibit 15.2.

the companies involved will be underpaid during inflation and overpaid during deflation.

In summary, conventional accounting statements cause the "good" years to look better and the "poor" years to look worse than they really are. This certainly has undesirable effects on the individual company and on the national economy as a whole. Distorted information at the company level often leads to decisions that have macroeconomic effects.[4]

15.3 Effect of Change in the Rate of Price Level Changes

It has been shown that inflation (deflation) causes bias in conventional reported profit. The degree of bias is influenced not only by the rate of price level changes, but by the changes in this rate as well. Three patterns of inflation rates are analyzed: constant, increasing, and decreasing.

To illustrate the effects of these patterns of change, the data related to the Manufacturing Equity Company are extended, as shown in Exhibit 15.4. The biased profit figures in Exhibit 15.4 are deflated in order to present inflationfree comparable data. These data are plotted in Exhibit 15.5, which shows that, as long as the inflation rate is constant (yearly inflation of 10% in years 2 to 4), the bias in profit reported by conventional accounting procedures is constant as well. If the rate of inflation increases (years 4 to 6), the bias becomes disproportionately greater. If the price level rises, but at a decreasing rate (years 7 to 9), the absolute bias decreases.

The analysis in Exhibit 15.3 (bias in reported profit over the assumed trade cycle) and that in Exhibit 15.5 (bias in reported profit as a result of changes in rate of inflation) can be consolidated. Consider the classical assumption of a sinoidal cycle, as depicted in Exhibit 15.6. The upper section of this exhibit is a graphical representation of the pattern of price level change during a sinoidal cycle. The lower section is similar to the middle section of Exhibit 15.3; it is a graphical display of the bias in reported profit during the phases of the cycle. Both cases rest on the assumption that the company is stable in physical assets, production, and sales and that the assets are replaced steadily in a stagger system.

The analysis in Exhibit 15.6 shows that, as long as the price level increases (inflation exists), conventional profit is upward biased (periods *a* and *b*). When the price level declines (deflation exists), conventional profit is downward biased (periods *c* and *d*). The effect of the pattern of the price level change on conventional reported profit is illustrated as well. The change in bias in conventional profit over time is determined by the rate of the price level change (the first-order differential). As long as the rate of price level change increases (period *a*, at a positive rate, and period *c*, at a negative rate), the bias increases (positively and negatively, respectively); when the rate decreases (periods *b* and *d*) the bias decreases.

The life span of assets, that is, the time lag between acquisition and realization, affects the magnitude of the bias in conventional reported profits: the longer the asset life (and the greater the inflation rate), the greater is the bias. The life span of assets also affects the change

Exhibit 15.4. Manufacturing Equity Company
Summary of Profit Figures for 10 Years

Year:	0	1	2	3	4	5	6	7	8	9
Price index:	100.00	110.00	121.00	133.10	146.41	168.37	202.05	242.46	278.82	306.71
Inflation rate (%):	—	10	10	10	10	15	20	20	15	10
Conventional profit	$20.00	$27.00	$32.20	$35.42	$38.96	$47.98	$62.73	$77.11	$84.05	$84.37
PLA profit	20.00	22.00	24.20	26.62	29.28	33.67	40.41	48.49	55.76	61.34
Difference (bias)	—	5.00	8.00	8.80	9.68	14.31	22.32	28.62	28.29	23.03
Deflating factor	1.000	0.909	0.826	0.751	0.683	0.594	0.495	0.412	0.359	0.326
Deflated bias	—	4.55	6.61	6.61	6.61	8.50	11.05	11.80	10.15	7.51

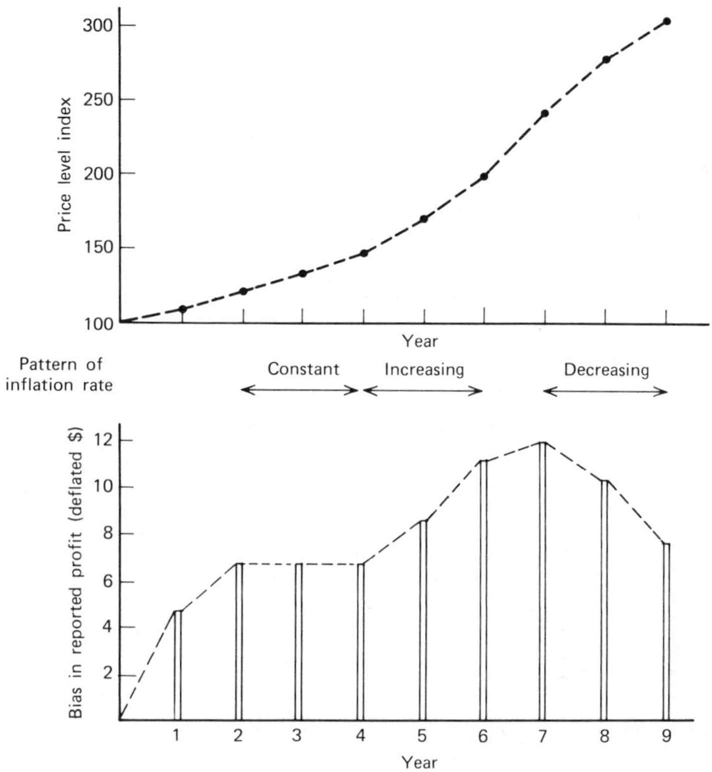

Exhibit 15.5. Manufacturing Equity Company
Inflation Rate and Bias in Conventional Profit*

*The biases for years 1 and 7 are inconsistent because of the transition in inflation rate.
Source: Data from Exhibit 15.4.

in the bias when the rate of inflation changes: the shorter the asset life (and the greater the change in the inflation rate), the more significant is the change in the bias in conventional reported profit.[5]

In summary, a change in the rate of inflation affects the bias in reported profit caused by conventional accounting procedures. When the inflation rate is increasing, the bias increases as well, and conventional financial statements feed the fires of overoptimism. When inflation continues, but at a decreasing rate, the bias in reported profit decreases and pessimism may set in, thus leading to decisions at the corporate level that may bring about the least desired results—a matter of overcorrection.

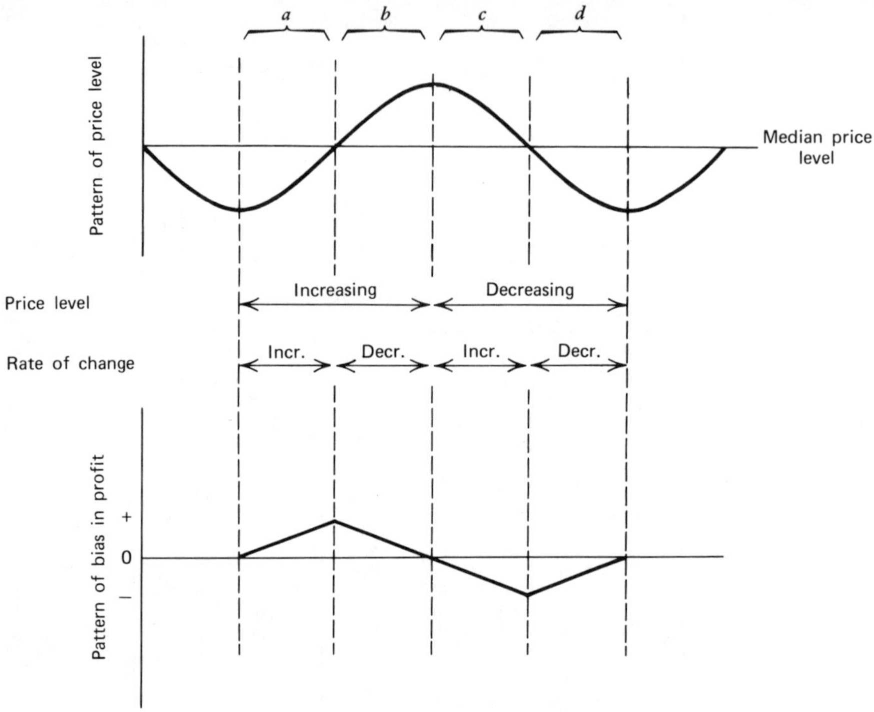

Exhibit 15.6. Bias in Conventional Profit over the Traditional Trade Cycle*

*Assuming a stable company with steady replacement of assets.

15.4 Leverage Loss under Deflationary Conditions

During a period of deflation the purchasing power of money increases; thus the reported PLA profit declines, even assuming stability in production and sales. In the illustration with 100% equity, the PLA pretax profit declined by the drop in the price level. In the more realistic case of financial leverage, deflationary conditions cause PLA profit to decrease more than is required by the drop in price level, as in the following example.

At the end of 19X3 the Manufacturing Leverage Company anticipated that inflationary conditions might not continue. Therefore it renegotiated the loan agreements and succeeded in reducing the nominal interest rate from 14% to 8%. To keep the accounting simple, it is assumed that the decrease affects the outstanding loan (Loan 5) as well. On January 1, 19X4, the price level fell by 9.09%. Relevant financial statements are presented in Exhibit 15.7.

The real effect of financial leverage during deflation is illustrated by the low PLA pretax profit in 19X4: $15.80 compared to $20.80 in 19X2. Not only is the absolute sum reduced, but also in relation to sales and equity profit is lower even than in 19X1 (7.2% and 31.9% as against 8.8% and 39.1%, respectively). This occurred despite the fact that the bank had immediately adjusted its interest rate to the 19X1 level.

Because of stability in production and sales, expected PLA pretax profit is $19.36 ($17.60 in 19X1, the base year, plus 10% PLA). Yet this figure is $3.56 above that computed in Exhibit 15.7. The decline in the PLA profit is due to two reasons: (1) a net restatement loss of $3.30, resulting from the fact that asset values declined by $8.25, of which only $4.95 was absorbed by the equity maintenance adjustment; and (2) interest of $0.26 on an extra loan, due to the fact that the price level and the PLA value of assets dropped on January 1, 19X4, while the loans (taken for the predeflationary higher asset values) are held until December 31, 19X4.

In summary, the decline in price level (9.09% in 19X4) led to a deflationary leverage loss ($3.56), whereas earlier the increase in price level (10% in 19X2) brought about inflationary leverage returns ($1.44). This discrepancy between returns and loss occurred despite the fact that the rate of interest decreased and increased, respectively, by 6 percentage points in each case.

The discussion and illustrations above assumed, for the sake of simplicity, that institutional restrictions on the rate of interest appear as a lag in the adjustment of the current rate of interest to the rate of price level change. In addition, interest charges lag because usually the terms of outstanding loans are not renegotiable when price level conditions change. The latter effect implies that the outstanding loans bear nonfloating interest rates in contrast to the previous assumption (upon which all the illustrations were based). This "rigidity" will increase the inflationary leverage returns or losses, thus augmenting the procycle tendency of profit under financial leverage.

Consider the Manufacturing Leverage Company, functioning under such conditions. Because of the assumed nonfloating interest rates, as calculated in Exhibit 15.8, total interest expenses are lower during inflationary, and higher during deflationary, periods than when interest rates on outstanding loans are floating. The difference in the interest expenses (between the two assumed conditions) should be added to the inflationary leverage returns, as follows:

	19X2	19X4
Inflationary returns (loss), conditions of floating rates	$1.44	$(3.56)
Difference in interest expenses (from Exhibit 15.8)	1.80	(2.18)
Total inflationary returns (loss), conditions of nonfloating rates	3.24	(5.74)

Exhibit 15.7. Manufacturing Leverage Company
Financial Statement for the Year 19X4
(9.09% Deflation, 100% Fixed Assets, 60% Equity, 8% Interest)

Balance Sheet as of December 31, 19X4

Assets					Liabilities and Equity				
12.31.19X3			12.31.19X4		12.31.19X3			12.31.19X4	
Conventional	PLA*		Conventional	PLA*	Conventional	PLA		Conventional	PLA
$55.00	$60.50r	Machine 4	—	—	$11.00	$11.00	Loan 4	—	—
						1.10	Loan 4a		—
60.50	60.50	Machine 5	$60.50	$55.00r	24.20	24.20	Loan 5	$12.10	$12.10
—	—	Machine 6	55.00	55.00	—	—	Loan 6	22.00	20.90
					35.20	36.30	Total liabilities	34.10	33.00
115.50	121.00	Assets, at cost	115.50	110.00	45.00	45.00	Equity	45.00	45.00
(27.50)	(30.25)	Accum. depr.	(30.25)	(27.50)	7.80	—	New shares	6.15	—
88.00	90.75		85.25	82.50	—	9.45	Equity maint. reserve	—	4.50
88.00	90.75		85.25	82.50	88.00	90.75		85.25	82.50

*The letter *r* indicates restated figure.

Exhibit 15.7. (continued)

Profit and Loss Statement for the Year 19X4

	Conventional		PLA	
Sales		$220.00		$220.00
Out-of-pocket costs	$143.00		$143.00	
Interest	2.82		2.90	
Depreciation	57.75		55.00	
		203.57		200.90
PLA operating profit		—		19.10
Asset restatement gains (losses)		—	(8.25)	
Equity maint. adjustment		—	4.95	
Net restatement loss		—		(3.30)
Profit tax and dividend		16.43		15.80

Sources and Uses Statement for the Year 19X4

Sources	Conventional	PLA	Uses	Conventional	PLA
Depreciation	$57.75	$55.00	Machine 6	$55.00	$55.00
Profit	16.43	15.80	Tax and dividend	16.43	15.80
Asset restatement	—	8.25	Equity maint.	—	4.95
			Share redemption	1.65	—
Loan 6	22.00	20.90	Loans repayment	23.10	24.20
	96.18	99.95		96.18	99.95

Exhibit 15.8. Manufacturing Leverage Company
Interest Charges under PLA Accounting, Assuming non-floating Interest Rates

			Loan Schedule				
12.31.19X1	Loan No.	Interest Rate (%)	12.31.X2	12.31.X3	12.31.X4	12.31.X5	12.31.X6
$10.00	Loan 2	8	—	—	—	—	—
20.00	Loan 3	8	$10.00	—	—	—	—
	Loan 3a	14	1.00	—	—	—	—
	Loan 4	14	22.00	$11.00	—	—	—
	Loan 4a	14	—	1.10	—	—	—
	Loan 5	14	—	24.20	$12.10	—	—
	Loan 6	8			20.90	$10.45	—
	Loan 7	8				19.55	$ 9.78
	Loan 8	8					20.22
30.00	Total loans		33.00	36.30	33.00	30.00	30.00
			Interest Charges on Former Year's Outstanding Loans				
			$0.80	$0.80	$ 1.54	$ 1.69	$ 0.84
			1.60	0.14	0.15	1.67	1.56
				3.08	3.39		
Total nonfloating charges			2.40	4.02	5.08	3.36	2.40
Total floating charges*			4.20	4.62	2.90	2.64	2.40
Difference			(1.80)	(0.60)	2.18	0.72	—

*As assumed and computed in all other illustrations.

The effect of nonfloating interest rates on profit is determined, under given conditions, by the data on which the loan was granted. Assume that inflation exists for a prolonged period, and that the rate of interest on new loans increases over time, as the rate of price level change increases. Under these conditions, the earlier the loan was taken, the lower is the rate of interest on the loan, and the greater are the borrower's inflationary leverage returns. When the rate of change in the price level decreases, the reverse is true.

Note that the reduced profit in 19X4 is based on the assumption that production and sales did not decline. When sales decline during a period of deflation, a company's leverage losses will be even greater. Those who remember the Great Depression are familiar with this phenomenon.

Although on the face of it interest rates (in the illustration) seem to move symmetrically over the trade cycle, actual compensation of debt capital is not symmetric. Whereas debt capital receives (at least partial) compensation for price level changes during inflationary periods, it usually does not participate in losses during deflationary periods.[6]

Suppose that a bank grants a $100 loan for 1 year which bears 8% interest per year with the principal linked to the price level index (Section 4.2). Suppose further that it is agreed that upon repayment, the loan will be renewed in an amount equal to principal, interest, and linkage paid. In Year 1, when the loan was originally granted, the price level index was constant; in Year 2, the index rose by 10%; and in Year 3, it fell by 9.09%, that is, back to the Year 1 level. The resultant payments are shown in the upper section of Exhibit 15.9.

Now assume that conditions are the same as above, but that the loan is not linked to price index. Instead, in Year 2 the bank raised the nominal interest rate to 14%, and in Year 3 lowered it again to 8%. The results are shown in the lower section of Exhibit 15.9. As can be seen, during the inflationary year (Year 2) actual compensation for the nonlinked loan was $15.12 instead of $19.64 required for full compensation. In Year 3, on the other hand, compensation for the nonlinked loan was $9.85 against $ −2.55 for the linked loan. Over the 3-year inflation–deflation cycle, total compensation for the nonlinked loan was 32.97%, whereas for the linked loan it was 25.09%. The internal rate of return[7] for the non-linked loan was about 10%, as compared with 8% for the linked loan.

This demonstrates another aspect of the profit-risk allocation of leverage financing. Debt capital did not participate fully in the gains of the inflationary period, but did not lose at all during the deflation.[8]

Exhibit 15.9. Loan Repayment under Two Schemes

Year:	1	2	3
Price index:	100.0	110.0	100.0
	Linked Loan		
Opening balance	$100.00	$108.00	$127.44
Interest for the year at 8%	8.00	8.64	10.21
Linkage for the year	—	10.80	(11.58)
Closing balance	108.00	127.44	126.07
	Nonlinked Loan		
Opening balance	100.00	108.00	123.12
Interest for the year			
At 8%	8.00	—	9.85
At 14%	—	15.12	—
	108.00	123.12	132.97

When price level linked loans are practiced, usually there is a "one-way" clause. If the index rises above the base index during the loan period, so does linkage; if the index falls below the base index, compensation remains as stipulated at the base. Deflationary loss is borne by equity. Creditors display downward rigidity in their income claims.[9]

15.5 Perturbation of Profit Measures Due to Price Level Changes

The effect of price level changes on PLA operating profit differs from the effect on PLA total profit because the latter includes restatement gains and losses whereas the former does not. The effect of price level changes on conventional profit differs from the two PLA measures, since the former includes realized restatement gains without deduction of expenses resulting from restatement of assets.

The three types of profit for the Manufacturing Leverage Company are summarized in Exhibit 15.10 and depicted in Exhibit 15.11. Comparing profit figures resulting from these three measures for the Manufacturing Leverage Company (Exhibit 15.10) reveals the following relations:

Comparison of Profit Measures

During Inflation	During Deflation
Conventional > PLA total	Conventional < PLA total
Conventional > PLA operating	Conventional < PLA operating
PLA total > PLA operating	PLA total < PLA operating

Exhibit 15.10. Manufacturing Leverage Company
Three Profit Measures for the Years 19X1–19X7

Year:	19X1	19X2	19X3	19X4	19X5	19X6	19X7
Price index:	100.0	110.0	121.0	110.0	100.0	100.0	100.0
Conventional profit	$17.60	$22.80	$27.72	$16.43	$ 9.52	$15.02	$17.60
PLA operating profit	17.60	17.80	19.58	19.10	17.36	17.60	17.60
Net restatement gains (loss)	—	3.00	3.30	(3.30)	(3.00)	—	—
PLA total profit	17.60	20.80	22.88	15.80	14.36	17.60	17.60

Source: Data from Appendix C.

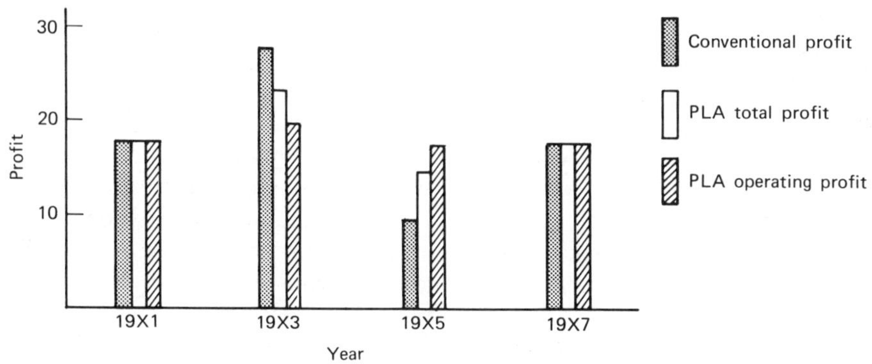

Exhibit 15.11. Manufacturing Leverage Company
Three Profit Figures over the Assumed Trade Cycle*

*The years 19X2, 19X4, and 19X6 are omitted because they are transitionary.
Source: Data from Exhibit 15.10.

These relations suit the Manufacturing Company's conditions, as well as most actual situations. Only if the company were highly leveraged, could PLA total profit be higher than conventional profit during inflation.

Price level adjusted operating profit is lower than conventional profit during inflation (and vice versa during deflation) since in the former case lagged costs are price level adjusted. It is also lower than PLA total profit during inflation (and vice versa during deflation) since net restatement gains resulting from the debt share of capital are not included.[10] It can be inferred from the respective differences during inflation and deflation that PLA operating profit is less perturbed by price level changes than is the other measure.

The sensitivity of a profit measure to price level changes is an important characteristic according to which the advantage or disadvantage of the measure can be judged. The less perturbed the measure is by price level change, the better it serves the objective of income (dividend) distribution.[11]

Perturbation of the three types of profit for the Manufacturing Leverage Company is measured by the annual amplitudes relative to the pre-price-level-change period (19X1). The extreme amplitudes are as follows:

	19X3	19X5
Conventional profit	30%	– 46%
PLA total profit	7	– 18
PLA operating profit	– 8	– 1

As can be seen, amplitudes over the trade cycle are lowest for the PLA operating profit; amplitudes are at the maximum for the conventional profit and in between for the PLA total profit.

The perturbation of conventional profit depends directly on the share of lagged cost that determines the realized restatement gains. The larger this variable, the larger is the bias in conventional profit and the larger the perturbation will be over the trade cycle. This effect is demonstrated by changing the given production function of the Manufacturing Leverage Company, by way of alterations in the assumed life span of assets.

Assume first that the company holds $75 worth of inventory of a 1-year cycle; during the year $75 worth of materials is used, all drawn from the opening inventory. Thus lagged cost is composed of $75 of materials rather than $50 of depreciation (the original figure); total restatement gains are realized, rather than 67% ($5 out of $7.50). Second, assume that the company holds $75 worth of nondepreciable assets (e.g., land). Thus lagged costs are not involved in production. The corresponding profit and loss statements over the assumed trade cycle are presented in Exhibit 15.12. As can be seen, the characteristics of lagged cost affect conventional profit considerably. The extreme amplitudes (relative to 19X1) are as follows:

	19X3	19X5
Original data	30%	– 46%
Short-lived assets	58	– 44
Long-lived assets	14	—

A simulation on the Manufacturing Leverage Company,[12] wherein the specific conditions are changed to higher and lower levels than those origi-

Exhibit 15.12. Manufacturing Leverage Companies
Profit and Loss Statements for the Years 19X1 – 19X6
Effects of the Production Function

Year:	19X1	19X2	19X3	19X4	19X5	19X6
Price index:	100.0	110.0	121.0	110.0	100.0	100.0
	*Short-Lived Assets (Inventory), Conventional Accounting**					
Sales	$200.00	$220.00	$242.00	$220.00	$200.00	$200.00
Out-of-pocket costs	105.00	115.50	127.05	115.50	105.00	100.00
Materials from inventory	75.00	75.00	82.50	90.75	82.50	75.00
Interest	2.40	4.20	4.62	2.90	2.64	2.40
	182.40	194.70	214.17	209.15	190.14	182.40
Profit	17.60	25.30	27.83	10.85	9.86	17.60
	Long-Lived Assets (Nondepreciable), Conventional Accounting†					
Sales	$200.00	$220.00	$242.00	$220.00	$200.00	$200.00
Out-of-pocket costs	180.00	198.00	217.80	198.00	180.00	180.00
Interest	2.40	4.20	4.20	4.20	2.40	2.40
	182.40	202.20	222.00	202.20	182.40	182.40
Profit	17.60	17.80	20.00	17.80	17.60	17.60
	Both Companies, PLA Accounting‡					
PLA operating profit	$17.60	$17.80	$19.58	$19.10	$17.36	$17.60
PLA total profit	17.60	20.80	22.88	15.80	14.36	17.60

*The respective balance sheets equal those under PLA accounting (Appendix C).
†The respective balance sheets equal that of 19X1.
‡Data from Exhibit 15.10.

nally assumed, shows that this result (the relatively low sensitivity of PLA operating profit to price level changes) is a general rule.

The simulation is based on the following data: (1) the rates of inflation (in 19X2 and 19X3) and of deflation (in 19X4 and 19X5) are changed from 10%: first to 5% and second to 15%; (2) the rate of interest movement in response to the rate of price level changes is revised from 8 %–14%–8% (14% in 19X2 and 19X3): first, to 8% throughout and second, to 8%–20%–8%; and (3) the financial leverage is changed from 60% equity: first to 100% and second, to zero. The results are presented in Exhibit 15.13.

Exhibit 15.13. Manufacturing Leverage Company
Amplitudes in Profit Measures over the Assumed Trade Cycle

	Variable				Extreme Amplitudes (%)		Relative to 19X1 Profit			
					Conventional Profit		PLA Total Profit		PLA Operating Profit	
					Inflation	Deflation	Inflation	Deflation	Inflation	Deflation
	Rate (%) of Price Change*									
	19X1	19X2,3	19X4,5	19X6						
	—	5	− 4.76	—	+11	−23	− 1	− 9	− 9	− 1
Original data:	—	10	− 9.09	—	+30	−46	+ 7	−18	− 8	− 1
	—	15	−13.04	—	+47	−70	+15	−28	− 7	− 2
	Production Function (Exhibit 15.12)									
	Lagged Costs		Realization							
	$ 0		$ 0	0%	+14	—	− 1	− 9	− 9	− 1
Original data:	50		5.0	67	+30	−46	+ 7	−18	− 8	− 7
	75		7.5	100	+58	−44	+15	−28	− 7	− 2
	Rate (%) of Interest*									
	19X1	19X2,3	19X4,5	19X6						
	8	8	8	8	+39	−46	+17	−18	+ 1	− 1
Original data:	8	14	8	8	+30	−46	+ 7	−18	− 8	− 1
	8	20	8	8	+21	−46	− 2	−18	−17	− 1
	Financial Leverage (% Equity)*									
			100		+33	−39	—	—	—	—
Original data:			60		+30	−46	+ 7	−18	− 8	− 1
			0		+24	−61	+23	−58	−25	− 4

*The respective computations are omitted to save space.

The main perturbation factors influencing conventional profit are the rate of price level change and the production function (share of lagged costs); the greater these variables, the larger are the amplitudes of reported profits over the cycle. The PLA operating and total profit figures are not affected by the production function, but they are affected by the rate of price level change. The amplitudes of PLA operating profit, due to price level changes, are usually negative (in relation to profit before the price level changed), especially during a period of inflation.

The lower PLA operating profit figure during inflation is caused by the increased rate of interest on debt, which is deducted from profit. The increased interest rate provides price level compensation to debt capital (recorded as expense), but price level gains (restatement gains) are not included in PLA operating profit. Therefore the amplitudes are affected by, and correlated to, both the rate of interest during inflation and the level of financial leverage (see the extreme case of zero equity). Since restatement gains are included in PLA total profit, its amplitudes are mainly positive during inflation and negative during deflation. These conclusions are summarized in Exhibit 15.14.

Using PLA operating profit as a measure of the results of company activity would reduce the procycle amplitudes that are embodied in conventional profit. Thus it would have important psychological effects at both company and national levels (see Section 15.2). It would also reduce the claims to profit by the various claimants during a period of inflation, but would increase them during deflation. This characteristic has an anticycle effect without depleting the company of resources beyond its real capability.

15.6 Profit Measure for Dividend Policy

The profit measure that serves as the basis for dividend policy should take into consideration the behavior of the claimants to profit (Section 2.3), as well as the changes in the dollar's purchasing power (price level). Neither the conventional nor the PLA total profit measure is suitable for this purpose, that is, for determining the sum that may be consumed. Conventional profit includes fictitious profit, and PLA total profit includes short-run inflationary leverage returns. For these reasons, they may cause excessive withdrawal of resources from the company during a period of inflation.

Price level adjusted operating profit meets the requirements stated above, both for 100% equity and for financial leverage. This is so

Exhibit 15.14. Effects of Change in Variables on Amplitudes in Profit Measures

	Correlation with Change in Variable		
Variable	Conventional Profit (large amplitude over trade cycle)	PLA Total Profit (medium amplitude over trade cycle)	PLA Operating Profit (small amplitude over trade cycle)
Rate of price change	Positive	Positive	—*
Portion of realization	Positive	—*	—*
Rate of interest	—*	Negative	Positive
Share of equity	—*	Negative	—*

*No significant effect and, in turn, no correlation.

because (1) the lagged costs are restated, making the reported profit price level adjusted, and (2) restatement gains (which originate from the debt share of capital) are not included, thereby setting aside reserves for restatement losses if these appear during a deflationary period.

The main advantage of PLA operating profit as a basis for dividend policy is that it is less affected by price level changes over the trade cycle than are other profit measures, as shown in Section 15.5.

Reporting PLA operating profit means that the net restatement gains resulting from financial leverage are excluded from the PLA profit and loss statement. These are transferred to the PLA balance sheet.[13]

In Section 2.1 it was shown that during a period of stable prices the conventional profit figure may serve as a good surrogate for economic profit as defined by Hicks. Over a period of price level changes, on the other hand, the best surrogate for economic profit is probably PLA operating profit. This figure is computed by following conventional accounting procedures, except for the restatement of historical costs in which there is a time lag between acquisition and realization (depreciation and materials drawn from inventory). For a given year the PLA operating profit figure does not coincide with the Hicksian definition (under financial leverage conditions). In the long run, however, considering the behavioral aspects of the claimants to profit, this measure will probably be in accordance with the economic concept. Using PLA operating profit to determine the sum that may be withdrawn from the company will avoid capital erosion during inflation; it will also preserve or even improve a company's liquidity.

NOTES

1. Some authorities (e.g., Lerner 1972) claim that deflation cannot exist at present because prices, especially those of the main resources (labor, management, capital), are rigid downward.
2. For a review of this subject see Ray (1960, Chapters 2 and 3) and Morley (1974, pp. 36–44).
3. For further discussion of this subject see Ray (1960, Chapters 4 and 5).
4. Let us quote early statements of three authorities on this subject (from Ray 1960, pp. 27, 5, 33, respectively):

   Schmidt, in 1929: "...apparent profit in periods of general increase in prices and apparent losses in periods of decreases in prices...."

   Canning, in 1933: "...belief in the accountants' figures leads to action that must increase the amplitude of the business cycle swings."

   Kuznets, in 1937: "...the disparity between real and apparent net income constitutes an important factor in business cycles."

   Actual biases in depreciation expenses in the United States during the corresponding period were as follows (Finley 1950, p. 10):

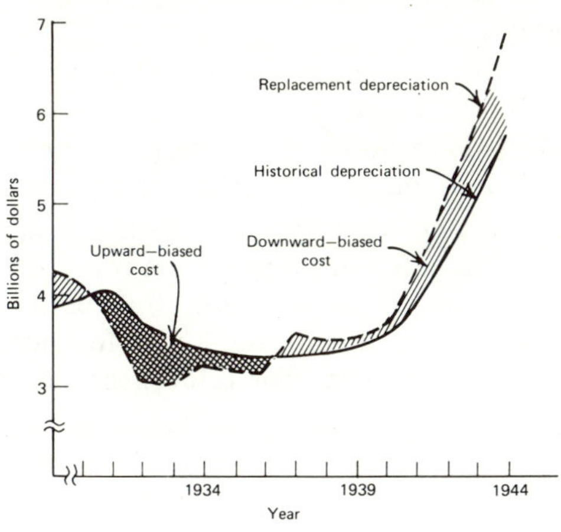

5. For details see Baxter (1969).
6. For studies of the relations between interest rates and price level changes see, for example, Roll (1972), Cargill and Meyer (1974), and Fama (1975).
7. The internal rate of return is the rate of discount that will bring the present value of the net cash flow to zero.
8. In terms of the formal presentation in Chapter 6:

$$[(i + h) < (i + p)(1 + i)]_{\text{in}} \quad \text{during prolonged inflation}$$

$$[(i + h) > (i + p)(1 + i)]_{\text{de}} \quad \text{during prolonged deflation}$$

and

$$[(h - p)(1 + i)]_{\text{de}} > [(h - p)(1 + i)]_{\text{in}}$$

9. Downward rigidity of the claimants to profit characterizes other suppliers of resources as well (Section 2.3).
10. These relations can be deduced from (6.6) and (6.14). During inflation the conventional profit is larger than the PLA operating profit by $p(A/L)$; during deflation it is smaller by $-p(A/L)$. The PLA total profit is larger than the PLA operating profit by $p(D-F)$ during inflation, and smaller by $-p(D-F)$ during deflation. The PLA total profit falls between the other two measures from the standpoint of perturbation.
11. When proportional income tax is levied on the "portubated" profit, it has a countercyclical effect on the national economy (Section 14.4).
12. Demonstrating this effect by simulation has been suggested by Dr. Leon Shashua.
13. Application of this procedure to the Manufacturing Leverage Company (Exhibit 4.5 and Appendix C) implies that \$3 in net restatement gains is excluded from the profit and loss statement. This sum substitutes for \$1 of Loan 3a and \$2 of Loan 4.

    It is interesting to note that Philips Electrical Industries of Holland excludes net restatement gains from reported profit during a period of inflation. On the other hand, it deducts the deflationary loss from reported profit during deflation, following the accounting principle of conservatism. For references, see Note 20, Chapter 3.

References

Baxter, W. T., "The Accountant's Contribution to the Trade Cycle," in R. H. Parker and G. C. Harcourt (eds.), *Readings in the Concept and Measurement of Income,* Cambridge University Press, London, 1969, pp. 215–229. Reprinted from *Economica,* Vol. XXII, 1955, pp. 99–112, Revised.

Cargill, T. F. and R. A. Meyer, "Interest Rates and Prices since 1950," *International Economic Review,* June 1974, pp. 458–471.

Fama, E., "Short-Term Interest Rates as Predictors of Inflation," *American Economic Review,* June 1975, pp. 269–282.

Finley, J. A., *Handling Higher Replacement Costs,* Studies in Business Policy No. 47, National Industrial Conference Board, New York, 1950.

Lerner, A. P., *Flation—Not Inflation of Prices, Not Deflation of Jobs,* Quadrangle Books, New York, 1972.

Morley, M. F., *The Fiscal Implications of Inflation Accounting,* Institute for Fiscal Studies and Institute of Chartered Accountants in ngland and Wales, London, 1974.

Ray, D. D., *Accounting and Business Fluctuations.* University of Florida Press, Gainesville, 1960.

Roll, R., "Interest Rates on Monetary Assets and Commodity Price Index Changes," *Journal of Finance,* May 1972, pp. 251–277.

Sixteen

Effects of Inflation on Financial Management

The discussion in this book has dealt with the effects of specific and general price level changes on conventional financial statements. Procedures for correcting the resulting distortions have been outlined. The aim has been to bring reported accounting into line with the economic concept of profit. To this end, the conventional profit figure has been analyzed to isolate various effects of price level changes. Understanding the subject may help corporate management to improve its decision making during a period of inflation. Proper inflation management can benefit a company or at least reduce the harmful effects of inflation on the company.

16.1 Damaging Effects of Inflation

> The anonymous author who first expressed the cause of inflation as too much money chasing too few goods still holds the prize for the best simple-minded truth on this subject. When the dollar value of what the nation is trying to spend exceeds the value of its capacity output, prices are bid up (Okun 1970, p. 7).

Inflation causes the measure of economic activities, that is, money, to shrink, not once, but continuously. In earlier days money was "debased" by clipping the coins; from the clippings, more coins could be minted.[1] In modern times money can be minted without clipping. Suppose that the foot measure was gradually reduced by removing an inch every so often, and lengths were measured by a 10-inch foot or a 5-inch foot; everything would be longer! This is recognized as absurd since it relates to engineering activities. The change in the measure of economic activity, on the other hand, is not seen as absurd because of the "money illusion."

A major damaging effect of inflation is the unjustified optimism caused by reporting fictitious profits. This affects every company and the national economy as well. The upward-biased reported profit may cause withdrawal of resources from the company beyond its economic capacity and impair managerial control.

In addition to the distortion of financial statements, inflation has some direct damaging effects.[2] It may cause overinvestment ("Buy now; it will cost more tomorrow!"), in contrast to the understatement of real asset depletion (understated depreciation expenses). This combination, overinvestment and underreservation of internal funds, may result in an exaggerated increase in financial leverage.

In fact, the source of new funds for nonfinancial corporations in the United States changed from 38% debt in 1965 to 53% in 1974.[3]

The increase in financial leverage may stem from management decisions to benefit from the inflationary leverage returns, taking advantage of the institutional restrictions on the rate of interest. It may stem also from capital erosion in the past, when inflation has existed for several years.

Another damaging effect of inflation is the distortion of plans, budgets, and sets of standards that were prepared in advance. Comparison of actual performance to the plan and standards is meaningless. Thus control of individual activities becomes difficult. The external increase in input prices often provides an alibi for internal inefficiency. For example, increased costs are blamed on inflation even when inputs are wasted.

Price level adjustments correct the main distortions that inflation causes in financial statements, as shown in this book. These adjustments are not, however, a panacea for the real ailments that are produced by inflation.

16.2 Inflationary Returns from Decisions on Capital Structure

Since the accounting data used by management are distorted, managerial decisions may also be distorted during a period of inflation.

On the other hand, a company may benefit (or reduce possible loss) from price level changes if management reckons with this additional variable in its decision making.

This section indicates how decisions on capital structure will affect future profit during a period of price level change. The subject resembles that discussed in Sections 14.1 and 14.2, which deal with the effects of capital and asset structures on conventional profit and tax payments.

If a company has adequate opportunities to invest additional capital in "price level linked" assets, it should increase its financial leverage (by nonlinked loans) as long as the additional debt capital generates inflationary leverage returns that compensate for the additional risk involved in increasing the financial leverage.[4] This holds if (1) inflation is expected to prevail (at the present or a higher rate) during the period for which the additional loan is taken, and (2) the terms of the loan are not renegotiable when price level conditions change.

The "inflationary" returns from financial leverage during a period of inflation involve an "inflationary" risk as well. The risk is that the rate of inflation may decline in the future or even that deflation may set in. If this happens, the inflationary leverage returns will vanish or may even change into deflationary leverage loss. In other words, the expected direction and rate of price level change must be considered when the volume of loans and their repayment schedule are decided upon.

Decision rules for borrowing during a period of price level change are based on two assumptions: (1) the rate of interest in the capital market adjusts itself (with some time lag) to the price level change (providing the lender with compensation for price level changes), and (2) the rate of interest on outstanding loans held by the company is not affected by price level changes.

Consider first an extreme and artificial case in which the direction of price level change (inflation or deflation) and its rate are expected to prevail continuously. Under these conditions the borrowing decision rules become simple, as summarized in Exhibit 16.1.

If it is expected that inflation will prevail forever at the present rate (or that the rate of inflation will even increase in the future), then the larger the financial leverage and the longer the repayment period of loans, the more inflationary leverage returns will be reaped by a company (provided that the capital is invested in price level linked assets). In the case of an increasing rate of inflation, the later the loan is taken, the higher will be its interest rate. Under these

Exhibit 16.1. Borrowing Decision Rules During A Period of Continuing Price Level Change

Type of Price Level Change	Volume and Length of Loans
Inflation	
Constant or increasing rate	Maximum
Decreasing rate	Minimum
Deflation	
Constant or increasing rate	Minimum
Decreasing rate	Maximum

conditions the earlier (nonlinked) loans are taken and invested (in price level linked assets), the greater will be a company's returns from inflation.

If the rate of inflation is expected to decrease, the shorter the repayment schedule, the lower will be the loss from the financial leverage because, at each loan renewal, the interest rate will be lower. If deflation is expected, then the lower the financial leverage, the better off the company will be.

Consider now a more realistic case, in which both direction and rate of price level change are not constant but rather change gradually over time. The rules concerning volume of loans, as listed in Exhibit 16.1, still hold; the rules concerning the length of the loans, however, change. When conditions suggest expanding financial leverage, the best expansion will be that which enables repayment of the loans before a downward change in the rate of price level increase occurs. This is illustrated on the traditional trade cycle as depicted in Exhibit 16.2.

The turning points of expanding and contracting financial leverage are not at the peak or trough of the cycle but rather at the points of change in the direction of the rate of price level change (points A and C in Exhibit 16.2). The periods during which financial leverage should be expanded or contracted depend on the rate of change of price level change (i.e., the second derivative of the price level). For example, increasing price level times increasing rate of change provides a positive effect (period a), suggesting leverage expansion.

Repayment of loans should be scheduled to occur before the rate of inflation starts to decline (point A). If loans must be taken after the rate of inflation declines, the shorter the repayment schedule, the better. Loans should be increased again as the rate of deflation starts to decline and the rate of interest is about to increase again.

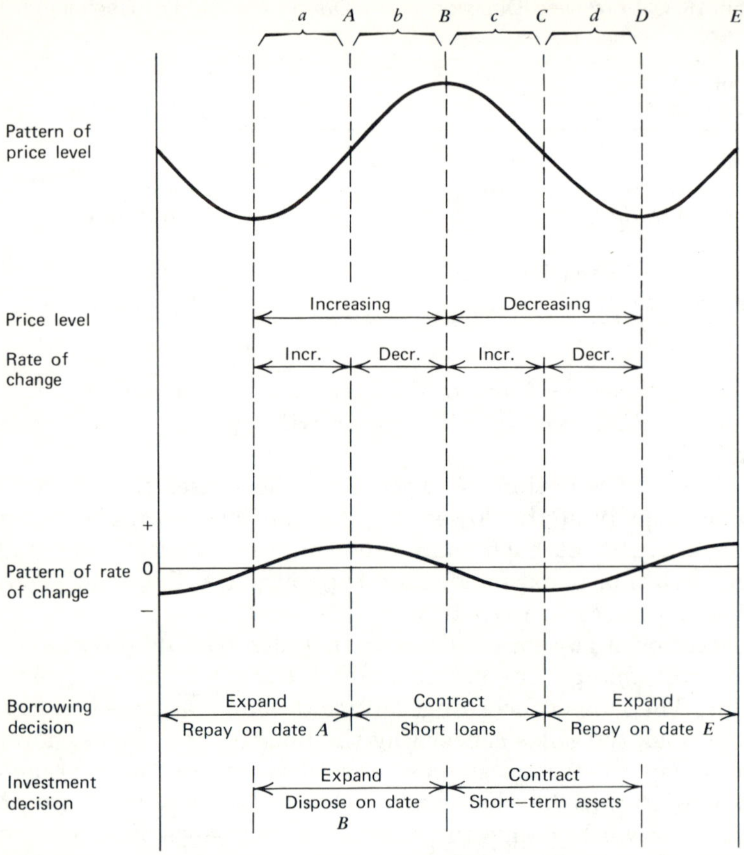

Exhibit 16.2. Borrowing and Investment Decision Rules over the Traditional Trade Cycle

16.3 Inflationary Returns from Decision on Asset Structure

In the preceding section it was assumed that the company has adequate opportunities to invest additional capital in "price level linked" assets. The lower the share of financial assets that are not price level linked, the better off the company will be during a period of inflation. The opposite holds during deflation.

Not only "price level linkage" but also asset life span has an effect on inflationary benefit. The historical costs of goods that stem from price level linked assets (i.e., lagged costs) are downward biased during inflation. As a result, conventional profit is upward biased—it includes fictitious profit. Unfortunately, some of this fictitious profit, as reported by conventional financial statements, is withdrawn from the company (by income taxes, bonuses, increased wages, etc.). Management decisions in regard to asset structure can reduce the share of fictitious profit in reported profit.

The share of fictitious profit in reported profit is composed of the realized asset restatement gains, which are determined by the life span of the assets. If a continuous period of inflation is assumed, the nonrealized portion of the asset restatement gains depends directly on the asset life span, as depicted in Exhibit 14.3.

The longer the life span of the assets, the longer is the realization span of the restatement gains, and the smaller is the per period realized portion. In turn, the upward bias in reported profit is smaller and so is the sum that is withdrawn from the company.[5] In this way the withdrawal of fictitious profit is postponed to the benefit of the company.[6] The ideal situation, from the company's point of view, occurs when the asset life span is infinite (e.g., land). In this case gains will be realized only upon sale of the asset.[7]

If inflation is expected to prevail forever, the longer the expected life span of assets, the better off the company will be (provided that these assets will be productive and will not become obsolete). During a period of deflation, if the company must acquire assets, it will benefit from acquiring short-lived ones so that assets at lower prices will earlier replace the existing ones. The relevant investment rules are as follows:

	Volume and Life Span of Assets
During inflation	Maximum
During deflation	Minimum

If deflation is expected to follow a period of inflation, the best assets to be purchased during inflation are those that will be disposed of when deflation is expected to start.

The investment rules indicated above can be applied to the traditional trade cycle, as shown in Exhibit 16.2. During a period of inflation, management should expand the volume of price level linked assets; during deflation it should contract their volume. Interestingly enough, the borrowing rules are not completely consistent with the investment rules, as shown in the lower section of Exhibit 16.2. During period a management should take loans (to be repaid on date A) and invest them in assets (to be disposed of on date B). During period b management should take short-term loans to finance the expansion in assets. During period *c* investment should not be undertaken, nor in period *d*. During period *d* management should expand borrowing but, on the other hand, should contract investment in price level linked assets.[8] This means that the company will benefit from taking loans to substitute equity during a period in which the rate of deflation declines.

This analysis suggests departure from some of the widespread rules of financial management. Management should develop a flexible financial leverage policy. Under given conditions, leverage should be expanded for expanding assets (period *a* in Exhibit 16.2) or for equity redemption (period *d*), taking into account the increased risk. The "current ratio" policy also must be more flexible. Under given conditions, fixed assets can be financed advantageously by short-term loans (period *b*), thus flouting current ratio doctrines. In other words, some of the accepted dogmas of financial management are too rigid during periods of price level changes.[9]

These rules are probably followed to some extent by many companies, causing cumulative effects on the national economy. During a period of inflation companies certainly expand investments and increase their financial leverage, not only because of expectations of higher sales but also out of speculative considerations, that is, to benefit from the changes in the capital and asset structures.

16.4 Correcting the Bias in Conventional Profit

When prices are stable, company profit, as computed by conventional accounting procedures, is consistent with the economic notion of profit, as defined by Hicks (Section 2.1). Therefore the profit figure, as reported by the conventional profit and loss statement, is suitable for all management decisions concerning the company as a whole.

Under conditions of inflation, however, conventional accounting profit ceases to be consistent with its economic counterpart. It is biased upward and therefore may mislead management. Several factors affect this bias, as summarized in Exhibit 16.3. Some of these factors are controllable by management (their effects are listed in the second column of the exhibit).

Correction of the distorted profit reported by conventional accounting procedures requires, as a first step, restatement of the company's assets. There are three major restatement methods. The uses of the figures resulting from the application of each of these methods are as follows:

Exhibit 16.3. Factors Affecting the Bias in Conventional Compared to PLA Profit During Continuing Inflation

Factor	Bias Is Larger When the Factor is:	Company is Benefited When the Factor Is:	Section in Which Factor Is Discussed
Inflation			
Rate	High		
Duration	Long		
Cost structure			
Share of lagged costs	High	Low	14.2, 15.5, 16.3
Captial structure			
Financial leverage	Low	High	4.5, 14.1, 16.2
Interest rate adjustment		Slow	
Age of loans		Old	16.2
Repayment schedule of loans		Long	16.2
Asset structure			
Share of financial assets		Low	4.6
Asset age	Old		14.2
Asset life span	Short	Long	14.2, 15.5, 16.3
Asset rate of growth	Low	High	
Costing method			
Depreciation	Large	Accelerated	14.3
Inventory	Large	LIFO	14.3

1. Restatement by a general price level index provides the basis for:
   a. Approximating the value of assets in current dollars.
   b. Determining standard lagged costs (depreciation, materials).
   c. Computing a proxy of company's economic profit.
   d. Determining the equity maintenance reserve.
2. Restatement by a specific price index provides the basis for:
   a. Approximating the value of assets in current cost figures.
   b. Approximating the lagged cost (depreciation, materials) in current figures.
   c. Calculating the terms of trade variance (in conjunction with point 1b).
3. Revaluation by appraisal provides an approximation of the value of fixed asset productive capacity. Revaluation of inventories in terms

of current market prices provides a close estimate of the real value of materials in inventory.

An important point to remember concerning asset restatement is that each method will result in a different figure of asset value. This "nonobjectivity" of revalued asset figures is often used as a major argument against PLA statements. In fact, the limited objectivity of asset values holds for conventional accounting statements as well.[10] The method of depreciation chosen and the estimated asset life assumed determine the recorded net value of assets; if the method is changed, the net asset value changes with it. Price level adjusted costs, arrived at by whatever logical method consistently applied, are closer approximations to "real" asset costs than the random mixture of historical figures that conventional accounting statements present.

16.5 Managerial Uses of Price Level Adjusted Profit Measures

Too often managers ask about profit as if the answer could be unique and unequivocal. This contradicts the simple rule that the specific use, for which the information is required, determines the relevant data to be supplied. The manager's question about the amount of profit must also define the purpose of the query. This is of special importance during a period of inflation when the profit measure calculated by conventional accounting practices diverges from its economic counterpart. The main managerial uses, coupled with a profit measure, are summarized in Exhibit 16.4[11]

Three types of PLA profit measures have been defined in this book: PLA total profit, PLA operating profit, and inflationfree profit. Additional profit measures relevant to an inflationary period have also been delineated: departmental profit, inflationary leverage returns, terms of trade variance, and projected operating cash flow. All of these are reviewed briefly below.

The PLA total profit is consistent with the Hicksian economic definition of the period profit. Thus this measure is suitable as a basis for levying income tax (Section 14.4). However, PLA total profit should not be used for dividend decisions or for adjudicating employees' wage claims, because it includes short-run inflationary leverage returns. Because of downward rigidity in dividends and wages, once these payments are raised during a period of inflation they are difficult to reduce when the rate of inflation decreases or inflation stops. During a period of continuous inflation (or, over a

Exhibit 16.4. Profit Analysis during Inflation
Manufacturing Leverage Company
Profit and Loss Statement for the Year 19X2

Type of Profit Measure	Managerial Use	Illustration		Source
Sales			$220.00	Exhibit 7.3
Less out-of-pocket costs			147.20	
OPERATING CASH FLOW	Investment analysis		72.80	
Less inventory price calculation			—	
Less conventional depreciation			(50.00)	
CONVENTIONAL PROFIT (Pretax)	Official report		22.80	Appendix C
Less PLA inventory adjustment			—	
Less PLA depreciation adjustment			(5.00)	
PLA OPERATING PROFIT	Dividend decisions		17.80	
Add asset restatement gains: Realized	Inflation management	$5.00		
Nonrealized		2.50		
Less equity maintenance adjustment		(4.50)		
Net restatement gains			3.00	
PLA TOTAL PROFIT	Tax basis		20.80	
Less inflationary leverage returns	Inflation management		(1.44)	Exhibit 7.8
INFLATIONFREE PROFIT	Performance evaluation		19.36	
Less cost of capital			(9.74)*	
DEPARTMENTAL PROFIT (Standard)†	Departmental analysis		9.62 ‡	
Add/less terms of trade variance	Inflation management		(0.96)	Exhibit 8.5
DEPARTMENTAL PROFIT (Actual)†			8.66	

*Imputed cost of capital (Exhibit 7.8)	$12.38
Imputed cost of debt (Exhibit 7.8)	2.64
Cost of capital	9.74

†The $9.62 departmental profit (of both departments in Exhibit 7.4) is considered in Exhibit 8.5 as a standard (the expected profit, assuming inflation). The terms of trade variance is $0.96; thus the actual departmental profit is $8.66 ($4.00 + $4.66).

‡Departmental profit ($9.62) plus equity returns ($11.18) provide PLA total profit ($20.80), as shown in Exhibit 7.4.

normal trade cycle), income distribution that is based on PLA total profit, may eventually lead to capital erosion. In other words, because of the behavioral aspects of profit claimants, PLA total profit is not consistent with long-run economic profit.

The PLA operating profit, on the other hand, is suitable for decisions regarding dividends (and employees' wage claims). This figure is lower than PLA total profit during inflation (the reverse holds for deflation), and it does not include nonrealized restatement gains. Furthermore, it is less sensitive to price level changes than either PLA total profit or conventional profit (Section 15.5). Taking into consideration the behavioral aspects of profit claimants, this measure is advantageous.

Inflationfree profit is equitable as a basis for income tax (Section 14.4) and is useful for performance evaluation of the company's operations, since it does not include inflationary leverage returns. These returns originate from external forces and financial decisions, not from operations.

Departmental profit is a better measure for performance evaluation since this figure takes into account the cost of equity capital. Also, this measure is free of biases caused by inflation (Section 7.3). Hence it should be used for decisions on and the control of specific activities at the departmental level, as well as aggregate operations.

The benefits that a company has gained from inflation can be estimated by three measures: (1) the ratio of nonrealized to realized asset restatement gains measures the benefit from asset structure during inflation—the higher this ratio, the lower is the withdrawal of fictitious profit from the company; (2) inflationary leverage returns measure the benefit from balance sheet composition; (3) terms of trade variance measure the benefit from speculation. It is important to isolate the terms of trade effect from operating profit during a period of inflation, when the prices of all or most commodities are on the increase, thereby obscuring the differentials involved.

Projected operating cash flow in both constant-price-level and nominal-price-level terms is required for investment analysis. Although the former method is simpler, it also has some drawbacks, since it ignores the effect of changes in the terms of trade and does not provide the data required for calculating income tax.

Inflation causes distortion of reported profit, and the correction of this distortion is costly. Moreover, there are several methods for correcting the distorted data, resulting in different profit measures (Exhibit 16.4). The appropriate method to choose in each case depends on the managerial use to be made of the resulting data.

16.6 Profit Level Adjustment Procedures to Be Applied in Practice

The diversified managerial activities require a variety of restatement value, cost, and profit measures. The relative efforts involved in calculating these measures are summarized in Exhibit 16.5. The importance of the specific measure in serving the specific use, on the one hand, and the effort required to supply it, on the other hand, should determine whether or not it should be calculated.

For practical purposes, calculation of at least three measures is recommended:

1. The *PLA* operating profit for the company as a whole, to be used as a substitute for the conventional profit figure.
2. The departmental profit, to be used for decisions on resource allocation, control, and performance evaluation at both departmental and company levels.
3. Inflationary leverage returns, to be used for evaluation of management decisions regarding inflation.

These measures provide information for the main managerial activities.

Exhibit 16.5. Efforts Involved in Calculating PLA Measures

Information Provided	Procedure or Measure	Relative Effort in Calculating
Asset value	Restatement by general index	Low
	Restatement by specific index	Intermediate
	Revaluation by appraisal	High
Inventory value	Revaluation by current market price	Low
	Restatement by general index	Intermediate
	Restatement by specific index	High
Profit for distribution	PLA operating profit	Low
	PLA total profit	Intermediate
	Inflationfree profit	High
Profit for performance evaluation	Inflationfree profit	Low
	Departmental profit	High
Inflation management evaluation	Inflationary leverage returns	Low
	Nonrealized to realized restatement gains	Intermediate
	Terms of trade variance	High
Cash flow for investment analysis	Constant-price-level data	Low
	Nominal-price-level data	High

The suggested adjustments should serve for internal purposes. A company should not provide external parties with PLA financial statements unless PLA procedures are practiced by a major share of organizations in the industry. During inflation both reported profit and financial ratios computed from PLA data are less optimistic than those based on conventional data. It is expected, therefore, that a company that publishes PLA financial statements will be graded too low.

Despite the widespread and continuous phenomenon of inflation, adjusted accounting procedures are not in common use. Nevertheless, in some countries adjustments are allowed or even compulsory; in others, they are recommended (see Section 1.5). The causes of the reluctance to accept adjusted accounting procedures during inflation can be found in behavioral reasoning. Conventional profit and loss statements record a larger "booty" to be divided among the members of the "coalition" which, according to Cyert and March (1963), constitute the business organization (Section 2.3). Government officials, elected representatives, and others are happy with the flourishing businesses reported by the upward-biased conventional statements, on the one hand, and the relatively low costs (as computed by conventional accounting procedures) of public utilities, government contracts and purchasing, and the like, on the other hand.

Sweeney states in the preface of the renewed version (1964) of his *Stabilized Accounting,* which appeared in the middle of the depression 1930s, that the book

> evoked theoretical attention and approval as a potentially usable tool....But it did not arouse any enthusiasm as a cure for "rubber dollar" errors in current accounting figures.
>
> The probable reason is not all mysterious. It is simply that a period of general economic depression does not cause much fault to be found with conventional accounting (although it should). For in such a time business profits become understated because revenues are charged with costs (especially of materials, merchandise, and depreciation) that should be restated in the lower price level of the depression period. Hence, income taxes become underpaid, union demands less troublesome, and dividends to stockholders lower. And yet despite such unsuccessful economic results, for which the unstabilized measuring unit is largely responsible, management can absolve itself from stockholder ire by blaming the depression.
>
> But a period of inflation causes business management to arise in unanimous protest. For then expenses become understated, profits and income taxes overstated, and union and stockholder desires insatiable. Business management is well informed, well financed, and well or-

> ganized. It likes to bask in the spurious glory of overstated profits—but likes to blast the accompanying excessive wages, income taxes, and dividends.

Recent developments in the United States and in Western European countries (Section 1.5), it is to be hoped, will make these criticisms obsolete.

Notes

1. It is interesting to note that inflation has existed for centuries:

   > In those days, fruit and other goods were cheap and much could be bought for the price of a penny. But in our times, when a penny will hardly buy anything at all, this ruling—a penny being the minimum value of an object to be admitted for litigation—should be restated. *(Me'irat Eynayim,* a commentary of *Shulchan Aruch,* sixteenth century).

   Y. Medan and A. Shmu'eli drew our attention to this source.
2. See Exhibit 1.9 for a list of damaging effects of inflation.
3. Jones (1975, p. 51; based on Federal Reserve Board figures).
4. It should be mentioned that during an extended period of inflation the conventional balance sheet causes downward bias of the real financial leverage (since asset restatement will inflate the equity).
5. This is shown formally by relation (6.6).
6. It is possible to compute the ratio of nonrealized to realized restatement gains for a given investment. Using this ratio for comparison of alternative sets of investments will provide a measure of the flow of realized inflationary returns, provided that inflation will prevail as long as the set of assets will exist.
7. Usually, the tax rate on asset appreciation is lower than corporate income tax. Thus not only is the tax on restatement gains being deferred, but the tax rate itself is also lower.
8. Comparison of the analysis in Exhibit 16.2 with that in Exhibit 15.6 shows that the investment rules correspond to the bias in conventional profit (expand when the bias is positive, contract when it is negative). The borrowing rules, on the other hand, correspond to the direction of price level change (expand when the direction is positive, contract when it is negative).

9. For example:

> To help stem illusory reported profits and improve cash flow, dozens of companies have recently switched to LIFO (last in, first out) accounting for inventories to match current inventory costs with revenues. But LIFO is not without its problems, particularly for capital-related matters. "It's a disaster for current ratios, working capital ratios, and bond indenture agreements," says FASB's Sprouse *(Business Week,* September 22, 1975).

10. See Note 6, Chapter 1, for references on the objectivity of revalued statements.
11. Graphical comparisons of the various profit measures are presented in Exhibits 4.6, 7.6, and 8.3.

References

Cyert, R. M. and J. G. March, *A Behavioral Theory of the Firm,* Prentice-Hall, Englewood Cliffs, N.J., 1963.

Jones, R. H., "Why Business Must Seek Tax Reform," *Harvard Business Review,* September–October 1975, pp. 49–55.

Okun, A. M., "Inflation: The Problems and Prospects before Us," in A. M., Okun, H. H. Fowler, and M. Gilbert, *Inflation: The Problems It Creates and the Policies It Requires,* New York University Press and University of London Press, New York and London, 1970, pp. 1–53.

Sweeney, H. W., *Stabilized Accounting,* Harper, New York, 1936 (revised, Holt, Rinehart & Winston, New York, 1964).

Appendix A

The Price System in Microcosm: A Prisoner-of-War Camp (Extracts)

The following is quoted from R. A. Radford, "The Price System in Microcosm: A P.O.W. Camp," in C. L. Harriss (ed.), *Selected Readings in Economics,* Prentice-Hall, Englewood Cliffs, N.J., 1958, pp. 69–79. This was originally an article in *Economica,* London, Vol. XII, No. 48, November 1945, pp. 189–201.

> After allowance has been made for abnormal circumstances, the social institutions, ideas and habits of groups in the outside world are to be found reflected in a Prisoner of War Camp. It is an unusual but a vital society. ... One aspect of social organization is to be found in economic activity. ...[It] came into existence not by conscious imitation but as a response to the immediate needs and circumstances.
>
> Between individuals there was active trading in all consumer goods and in some services. Most trading was for food against cigarettes or other foodstuffs, but cigarettes rose from the status of a normal commodity to that of currency.
>
> ...There was a lively trade in all commodities and their relative values were well known, and expressed not in terms of one another—one didn't quote bully in terms of sugar—but in terms of cigarettes. The cigarette became the standard of value. ... Everyone, including non-smokers, was willing to sell for cigarettes, using them to buy at another time and place. Cigarettes became the normal currency.
>
> ...[In] our...closed economy...a market came into spontaneous operation, and prices were fixed by the operation of supply and demand. Actually there was

[also] an embryo labor market. Even when cigarettes were not scarce, there was usually some unlucky person willing to perform services for them.

One trader in food and cigarettes, operating in a period of dearth, enjoyed a high reputation. His capital, carefully saved, was originally about 50 cigarettes, with which he bought rations on issue days and held them until the price rose just before the next issue. ... He kept himself smoking steadily—his profits—while his capital remained intact.

Although cigarettes as currency exhibited certain peculiarities, they performed all the functions of a metallic currency as a unit of account, as a measure of value ... They were homogeneous, reasonably durable, and of convenient size for the smallest or, in packets, for the largest transactions. Incidentally, they could be clipped or sweated by rolling them between the fingers so that tobacco fell out.

...Our economy was repeatedly subject to deflation and to periods of monetary stringency. While the Red Cross issue of 50 or 25 cigarettes per man per week came in regularly, and while there were fair stocks held, the cigarette currency suited its purpose admirably. But when the issue was interrupted, stocks soon ran out, prices fell, trading declined in volume and became increasingly a matter of barter. This deflationary tendency was periodically offset by the sudden injection of new currency. Private cigarette parcels arrived in a trickle throughout the year, but the big numbers came in quarterly when the Red Cross received its allocation of transport. Several hundred thousand cigarettes might arrive in the space of a fortnight. Prices soared, and then began to fall, slowly at first but with increasing rapidity as stocks ran out, until the next big delivery. Most of our economic troubles could be attributed to this fundamental instability.

The general price level was affected by other factors. An influx of new prisoners, proverbially hungry, raised it. Heavy air raids in the vicinity of the camp probably increased the non-monetary demand for cigarettes and accentuated deflation. ...Before breakfast, one morning in March of this year, a rumour of the arrival of...cigarettes was circulated. Within ten minutes I sold a treacle ration for four cigarettes (hitherto offered in vain for three), and many similar deals went through. By 10 o'clock the rumour was denied, and treacle that day found no more buyers even at two cigarettes.

More interesting than changes in the general price level were changes in the price structure. Changes in the supply of a commodity, in the German ration scale or in the make-up of Red Cross parcels, would raise the price of one commodity relative to others. Tins of oatmeal, once a rare and much sought after luxury in the parcels, became a commonplace in 1943, and the price fell. In hot weather the demand for cocoa fell, and that for soap rose.

In August, 1944, the supplies of parcels and cigarettes were both halved. Since both sides of the equation were changed in the same degree, changes in prices were not anticipated. But this was not the case: the non-monetary demand for cigarettes was less elastic than the demand for food, and food prices fell a little.

To increase and facilitate trade, ...a paper currency was organized by the Restaurant and the Shop. The Shop bought food on behalf of the Restaurant with paper notes and the paper was accepted equally with the cigarettes in the Restaurant or Shop, and passed back to the Shop to purchase more food. The Shop acted as a bank of issue. The paper money was backed 100 per cent by food; hence its name, the Bully Mark [BMK.]

Originally one BMK. was worth one cigarette and for a short time both circulated freely inside and outside the Restaurant. ... However the BMK. was tied to food, but not to cigarettes: as it was issued against food...prices of both food and BMK.s could and did fluctuate with the supply of cigarettes ....

In August parcels and cigarettes were halved and the Camp was bombed. ... The food and cigarette shortage became increasingly acute and people were unwilling to convert such valuable goods into paper [BMK.] and to hold them for luxuries like snacks and tea [in the Restaurant].

There was a strong feeling that everything had its "just price" in cigarettes. ... This price was...pretty closely known. It can best be defined as the price usually fetched by an article in good times when cigarettes were plentiful. The "just price" changed slowly; it was unaffected by short-term variations in supply... .

As soon as prices began to fall with a cigarette shortage, a clamor arose, particularly against those who held reserves and who bought at reduced prices. Sellers at cut prices were criticized and their activities referred to as the black market. In every period of dearth the explosive question of "should non-smokers receive a cigarette ration?" was discussed to profitless length.

The popularity of the price-fixing scheme, and such success as it enjoyed, were undoubtedly the result of this body of [public] opinion. On several occasions the fall of prices was delayed by the general support given to the recommended scale. The onset of deflation was marked by a period of sluggish trade; prices stayed up but no one bought. Then prices fell on the black market, and the volume of trade revived in that quarter. Even when the recommended scale was revised, the volume of trade in the Shop would remain low. Opinion was always overruled by the hard facts of the market. ... Prices moved with the supply of cigarettes, and refused to stay fixed in accordance with a theory of ethics.

Appendix B

Recent American Declarations on PLA and Replacement-Cost Procedures (Extracts)

SECURITIES EXCHANGE COMMISSION RULE 3-17, REGULATION S-X CURRENT REPLACEMENT COST INFORMATION

Notice of Adoption of Amendments to Regulation S-X Requiring Disclosure of Certain Replacement Cost Data*

The new rule as adopted requires registrants who have inventories and gross property, plant and equipment which aggregate more than $100 million and which comprise more than 10% of total assets to disclose the estimated current replacement cost of inventories and productive capacity at the end of each fiscal year for which a balance sheet is required and the approximate amount of cost of sales and depreciation based on replacement cost for the two most recent full fiscal years. In addition, registrants are required to disclose the methods used in determining these amounts and to furnish any additional information of which management is aware and believes is necessary to prevent the information from being misleading. This information may be presented either in a footnote to the financial statements or in a separate section of the financial statements following the notes. In either place, the information may be designated as "unaudited."

In requiring these data, the Commission is aware that it is requiring

**Accounting Series,* Rel. No. 190/March 23, 1976

companies to make disclosures of costs which cannot be calculated with precision. They must be estimated on the basis of numerous assumptions which may vary over time and from company to company and through the use of techniques which are not so fully developed that they can be standardized at the present time, if ever. This is because estimates of current replacement cost must be made within the framework of each registrant's economic situation and because there are difficult conceptual and empirical judgments which must be made in the light of different specific factual circumstances in developing the data. Nevertheless, the Commission believes that such data are important and useful to investors and are not otherwise obtainable. It feels that imprecision, if properly explained, will not make the data misleading. The Commission encourages registrants to supplement the required disclosures with information which management believes will be helpful to investors in understanding the impact of price changes and other current economic conditions on reported results.

The Commission's judgment that delay is not appropriate is based on a number of factors. First, it believes that under current economic conditions, data about the impact of changes in the prices of specific goods and services on business firms is of great significance to investors in developing an understanding of the current operations of any firm. While the current general rate of inflation has been reduced from 1974 levels, it is still at a level such that unsupplemented historical cost based data do not adequately reflect current business economics. Further, in an inflationary economy specific costs and prices which may affect a business change more rapidly than the general price level. These factors make the impact of delay more severe than would be the case in a time of price stability.

In addition, as a practical matter, it would never be possible for the Commission to anticipate every possible circumstance that may be faced in the application of this new disclosure rule. This is particularly true since the rule covers new ground and requires subjective judgments in its application. Accordingly, the Commission believes that various approaches taken in implementing the rule should be viewed as experimental, and that alternative approaches will be acceptable as long as the methods used are fully described and are applied in good faith and with reasonable care. There does not seem to be any persuasive reason, therefore, to deny these data to investors while experimentation in alternative techniques takes place.

Nevertheless, the Commission recognizes that it is important that registrants receive guidance on implementation problems and that experience in this regard is shared. Accordingly, it has determined to appoint an advisory committee composed of persons working with the problems of implementation to meet on a regular basis with the staff of the Commission to consider problems raised by registrants in complying with the rule.

In addition to its own efforts, the Commission believes that it would be useful for industry groups and associations to consider specialized problems in the application of replacement cost concepts to their areas of interest. In this connection, such groups may undertake to develop specific price indices applicable to particular classes of assets and suggest uniform industry-wide reporting approaches. The Commission staff would be willing to lend such assistance as it can to such efforts.

Analysis of Costs and Benefits. The release which accompanied the proposed rules specifically requested data as to the cost of compliance. Many respondents expressed concern about costs, but only a small number made specific estimates. Those estimates varied widely, and in general the cost estimates supplied by companies which had implemented replacement cost systems or undertaken pilot studies were substantially below those which had not. This suggests that as companies take steps to implement the rules adopted herein, they will find that the cost of compliance will be less than that estimated. Nevertheless, the Commission recognizes that the cost of implementing this rule will be significant, particularly in the first year of preparing the necessary data. It also seems clear that the cost will be proportionately higher for small companies with less sophisticated accounting systems.

The unaudited footnote or separate section of the financial statements containing the data will be a part of financial statements reported on by independent accountants. Accordingly, the independent accountant will be associated with the replacement of cost information even though it is unaudited. The Commission urges the Auditing Standards Executive Committee of the American Institute of Certified Public Accountants to develop appropriate standards applicable to the auditor in the case of such association.

In December 1974, the FASB issued an exposure draft of a statement which would require financial statements to include supplemental data in which historical costs were adjusted for changes in the general price level. In the Commission's proposal, it noted that general price level adjustments might be used either with historical cost or current replacement cost financial data. Accordingly, it did not and does not view its proposal as competitive with that of the FASB. In fact, in implementing the Commission's rule, some registrants may wish to use data regarding changes in the general price level as part of the analysis of reasons for changes in replacement costs. At the present time, however, the Commission does not propose to require the presentation of data restated for changes in the general purchasing power of the monetary unit.

Similarly, the Commission does not believe its new requirements prejudge any conclusions which may arise from the FASB's study of the conceptual framework of financial statements. As it noted in its original proposal, the Commission believes that fundamental changes in the basic accounting model should come about only after careful study by the FASB. It believes that experimentation with replacement cost information of the sort that will result from the implementation of this rule will materially assist the FASB in its study as well as providing meaningful supplemental disclosure to investors in the interim.

Effective Date of Regulation S-X Amendments. The Commission has determined to make Rule 3-17 of Regulation S-X effective for financial statements covering fiscal years ending on or after December 25, 1976, with the exception that it shall not apply to the mineral resource assets of companies engaged in the extractive industries prior to fiscal years ending on or after December 25, 1977, nor shall it apply to the assets located outside the North American continent and the countries of the European Economic Community prior to fiscal years ending on or after December 25, 1977, provided that the historical cost and a description of any such assets excluded from the supplemental replacement cost data are disclosed.

Regulation S-X: Rule 3-17. Current Replacement Cost Information. (New Rule)

Statement of Objectives. The purpose of this rule is to provide information to investors which will assist them in obtaining an understanding of the current costs of operating the business which cannot be obtained from historical cost financial statements taken alone. Such information will necessarily include subjective estimates and it may be supplemented by additional disclosures to assist investors in understanding the meaning of the data in particular company situations. A secondary purpose is to provide information which will enable investors to determine the current cost of inventories and productive capacity as a measure of the current economic investment in these assets existing at the balance sheet date.

Exemption. This rule shall not apply to any person where the total of inventories and gross property, plant and equipment (i.e., before deducting accumulated depreciation, depletion and amortization) as shown in the consolidated balance sheet at the beginning of the most recently completed fiscal year is less than $100 million or where the total of inventories and gross property, plant and equipment is less than 10 percent of the total assets of the person as shown in the consolidated balance sheet at the beginning of the most recently completed fiscal year.

The information set forth below shall be shown in a note to the financial statements or as part of a separate section of the financial statements following the notes. The note or the separate section may be designated "unaudited."

(a) The current replacement cost of inventories at each fiscal year end for which a balance sheet is required shall be stated. If current replacement cost exceeds net realizable value at that date, that fact shall be stated and the amount of the excess disclosed.

(b) For the two most recent fiscal years, state the approximate amount which cost of sales would have been if it had been calculated by estimating the current replacement cost of goods and services sold at the times when the sales were made.

(c) State the estimated current cost of replacing (new) the productive capacity together with the current depreciated replacement cost of the productive capacity on hand at the end of each fiscal year for which a balance sheet is required. For purposes of this rule, assets held under financing leases as defined in Rule 3-16(q) shall be included in productive capacity. In the case of any major business segments which the company does not intend to maintain beyond the economic lives of existing assets, the disclosures set forth in Rules 3-17(c) and (d) are not required provided full disclosure of the facts, amounts and circumstances is made.

(d) For the two most recent fiscal years, state the approximate amount of depreciation, depletion and amortization which would have been recorded if it were estimated on the basis of average current replacement costs of productive capacity. For purposes of this calculation, economic lives and salvage values currently used in calculating historical cost depreciation, depletion or amortization shall generally be used. For assets being depreciated, depleted or amortized on a time expired basis, the straight-line method shall be used in making this calculation. For assets depreciated, depleted or amortized on any other basis (such as use), that basis shall be used for this calculation.

(e) Describe the methods used in determining the amounts disclosed in items (a) through (d) above. Describe what consideration, if any, was given in responding to items (a) and (b) to the related effects on direct labor costs, repairs and maintenance, utility and other indirect costs as a result of the assumed replacement of productive capacity. Where the economic lives or salvage values currently used in historical cost financial statements are not used in (d) above, an explanation of other bases used and the reasons therefore shall be disclosed. If depreciation, depletion or amortization expense is a component of inventory cost or cost of sales, indicate that fact and cross-reference the answer for this item in item (b) in order to avoid potential duplication in the use of these data.

(f) Furnish any additional information—such as the historical customary relationships between costs changes and changes in selling prices, the difficulty and related costs (such as those related to environmental regulations) which might be experienced in replacing productive capacity—of which management is aware and which it believes is necessary to prevent the above information from being misleading.

* * *

This amendment to Regulation S-X is adopted pursuant to Sections 6, 7, 8, 10 and 19 (a) of the Securities Act of 1933; Sections 12, 13, 15(d) and 23(a) of the Securities Exchange Act of 1934; and Sections 6(b), 14 and 20(a) of the Public Utility Holding Company Act of 1935.

Rule 3-17 of Regulation S-X is effective for financial statements for fiscal years ending on or after December 25, 1976, except that the rule shall be initially applicable to the mineral resource assets of registrants engaged in the extractive industries and to registrants' assets located outside the North American continent and the countries of the European Economic Community in financial statements for fiscal years ending on or after December 25, 1977; provided that the historical cost and a description of any such assets excluded from the supplemental replacement cost data are disclosed.

Accounting Series Release No. 190—Relating to Amendments to Regulation S-X Requiring Disclosure of Replacement Cost Data (Rule 3-17)*

Question

What is the definition of replacement cost?

Interpretive Response

For purposes of this rule, replacement cost is the lowest amount that would have to be paid in the normal course of business to obtain a new asset of equivalent operating or productive capability. In the case of depreciable, depletable or amortizable assets, replacement cost (new) and depreciated replacement cost should be distinguished. Replacement cost (new) is the total estimated current cost of replacing total productive capacity at the end of the year while depreciated replacement cost is the replacement cost (new) adjusted for the already expired service potential of such assets.

Question

What is the definition of productive capacity?

Interpretive Response

Productive capacity is a measurement of a company's ability to produce and distribute. The productive capacity of a manufacturer would be measured by the number of units it can presently produce and distribute within a particular time frame, in the case of a telephone company, for example, it would be a measurement of the number of telephone calls it can presently complete within a certain time frame.

Question

What approach to replacement cost is contemplated by the rule?

Interpretive Response

There is no simple concept of replacement cost which will be applicable in every circumstance. In general, replacement cost of productive capacity means the cost of replacing capacity within the existing business framework of the entity. Thus replacement cost does not generally contemplate a single time complete replacement of each of the specific totally ignoring the structure of the business as it exists. Neither does it mean replacement of each of the specific assets currently owned unless that is the way in which the business generally replaces its capacity. Rather, replacement costs should be based on the entity's normal approach to replacement of capacity.

Question

Does this approach require the re-engineering of productive capacity so as to determine replacement cost?

Interpretive Response

Some re-engineering would normally be necessary even though a complete re-engineering of the entire productive capacity would seldom be required.

In requiring registrants to report the replacement cost of their productive

**Staff Accounting Bulletin,* Release No. 7/March 23, 1976
Topic 6 Interpretations of Accounting Series Releases

capacity, it was not the Commission's intent to require a *de novo* approach to their business. Beside being impractical it would be unrealistic in that the productive capacity would rarely be replaced in that fashion. One major public utility described their approach (which the staff believes is reasonable) as follows.

In determining replacement cost data, these companies performed an asset-by-asset evaluation to determine the appropriate replacement vehicle. It was assumed that each asset was replaced with the most up-to-date plant available on December 31, 1974. No attempt was made to re-engineer or re-design the existing plant as a total integrated system since the assumptions underlying such an approach would be totally unrealistic, i.e., future replacement of plant will occur on an asset-by-asset basis and not in totallity. The approach followed results in replacement cost data which realistically measures the economic worth of our productive capacity.

In those situations where management intends to replace existing productive capacity through consolidation of operating units, then the replacement cost data should reflect this intent.

Question

Is a single number required to be presented in answer to the required amount?

Interpretive Reponse

No Data may be stated in terms of ranges. Where necessitated by the degree of uncertainty, registrants should supplement the description of methods used with discussion of the facts causing the inherent imprecision of the data.

Question

Should the company use the contract price or current market price in arriving at the current replacement cost of its total inventory?

Interpretive Response

If the contract runs for a long term (e.g., more than two years beyond the balance sheet date), the company should use the contract price in the calculation. It should disclose the nature and terms of the contract if the inventory acquired is a substantial input to the production process. If the supply contract has only a short time to run and the price paid varies materially from year-end market prices, the year-end market prices should be used in determining replacement cost.

Question

Is it acceptable to compute replacement cost basis cost of sales on the basis of year-end costs?

Interpretive Response

Computing cost of goods sold on the basis of end-of-period replacement cost of all goods sold during the period will not meet the objectives of this disclosure since it would not provide information about the relationships between sales during the reporting period and cost of sales at the time when such sales were made and thus would not indicate the impact of price changes on operations during the period. To the extent that the relationships which exist on a replacement cost basis during the period are not indicative of the relationships existing at the end of the period or which are anticipated, such facts should be disclosed.

Question
Is it acceptable to estimate replacement cost data for cost of sales on the basis of average cost levels throughout the year rather than by trying to calculate replacement cost at the time sales were made?
Interpretive Response
Yes. Various methods of estimating and approximating may be appropriate based on the facts of each case. Registrants should disclose their methods of estimation.

Question
Where historical cost depreciation is calculated on an accelerated basis can the replacement cost depreciation also be calculated on the same basis?
Interpretive Response
Depreciation expense calculated on an accelerated basis may be disclosed, but the amount calculated on a straight line basis must also be presented.

Question
When replacement cost for the current year is different from the previous year, should the prior year's depreciation on a replacement cost basis be restated?
Interpretive Response
No. Although total depreciation may need to be adjusted to arrive at depreciated replacement cost, (as required by Rule 3-17(c)), the amount shown for the preceding year, based on that year's current replacement cost, should not be restated.

Question
Can average current replacement cost depreciation be calculated using beginning and end of year amounts for depreciable productive capacity?
Interpretive Response
Yes, and approximations may be used for assets acquired during the period.

Question
Rule 3-17 only requires replacement cost data related to certain assets. Is it permissible to supplement such data with general price level information on monetary assets and liabilities or to include complete or condensed financial statements restated in units of general purchasing power of selected data taken from such restated statements?
Interpretive Response
In issuing Rule 3-17 it is not the Commission's intent to preclude registrants from presenting financial data in units of general purchasing power. If management believes such information is useful it may be included, either in

statement or capsule form. Management may also wish to state separately that portion of the change in the replacement cost of inventory or property, plant and equipment that can be computed by reference to a change in the general purchasing power of the currency unit.

Question
How should replacement cost calculations to be made for foreign entities?
Interpretive Response
In the case of entities whose operations are denominated in foreign currencies, replacement cost calculations should be made on the basis of current costs in those currencies. In translating those data for purposes of the disclosures required under this rule, the exchange rate at the balance sheet date should be used for asset balances while the rates during the period should be used for computing expenses recognized during that period.

COST ACCOUNTING STANDARDS BOARD [4 CFR PART 413] ADJUSTMENT OF HISTORICAL DEPRECIATION COSTS FOR INFLATION, OCTOBER 9, 1975

The proposed Standard reads as follows:

Part 413 Cost Accounting Standard Adjustment of Historical Depreciation Costs for Inflation

Sec.
413.10 General applicability.
413.20 Purpose.
413.30 Definitions.
413.40 Fundamental requirement.
413.50 Techniques for application.
413.60 Illustrations.
413.70 Exemptions.
413.80 Effective date.

Authority. Sec. 719 of the Defense Production Act of 1950, as amended, Public Law 91-379, 50 USC App. 2166.

§413.10 General applicability.
General applicability of this Cost Accounting Standard is established by §331.30 of the Board's regulations on applicability, exemption, and waiver of the requirement to include the Cost Accounting Standards contract clause in negotiated defense prime contracts and subcontracts (4 CFR 331.30).

§413.20 Purpose.
The purpose of this Standard is to establish the principle that price-level adjustments are relevant in the determination of contract costs. The Standard provides criteria for the determination of an adjustment to be made to the recorded depreciation expense which was based on the historical acquisition

cost of depreciable assets. This adjustment will be a part of contract cost. Recognition of price-level adjustments, determined in accordance with the provisions of this Standard, will improve the economic usefulness of cost measurements for pricing purposes. This Standard is based on the techniques available at the time of promulgation. When improved techniques for dealing with the impact of inflation are developed, this Standard may be modified.

§413.40 *Fundamental requirements.*

(a) An inflation-related adjustment for depreciation shall be computed using an appropriate index annually at the end of each cost accounting period. The contractor shall: (1) Establish vintage groups of depreciable assets; (2) compute the depreciation expense based on historical costs for each group; (3) determine the percentage change in the index from each group's base year to the current year; and (4) determine the total inflation-related adjustment for the depreciation expense.

(b) The inflation-related adjustment for depreciation shall be allocated to final cost objectives in proportion to the assignment of the depreciation expense on which it is based.

(c) The inflation-related adjustment for depreciation shall be computed only on those tangible capital assets of a domestic concern whose service lives have been established in accordance with the provisions of Part 409 of the Cost Accounting Standards Board's rules and regulations and substantiated in accordance with §409.50 (e) thereof.

§413.50 *Techniques for application.*

(a) Records shall be maintained in sufficient detail to support the computation of the depreciation adjustment and permit audit verification.

(b) The annual average of the Gross National Product Implicit Price Deflator (GNP deflator) shall be used as the appropriate index. The GNP deflator is published by the Bureau of Economic Analysis of the U.S. Department of Commerce.

(c) Vintage groups of depreciable assets by year of acquisition (base year) shall be established.

(d) Annually the depreciation adjustment required by §413.40 (a) shall be computed by indexing the depreciation expense based on historical cost for each vintage group for the percentage change from that group's base year in the GNP deflator.

(e) The depreciation adjustment for each vintage group will be calculated in accordance with the following formula:

$$\text{Historical cost-based depreciation} \times \left(\frac{\text{Index for current year}}{\text{Index for base year}} - 1.0 \right)$$

Appendix C

Manufacturing Companies Summary of Financial Statement for the Years 19X1 – 19X7

Year	Price index
19X1	100.0
19X2	110.0
19X3	121.0
19X4	110.0
19X5	100.0
19X6	100.0
19X7	100.0

Manufacturing Equity Company
(100% Fixed Assets, 100% Equity)

Balance Sheets as of December 31, 19X1-19X7

12.31.19X1 Conv.& PLA	Assets	12.31.19X2 Conv.	12.31.19X2 PLA	12.31.19X3 Conv.	12.31.19X3 PLA	12.31.19X4 Conv.	12.31.19X4 PLA	12.31.19X5 Conv.	12.31.19X5 PLA	12.31.19X6 Conv.	12.31.19X6 PLA	12.31.19X7 Conv.	12.31.19X7 PLA
$50.00	Machine 2												
50.00	" 3	$50.00	$55.00^r										
	" 4	55.00	55.00	$55.00	$60.50^r								
	" 5			60.50	60.50	$60.50	$55.00^r						
	" 6					55.00	55.00	$55.00	$50.00^r				
	" 7							50.00	50.00	$50.00	$50.00		
	" 8									50.00	50.00	$50.00	$50.00
	" 9											50.00	50.00
100.00	Assets, at cost	105.00	110.00	115.50	121.00	115.50	110.00	105.00	100.00	100.00	100.00	100.00	100.00
(25.00)	Accum. depreciation	(25.00)	(27.50)	(27.50)	(30.25)	(30.25)	(27.50)	(27.50)	(25.00)	(25.00)	(25.00)	(25.00)	(25.00)
75.00		80.00	82.50	88.00	90.75	85.25	82.50	77.50	75.00	75.00	75.00	75.00	75.00
	Liabilities & Equity												
$75.00	Equity	$75.00	$75.00	$75.00	$75.00	$75.00	$75.00	$75.00	$75.00	$75.00	$75.00	$75.00	$75.00
-	New shares	5.00	-	13.00	-	10.25	-	2.50	-	-	-	-	-
-	Equity maintenance	-	7.50	-	15.75	-	7.50	-	-	-	-	-	-
75.00		80.00	82.50	88.00	90.75	85.25	82.50	77.50	75.00	75.00	75.00	75.00	75.00

Profit & Loss Statements for the Years 19X1-19X7

19X1 Conv.& PLA		19X2 Conv.	19X2 PLA	19X3 Conv.	19X3 PLA	19X4 Conv.	19X4 PLA	19X5 Conv.	19X5 PLA	19X6 Conv.	19X6 PLA	19X7 Conv.	19X7 PLA
$200.00	Sales	$220.00	$220.00	$242.00	$242.00	$220.00	$220.00	$200.00	$200.00	$200.00	$200.00	$200.00	$200.00
(130.00)	O.O.P.C.	(143.00)	(143.00)	(157.30)	(157.30)	(143.00)	(143.00)	(130.00)	(130.00)	(130.00)	(130.00)	(130.00)	(130.00)
(50.00)	Depreciation	(50.00)	(55.00)	(52.50)	(60.50)	(57.75)	(55.00)	(57.75)	(50.00)	(52.50)	(50.00)	(50.00)	(50.00)
20.00	Profit = tax & dividend	27.00	22.00	32.20	24.20	19.25	22.00	12.25	20.00	17.50	20.00	20.00	20.00

Manufacturing Leverage Company
(100% Fixed Assets, 60% Equity)

Balance Sheets as of December 31, 19X1-19X7

12.31.19X1	Assets	12.31.19X2		12.31.19X3		12.31.19X4		12.31.19X5		12.31.19X6		12.31.19X7	
Conv. 1 PLA		Conv.	PLA	Conv.	PLA	Conv.	PLA	Conv.	PLA	Conv.	PLA	Conv.	PLA
$50.00	Machine 2	-	-	-	-	-	-						
50.00	" 3	$50.00	$55.00[r]	-	-	-	-						
	" 4	55.00	55.00	$55.00	$60.50[r]	-	-						
	" 5	-	-	60.50	60.50	$60.50	$55.00[r]						
	" 6	-	-	-	-	55.00	55.00	$55.00	$50.00[r]				
	" 7	-	-	-	-	-	-	50.00	50.00	$50.00	$50.00		
	" 8	-	-	-	-	-	-	-	-	50.00	50.00	$50.00	$50.00
	" 9	-	-	-	-	-	-	-	-	-	-	50.00	50.00
100.00	Assets, at cost	105.00	110.00	115.50	121.00	115.50	110.00	105.00	100.00	100.00	100.00	100.00	100.00
(25.00)	Accum. depreciation	(25.00)	(27.50)	(27.50)	(30.25)	(30.25)	(27.50)	(27.50)	(25.00)	(25.00)	(25.00)	(25.00)	(25.00)
75.00		80.00	82.50	88.00	90.75	85.25	82.50	77.50	75.00	75.00	75.00	75.00	75.00

	Liabilities & Equity												
$10.00	Loan 2												
20.00	" 3	$10.00	$10.00										
	" 3a		1.00										
	" 4	22.00	22.00	$11.00	$11.00								
	" 4a				1.10								
	" 5			24.20	24.20	$12.10	$12.10						
	" 6					22.00	20.90	$11.00	$10.45				
	" 7							20.00	19.55	$10.00	$9.78		
	" 8									20.00	20.22	$10.00	$10.11
	" 9											20.00	19.89
30.00	Total liabilities	32.00	33.00	35.20	36.30	34.10	33.00	31.00	30.00	30.00	30.00	30.00	30.00
45.00	Equity	45.00	45.00	45.00	45.00	45.00	45.00	45.00	45.00	45.00	45.00	45.00	45.00
-	New shares	3.00	-	7.80	-	6.15	-	1.50	-	-	-	-	-
-	Equity maintenance	-	4.50	-	9.45	-	4.50	-	-	-	-	-	-
75.00		80.00	82.50	88.00	90.75	85.25	82.50	77.50	75.00	75.00	75.00	75.00	75.00

Profit & Loss Statements for the Years 19X1 - 19X7

19X1		19X2				19X3				19X4			
Conv.& PLA		Conventional		P L A		Conventional		P L A		Conventional		P L A	
$200.00	Sales		$220.00		$220.00		$242.00		$242.00		$220.00		$220.00
(130.00)	O.O.P.C.	$143.00		$143.00		$157.30		$157.30		$143.00		$143.00	
(2.40)	Interest	4.20		4.20		4.48		4.62		2.82		2.90	
(50.00)	Depreciation	50.00		55.00		52.50		60.50		57.75		55.00	
			197.20		202.20		214.28		222.42		203.57		200.90
17.60	PLA operating profit				17.80				19.58				19.10
	Asset restatement gains			7.50				8.25				(8.25)	
	Equity maintenance			(4.50)				(4.95)				4.95	
—			—		3.00		—		3.30		—		(3.30)
17.60	Profit = tax & dividend		22.80		20.80		27.72		22.88		16.43		15.80
17.60	Inflation-free profit				19.36				21.30				19.36
-	Inflationary leverage returns				1.44				1.58				(3.56)

	19X5				19X6				19X7			
	Conventional		PLA		Conventional		PLA		Conventional		PLA	
Sales		$200.00		$200.00		$200.00		$200.00		$200.00		$200.00
O.O.P.C.	$130.00		$130.00		$130.00		$130.00		$130.00		$130.00	
Interest	2.73		2.64		2.48		2.40		2.40		2.40	
Depreciation	57.75		50.00		52.50		50.00		50.00		50.00	
		190.48		182.64		184.98		182.40		182.40		182.40
PLA operating profit				17.36				17.60				17.60
Asset restatement gains			(7.50)									
Equity maintenance			4.50									
				(3.00)								
Profit = tax & dividend		9.52		14.36		15.02		17.60		17.60		17.60
Inflation-free profit				17.60				17.60				17.60
Inflationary leverage returns				(3.24)				-				-

Appendix D

A Comprehensive Illustration of Company Price Level Adjusted Financial Statements

The illustration in this appendix is a comprehensive demonstration of the major points that were presented individually in various sections of this book. It includes the following:

1. A company that is financed partly by equity and partly by debt capital.
2. The company owns assets of various kinds—fixed, inventory, and financial.
3. Changes in the price level are gradual throughout the year.
4. Stable, increasing, and decreasing price levels are demonstrated.
5. Multiyear comparisons between conventional and PLA financial statements, as well as calculation of inflationfree profit, are given.

Departmental profit statements and the measurement of specific price level changes are not included in this illustration.

Assume a company financed 60% by equity. Of its fixed assets, 40% are financed by long-term (L.T.) loans which are granted with the purchase of a new machine. The repayment schedule calls for quarterly installments so that at the end of each period the outstanding balance of each loan is equivalent to 40% of the net value of the asset it financed. The preinflation interest rate on these loans is 10%. As inflation sets in, the interest rate is raised to 15% per annum; for the sake of simplicity it is assumed that this change affects outstanding loans as well. When deflation occurs, the interest rate drops to 10%, again including outstanding loans. The remainder of the financing is by short-term (S.T.) loans bearing the same interest rate as the long-term loans. During years of price level changes, the statements presenting PLA data include changes in long-term loans parallel to the restatement of the fixed assets. To facilitate comparison between conventional and PLA statements, total outstanding debt has been kept equal in these two sets of statements.

The company owns eight identical machines, which are depreciated quarterly, straight line over a period of 2 years; salvage value is assumed to be zero. The age of the machines is staggered so that each quarter one machine is fully depreciated; it is then dropped from the books and from production. Since the company aims at overall stability, it renews its stock of fixed assets by buying a new machine each quarter.

The company also holds a long-term investment, say unquoted shares in another firm. In addition, it holds inventory equivalent to 4 1/2 months of input usage, which is represented here by out-of-pocket costs. Again for simplicity, it is assumed that this inventory is homogeneous as to use and price. The company grants credit to its customers; part of this customer credit bears interest equivalent to the rate paid by the company to banks. Cash equivalent to $50 is retained by the company.

It is assumed that each year the company produces and sells 100 units of its product. The out-of-pocket costs represent all expenses other than depreciation and interest; the physical quantities of inputs per unit of product remain unchanged throughout the illustration, so that changes in costs are due to price changes only.

The company compiles quarterly financial statements. At the end of each quarter it immediately pays a cash dividend equal to after-tax profit, and buys a new machine to replace the one that is fully depreciated. All other transactions—receipt and payment of loans, purchases, sales, and customer payments—also take place on the last day of each quarter.

During 19X1 the price level remained stable. In 19X2 it rose 10% over the years; prices continued to creep up at this rate during 19X3. From the beginning of 19X4, however, they dropped gradually by 9.09%, so that by the end of that year they had returned to the level of the end of 19X2. Specifically, the relevant price indices are as follows:

Date	Price index	Date	Price index
12.31.X1	100.00	9.30.X3	118.16
3.31.X2	102.41	12.31.X3	121.00
6.30.X2	104.88	3.30.X4	118.16
9.30.X2	107.40	6.30.X4	115.36
12.31.X2	110.00	9.30.X4	112.66
3.31.X3	112.66	12.31.X4	110.00
6.30.X3	115.36		

For each year, final financial statements—balance sheet, profit and loss statement, and sources and uses statement—are presented by conventional and PLA procedures. To clarify, the data basis of these statements, quarterly profit and loss statements, inventory calculations, and fixed asset schedules are also given. Further calculations, such as long-term loans, interest, and asset restatement, can be derived from these auxiliary data.

Balance Sheet as of December 31, 19X2

12. 31. 19X1 Conventional & PLA	Assets	12 . 31 . 19X2 Conventional	12 . 31 . 19X2 PLA	12. 31. 19X1 Conventional & PLA	Liabilities & Equity	12 . 31 .19X2 Conventional	12 . 31 .19X2 PLA
$ 50.00	Cash	$55.00	$55.00	$170.00	S.T. loans	$191.67	$187.00
50.00	Payables	55.00	55.00	90.00	L.T. loans	94.33	99.00
300.00	Inventory	326.11	330.00	260.00	Total debt	286.00	286.00
400.00	Total current assets	436.11	440.00				
				390.00	Equity	390.00	390.00
25.00	L.T. investment	25.00	27.50		New equity	20.94	-
					Equity maintenance adjustment		39.00
400.00	Equipment	412.36	440.00	390.00	Total equity	410.94	429.00
(175.00)	Accumulated depreciation	(176.53)	(192.50)				
225.00	Net fixed assets	235.83	247.50				
650.00	Total assets	696.94	715.00	650.00	Total liabilities & equity	696.94	715.00

Profit & Loss Statement for the Year 19X2

19X1 Conventional & PLA		Conventional		PLA	
$900.00	Sales		$955.56		$955.56
(600.00)	O.O.P.C.	$610.94		$637.05	
(200.00)	Depreciation	201.52		212.35	
(26.00)	Interest paid	41.40		41.40	
4.00	received	(6.37)		(6.37)	
(822.00)	Total expenses		847.49		884.43
78.00	PLA operating profit				71.13
	Asset restatement gains			55.00	
	Equity maintenance adjustment			39.00	
	Net restatement gains				16.00
78.00	Profit = tax & dividend		108.07		87.13

Sources & Uses Statement for the Year 19X2

Sources	Conventional	PLA	Uses	Conventional	PLA
Depreciation	$201.52	$212.35	New machine	$212.35	$212.35
Profit	108.07	87.13	Tax & dividend	108.07	87.13
New equity	20.94		Cash increase	5.00	5.00
			Payables increase	5.00	5.00
			Inventory increase	26.11	-
Equity maintenance adjustment		39.00	Inventory restatement		30.00
			Fixed assets restatement		22.50
			L.T. investment restatement		2.50
New S.T. loans	21.67	17.00			
New L.T. loans	84.94	93.94	L.T. loans paid	80.61	84.94
	437.14	449.42		437.14	449.42

Fixed Assets Schedule for the Year 19X2

12.31.X1	Date	3.31.X2	6.30.X2	9.30.X2	12.31.X2	Total
Conventional Accounting						
	No.Machine					
$ 6.25	1	–	–	–	–	
12.50	2	$ 6.25	–	–	–	
18.75	3	12.50	$ 6.25	–	–	
25.00	4	18.75	12.50	$ 6.25	–	
31.25	5	25.00	18.75	12.50	$ 6.25	
37.50	6	31.25	25.00	18.75	12.50	
43.75	7	37.50	31.25	25.00	18.75	
50.00	8	43.75	37.50	31.25	25.00	
	9	51.21	44.81	38.41	32.01	
	10		52.44	45.89	39.33	
	11			53.70	46.99	
	12				55.00	
225.00	Total net	226.21	228.50	231.76	235.83	
175.00	Acc. dep.	175.00	175.15	175.60	176.53	
400.00	Total gross	401.21	403.65	407.36	412.36	
Current depreciation		50.00	50.15	50.45	50.92	$201.52
PLA accounting:						
400.00	Total gross	409.64	419.51	429.62	440.00	
(175.00)	Acc. dep.	(179.22)	(183.54)	(187.96)	(192.50)	
225.00	Total net	230.42	235.97	241.66	247.50	
Current depreciation		51.21	52.44	53.70	55.00	

Inventory Calculations for the Year 19X2

Date	3.31.X2	6.30.X2	9.30.X2	12.31.X2	Total
Conventional accounting					
Opening	$300.00	$303.62	$310.94	$318.43	
Use	(150.00)	(150.00)	(153.62)	(157.32)	(610.94)
Buy	153.62	157.32	161.11	165.00	637.05
Closing	303.62	310.94	318.43	326.11	
PLA accounting					
Opening	300.00	307.26	314.64	322.24	
Restatement	7.26	7.38	7.60	7.76	30.00
Use	(153.62)	(157.32)	(161.11)	(165.00)	(637.05)
Buy	153.62	157.32	161.11	165.00	637.05
Closing	307.26	314.64	322.24	330.00	

Interim Profit & Loss Statement for the Year 19X2

Date	3.31.X2	6.30.X2	9.30.X2	12.31.X2	Total
Conventional accounting					
Sales	$230.42	$235.98	$241.66	$247.50	$955.56
O.O.P.C.	(150.00)	(150.00)	(153.62)	(157.32)	(610.94)
Depreciation	(50.00)	(50.15)	(50.45)	(50.92)	(201.52)
Interest paid	(9.98)	(10.22)	(10.47)	(10.73)	(41.40)
received	1.54	1.57	1.61	1.65	6.37
Total expenses	(208.44)	(208.80)	(212.93)	(217.32)	(847.49)
Profit = tax & dividend	21.98	27.18	28.73	30.18	108.07
PLA accounting					
Sales	230.42	235.98	241.66	247.50	955.56
O.O.P.C.	(153.62)	(157.32)	(161.11)	(165.00)	(637.05)
Depreciation	(51.21)	(52.44)	(53.70)	(55.00)	(212.35)
Interest paid	(9.98)	(10.22)	(10.47)	(10.73)	(41.40)
received	1.54	1.57	1.61	1.65	6.37
Total expenses	(213.27)	(218.41)	(223.67)	(229.08)	(884.43)
Operating profit	17.15	17.57	17.99	18.42	71.13
Asset restatement gains	13.25	13.57	13.91	14.27	55.00
Equity maintenance	(9.40)	(9.62)	(9.88)	(10.10)	(39.00)
Net restatement gains	3.85	3.95	4.03	4.17	16.00
Profit = tax & dividend	21.00	21.52	22.02	22.59	87.13

Balance Sheet as of December 31, 19X3

12.31.19X2 Conventional	12.31.19X2 PLA	Assets	12.31.19X3 Conventional	12.31.19X3 PLA	12.31.19X2 Conventional	12.31.19X2 PLA	Liabilities & Equity	12.31.19X3 Conventional	12.31.19X3 PLA
$ 55.00	$55.00	Cash	$60.50	$ 60.50	$191.67	$187.00	S.T. loans	$211.47	$205.70
55.00	55.00	Payables	60.50	60.50	94.33	99.00	L.T. loans	103.13	108.90
326.11	330.00	Inventory	358.73	363.00	286.00	286.00	Total debt	314.60	314.60
436.11	440.00	Total current assets	479.73	484.00					
					390.00	390.00	Equity	390.00	390.00
25.00	27.50	L.T. investment	25.00	30.25	20.94	-	New equity	57.95	
						39.00	Equity maintenance adj.	-	81.90
412.36	440.00	Equipment	445.95	484.00	410.94	429.00	Total equity	447.95	471.90
(176.53)	(192.50)	Accumulated depreciation	(188.13)	(211.75)					
235.83	247.50	Net fixed assets	257.82	272.25					
696.94	715.00	Total assets	762.55	786.50	696.94	715.00	Total liabilities & equity	762.55	786.50

Profit & Loss Statement for the Year 19X3

19X2 Conventional	19X2 PLA		Conventional		PLA	
$955.56	$955.56	Sales		$1051.11		$1051.11
(610.94)	(637.05)	O.O.P.C.	$668.14		$700.76	
(201.52)	(212.35)	Depreciation	211.60		233.59	
(41.40)	(41.40)	Interest paid	45.55		45.55	
6.37	6.37	Received	(7.01)		(7.01)	
(847.49)	(884.43)	Total expenses		918.28		972.89
108.07	71.13	PLA operating profit				78.22
	55.00	Asset restatement gains			60.50	
	(39.00)	Equity maintenance adjustment			(42.90)	
	16.00	Net restatement gains				17.60
108.07	87.13	Profit = tax & dividend		112.83		95.82

Sources & Uses Statement for the Year 19X3

Sources	Conventional	PLA	Uses	Conventional	PLA
Depreciation	$211.60	$233.59	New machines	$233.59	$233.59
Profit	112.83	95.82	Tax & dividend	112.83	95.82
New equity	37.01	-	Cash increase	5.50	5.50
			Payables increase	5.50	5.50
			Inventory increase	32.62	
Equity maintenance adjustment	-	42.90	" restatement		33.00
			Fixed assets restatement		24.75
			L.T. investment "		2.75
New S.T. loans	19.80	18.70			
New L.T. "	93.44	103.34	L.T. loans paid	84.64	93.44
	474.68	494.35		474.68	494.35

Fixed Assets Schedule for the Year 19X3

12.31.19X2	Date	3.31.X3	6.30.X3	9.30.X3	12.33.X3	Total
Conventional accounting						
	No. Machine					
$ 6.25	5	-	-	-	-	
12.50	6	$ 6.25	-	-	-	
18.75	7	12.50	$ 6.25	-	-	
25.00	8	18.75	12.50	$ 6.25	-	
32.01	9	25.61	19.20	12.80	$ 6.40	
39.33	10	32.77	26.22	19.66	13.11	
46.99	11	40.28	33.57	26.86	20.14	
55.00	12	48.13	41.25	34.38	27.50	
-	13	56.33	49.29	42.25	35.21	
-	14	-	57.68	50.47	43.26	
-	15	-	-	59.08	51.70	
-	16	-	-	-	60.50	
235.83	Total net	240.62	245.96	251.75	257.82	
(176.53)	Acc. dep.	(178.07)	(180.41)	(183.70)	(188.13)	
412.36	Total gross	418.69	426.37	435.45	445.95	
Current depreciation		51.54	52.34	53.29	54.43	$211.60
PLA accounting						
440.00	Total gross	450.62	461.50	472.60	484.00	
(192.50)	Acc. dep.	(197.15)	(201.91)	(206.77)	(211.75)	
247.50	Total net	253.47	259.59	265.83	272.25	
Current depreciation		56.33	57.68	59.08	60.50	233.59

Inventory Calculations for the Year 19X3

Date	3.31.X3	6.30.X3	9.30.X3	12.31.X3	Total
Conventional accounting					
Opening	$326.11	$333.98	$342.03	$350.28	
Use	(161.11)	(165.00)	(168.98)	(173.05)	($668.14)
Buy	168.98	173.05	177.23	181.50	700.76
Closing	333.98	342.03	350.28	358.73	
PLA accounting					
Opening	330.00	337.97	346.12	354.45	
Restatement	7.97	8.15	8.33	8.55	33.00
Use	(168.98)	(173.05)	(177.23)	(181.50)	(700.76)
Buy	168.98	173.05	177.23	181.50	700.76

Interim Profit & Loss Statement for the Year 19X3

Date	3.31.X3	6.30.X3	9.30.X3	12.31.X3	Total 19X3
Conventional accounting					
Sales	$253.46	$259.57	$265.83	$272.25	$1051.11
O.O.P.C.	(161.11)	(165.00)	(168.98)	(173.05)	(668.14)
Depreciation	(51.54)	(52.34)	(53.29)	(54.43)	(211.60)
Interest paid	(10.98)	(11.25)	(11.52)	(11.80)	(45.55)
received	1.69	1.73	1.77	1.82	7.01
Total expenses	(221.94)	(226.86)	(232.02)	(237.46)	(918.28)
Profit = tax & dividend	31.52	32.71	33.81	34.79	112.83
PLA accounting					
Sales	253.46	259.57	265.83	272.25	1051.11
O.O.P.C.	(168.98)	(173.05)	(177.23)	(181.50)	(700.76)
Depreciation	(56.33)	(57.68)	(59.08)	(60.50)	(233.59)
Interest paid	(10.98)	(11.25)	(11.52)	(11.80)	(45.55)
received	1.69	1.73	1.77	1.82	7.01
Total expenses	(234.60)	(240.25)	(246.06)	(251.98)	(972.89)
Operating profit	18.86	19.32	19.77	20.27	78.22
Asset restatement gains	14.59	14.97	15.28	15.66	60.50
Equity maintenance	(10.36)	(10.61)	(10.84)	(11.09)	(42.90)
Net restatement gains	4.23	4.36	4.44	4.57	17.60
Profit = tax & dividend	23.09	23.68	24.21	24.84	95.82

Balance Sheet as of December 31, 19X4

Assets					Liabilities & Equity				
12 . 31 . 19X3			12 . 31 . 19X4		12 . 31 . 19X3			12 . 31 . 19X4	
Conventional	PLA		Conventional	PLA	Conventional	PLA		Conventional	PLA
$ 60.50	$60.50	Cash	$61.61	$55.00	$211.47	$205.70	S.T. loans	$182.68	$187.00
60.50	60.50	Payables	55.00	55.00	103.13	108.90	L.T. loans	103.32	99.00
358.73	363.00	Inventory	333.98	330.00	314.60	314.60	Total debt	286.00	286.00
479.73	484.00	Total current assets	450.59	440.00					
					390.00	390.00	Equity	390.00	390.00
25.00	30.25	L.T. investment	25.00	27.50	57.95	-	New equity	57.95	-
					-	81.90	Equity maintenance adj.	-	39.00
445.95	484.00	Equipment	461.69	440.00	447.95	471.90	Total equity	447.95	429.00
(188.13)	(211.75)	Accumulated depreciation	(203.33)	(192.50)					
257.82	272.25	Net fixed assets	258.36	247.50					
762.55	786.50	Total assets	733.95	715.00	762.55	786.50	Total liabilities & equity	733.95	715.00

Profit & Loss Statement for the Year 19X4

19X3 Conventional	19X3 PLA		Conventional		PLA	
$1051.11	$1051.11	Sales		$1026.36		$1026.36
(668.14)	(700.76)	O.O.P.C.	$709.01		$684.26	
(211.60)	(233.59)	Depreciation	227.55		228.09	
(45.55)	(45.55)	Interest paid	29.65		29.65	
7.01	7.01	received	(4.56)		(4.56)	
(918.28)	(972.89)	Total expenses		961.65		937.44
112.83	78.22	PLA operating profit				88.92
	60.50	Asset restatement loss			(60.50)	
	(42.90)	Equity maintenance adjustment			42.90	
	17.60	Net restatement loss				(17.60)
112.83	95.82	Profit = tax & dividend		64.71		71.32

Sources & Uses Statement for the Year 19X4

Sources	Conventional	PLA	Uses	Conventional	PLA
Depreciation	$227.55	$228.09	New machine	$228.09	$228.09
Profit	64.71	71.32	Tax & dividend	64.71	71.32
			Cash increase	1.11	-
Cash decrease	-	5.50			
Payables decrease	5.50	5.50			
Inventory "	24.75	-			
Inventory restatement loss		33.00	Equity maintenance adj.	-	42.90
Fixed assets " "		24.75			
L.T. investment " "		2.75			
New L.T. loans	91.23	91.23	L.T. loans paid	91.04	101.13
			S.T. loans paid	28.79	18.70
	413.74	462.14		413.74	462.14

Fixed Assets Schedule for the Year 19X4

12.31.19X3	Date	3.30.X4	6.30.X4	9.30.X4	12.31.X4	Total
Conventional accounting						
	No. Machine					
$ 6.40	9	–	–	–	–	
13.11	10	$ 6.55	–	–	–	
20.14	11	13.43	$ 6.71	–	–	
27.50	12	20.63	13.75	$ 6.88	–	
35.21	13	28.17	21.12	14.08	$ 7.04	
43.26	14	36.06	28.85	21.64	14.43	
51.70	15	44.31	36.93	29.54	22.16	
60.50	16	52.94	45.38	37.81	30.25	
–	17	59.08	51.70	44.31	36.93	
–	18	–	57.68	50.47	43.26	
–	19	–	–	56.33	49.29	
–	20	–	–	–	55.00	
257.82	Total net	261.17	262.12	261.06	258.36	
(188.13)	Acc. dep.	(192.65)	(196.94)	(200.62)	(203.33)	
445.95	Total gross	453.82	459.06	461.69	461.69	
Current depreciation		55.73	56.73	57.39	57.70	$227.55
PLA accounting						
484.00	Total gross	472.60	461.50	450.62	440.00	
(211.75)	Acc. dep.	(206.77)	(201.91)	(197.15)	(192.50)	
272.25	Total net	265.83	259.59	253.47	247.50	
Current depreciation		59.08	57.68	56.33	55.00	228.09

Inventory Calculations for the Year 19X4

Date	3.31.X4	6.30.X4	9.30.X4	12.31.X4	Total
Conventional accounting					
Opening	$358.73	$358.73	$350.28	$342.03	
Use	177.23	181.50	177.23	173.05	$709.01
Buy	177.23	173.05	168.98	165.00	684.26
Closing	358.73	350.28	342.03	333.98	
PLA accounting					
Opening	363.00	354.45	346.12	337.97	
Restatement	(8.55)	(8.33)	(8.15)	(7.97)	(33.00)
Use	(177.23)	(173.05)	(168.98)	(165.00)	(684.26)
Buy	177.23	173.05	168.98	165.00	684.26
Closing	354.45	346.12	337.97	330.00	

Interim Profit & Loss Statement for the Year 19X4

Date	3.31.X4	6.30.X4	9.30.X4	12.30.X4	Total
Conventional accounting					
Sales	$265.83	$259.57	$253.46	$247.50	$1026.36
O.O.P.C.	(177.23)	(181.50)	(177.23)	(173.05)	(709.01)
Depreciation	(55.73)	(56.73)	(57.39)	(57.70)	(227.55)
Interest paid	(7.68)	(7.50)	(7.32)	(7.15)	(29.65)
received	1.18	1.15	1.13	1.10	4.56
Total expenses	(239.46)	(244.58)	(240.81)	(236.80)	(961.65)
Profit = tax & dividend	26.37	14.99	12.65	10.70	64.71
PLA accounting					
Sales	265.83	259.57	253.46	247.50	1026.36
O.O.P.C.	(177.23)	(173.05)	(168.98)	(165.00)	(684.26)
Depreciation	(59.08)	(57.68)	(56.33)	(55.00)	(228.09)
Interest paid	(7.68)	(7.50)	(7.32)	(7.15)	(29.65)
received	1.18	1.15	1.13	1.10	4.56
Total expenses	(242.81)	(237.08)	(231.50)	(226.05)	(937.44)
Operating profit	23.02	22.49	21.96	21.45	88.92
Asset restatement loss	(15.66)	(15.28)	(14.97)	(14.59)	(60.50)
Equity maintenance	11.09	10.84	10.61	10.36	42.90
Net restatement loss	(4.57)	(4.44)	(4.36)	(4.23)	(17.60)
Profit = tax & dividend	18.45	18.05	17.60	17.22	71.32

Profit and Loss Statements for the Years 19X2-19X4

	19X2		19X3		19X4	
Sales	$955.56		$1051.11		$1026.36	
O.O.P.C.	(637.05)		(700.76)		(684.26)	
Depreciation	(212.35)		(233.59)		(228.09)	
Imputed interest paid	(27.61)		(30.37)		(29.65)	
received	4.24		4.67		4.56	
Inflation free profit		$82.79		$91.06		$88.92
Net restatement gains (loss)	16.00		17.60		(17.60)	
Leverage gains paid to lenders	(11.66)		(12.84)		-	
Inflationary leverage returns (loss)		4.34		4.76		(17.60)
PLA total profit		87.13		95.82		71.32
PLA operating profit		71.13		78.22		88.92
Conventional profit		108.07		112.83		64.71

Profit Analysis for the Years 19X2-19X4

		19X2	19X3	19X4
Inflation-free profit	to sales	8.66%	8.66%	8.66%
	to equity	19.30%	19.30%	20.73%
PLA total profit	to sales	9.12%	9.12%	6.95%
	to equity	20.31%	20.31%	16.62%
PLA operating profit	to sales	7.44%	7.44%	8.66%
	to equity	16.58%	16.58%	20.73%
Conventional profit	to sales	11.31%	10.73%	6.30%
	to equity	26.30%	25.19%	14.45%

Appendix E

Restatement Tables

E-1. Restatement Coefficients for Fixed Asset Gross Value and Depreciation (R_{gross})*

	p											
n	2	4	6	8	10	12	15	20	25	30	40	*n*
2	1.030	1.060	1.091	1.122	1.152	1.183	1.230	1.309	1.389	1.470	1.633	2
3	1.040	1.081	1.122	1.164	1.206	1.249	1.314	1.424	1.537	1.652	1.888	3
4	1.051	1.102	1.154	1.208	1.262	1.317	1.401	1.545	1.694	1.847	2.163	4
5	1.061	1.123	1.187	1.252	1.319	1.387	1.492	1.672	1.859	2.053	2.457	5
6	1.071	1.145	1.220	1.298	1.378	1.459	1.585	1.804	2.033	2.270	2.768	6
7	1.082	1.166	1.254	1.345	1.438	1.534	1.683	1.942	2.214	2.498	3.093	7
8	1.092	1.188	1.288	1.392	1.500	1.610	1.783	2.085	2.403	2.735	3.433	8
9	1.103	1.210	1.323	1.441	1.563	1.689	1.886	2.233	2.599	2.981	3.783	9
10	1.113	1.233	1.359	1.490	1.627	1.770	1.993	2.385	2.801	3.235	4.143	10
12	1.135	1.279	1.431	1.592	1.761	1.937	2.214	2.703	3.221	3.761	4.886	12
14	1.156	1.325	1.506	1.698	1.900	2.112	2.446	3.037	3.661	4.309	5.651	14
16	1.178	1.373	1.583	1.808	2.045	2.294	2.687	3.383	4.116	4.873	6.430	16
18	1.201	1.422	1.662	1.921	2.195	2.483	2.937	3.740	4.583	5.448	7.217	18
20	1.223	1.472	1.744	2.037	2.349	2.678	3.195	4.107	5.058	6.032	8.010	20
22	1.246	1.522	1.827	2.157	2.508	2.878	3.460	4.481	5.541	6.621	8.805	22
25	1.281	1.600	1.956	2.342	2.754	3.187	3.867	5.053	6.274	7.511	10.002	25
30	1.340	1.735	2.179	2.665	3.182	3.724	4.569	6.025	7.509	9.003	12.000	30
35	1.400	1.875	2.414	3.003	3.629	4.281	5.290	7.012	8.754	10.501	14.000	35
40	1.462	2.021	2.658	3.354	4.090	4.852	6.022	8.005	10.001	12.000	16.000	40
45	1.526	2.172	2.912	3.716	4.563	5.433	6.763	9.002	11.250	13.500	18.000	45
50	1.591	2.328	3.172	4.087	5.043	6.021	7.507	10.001	12.500	15.000	20.000	50

p = inflation rate, % per period
n = life span, periods
*Assuming zero rate of growth

E-2. Restatement Coefficients for Fixed Asset Net Value (R_{net})*

n	p = 2	4	6	8	10	12	15	20	25	30	40	n
2	1.026	1.053	1.080	1.107	1.134	1.161	1.202	1.271	1.339	1.408	1.547	2
3	1.033	1.067	1.101	1.135	1.169	1.204	1.256	1.343	1.431	1.520	1.701	3
4	1.039	1.081	1.122	1.163	1.205	1.247	1.310	1.417	1.526	1.636	1.860	4
5	1.046	1.094	1.143	1.191	1.240	1.290	1.365	1.493	1.623	1.755	2.024	5
6	1.053	1.108	1.164	1.220	1.277	1.334	1.422	1.570	1.722	1.877	2.192	6
7	1.060	1.122	1.185	1.249	1.314	1.379	1.479	1.649	1.823	2.001	2.364	7
8	1.067	1.136	1.207	1.278	1.351	1.425	1.537	1.730	1.927	2.128	2.540	8
9	1.074	1.150	1.228	1.308	1.388	1.471	1.596	1.811	2.032	2.257	2.719	9
10	1.081	1.165	1.250	1.337	1.427	1.517	1.656	1.894	2.139	2.388	2.900	10
12	1.095	1.193	1.294	1.398	1.504	1.612	1.778	2.063	2.357	2.656	3.269	12
14	1.109	1.222	1.339	1.459	1.583	1.709	1.903	2.237	2.580	2.930	3.645	14
16	1.123	1.251	1.384	1.522	1.663	1.808	2.031	2.413	2.807	3.208	4.026	16
18	1.137	1.281	1.430	1.586	1.745	1.909	2.161	2.593	3.038	3.491	4.411	18
20	1.151	1.310	1.477	1.650	1.828	2.011	2.292	2.776	3.272	3.776	4.799	20
22	1.165	1.341	1.524	1.715	1.913	2.115	2.426	2.961	3.508	4.064	5.189	22
25	1.187	1.386	1.596	1.815	2.041	2.273	2.630	3.242	3.866	4.499	5.778	25
30	1.223	1.464	1.718	1.985	2.260	2.543	2.976	3.717	4.470	5.231	6.764	30
35	1.260	1.543	1.844	2.159	2.485	2.818	3.329	4.199	5.080	5.968	7.754	35
40	1.297	1.623	1.972	2.337	2.713	3.099	3.687	4.685	5.694	6.709	8.747	40
45	1.335	1.705	2.102	2.517	2.946	3.383	4.049	5.175	6.311	7.452	9.741	45
50	1.373	1.788	2.234	2.701	3.181	3.669	4.413	5.667	6.929	8.196	10.737	50

p = inflation rate, % per period
n = life span, periods
* Assuming zero rate of growth.

E-3. Restatement Coeeficients for Inventories and for Materials Used When the FIFO Method is Practiced (R_{gross})*

n	p = 0.1	0.2	0.3	0.4	0.5	0.6	0.7	0.8	0.9	1.0	n
1	1.001	1.002	1.003	1.004	1.005	1.006	1.007	1.008	1.009	1.010	1
2	1.001	1.003	1.004	1.005	1.007	1.008	1.009	1.011	1.012	1.013	2
3	1.002	1.003	1.005	1.007	1.008	1.010	1.012	1.013	1.015	1.017	3
4	1.002	1.004	1.006	1.008	1.010	1.012	1.014	1.016	1.018	1.020	4
5	1.002	1.005	1.007	1.009	1.012	1.014	1.016	1.019	1.021	1.023	5
6	1.003	1.005	1.008	1.011	1.013	1.016	1.019	1.021	1.024	1.027	6
7	1.003	1.006	1.009	1.012	1.015	1.018	1.021	1.024	1.027	1.030	7
8	1.003	1.007	1.010	1.013	1.017	1.020	1.023	1.027	1.030	1.034	8
9	1.004	1.007	1.011	1.015	1.018	1.022	1.026	1.029	1.033	1.037	9
10	1.004	1.008	1.012	1.016	1.020	1.024	1.028	1.032	1.036	1.040	10
11	1.004	1.009	1.013	1.017	1.022	1.026	1.031	1.035	1.039	1.044	11
12	1.005	1.009	1.014	1.019	1.023	1.028	1.033	1.038	1.042	1.047	12
13	1.005	1.010	1.015	1.020	1.025	1.030	1.035	1.040	1.045	1.050	13
14	1.005	1.011	1.016	1.021	1.027	1.032	1.038	1.043	1.048	1.054	14
15	1.006	1.011	1.017	1.023	1.028	1.034	1.040	1.046	1.052	1.057	15

p = inflation rate, % per period
n = life span, periods
*Assuming zero rate of growth

n	p = 1.1	1.2	1.3	1.4	1.5	1.6	1.7	1.8	1.9	2.0	n
1	1.011	1.012	1.013	1.014	1.015	1.016	1.017	1.018	1.019	1.020	1
2	1.015	1.016	1.017	1.019	1.020	1.021	1.023	1.024	1.025	1.027	2
3	1.018	1.020	1.022	1.023	1.025	1.027	1.028	1.030	1.032	1.033	3
4	1.022	1.024	1.026	1.028	1.030	1.032	1.034	1.036	1.038	1.040	4
5	1.026	1.028	1.030	1.033	1.035	1.038	1.040	1.042	1.045	1.047	5
6	1.029	1.032	1.035	1.038	1.040	1.043	1.046	1.048	1.051	1.054	6
7	1.033	1.036	1.039	1.042	1.045	1.048	1.051	1.054	1.058	1.061	7
8	1.037	1.040	1.044	1.047	1.050	1.054	1.057	1.061	1.064	1.067	8
9	1.041	1.044	1.048	1.052	1.056	1.059	1.063	1.067	1.071	1.074	9
10	1.044	1.048	1.052	1.057	1.061	1.065	1.069	1.073	1.077	1.081	10
11	1.048	1.053	1.057	1.061	1.066	1.070	1.075	1.079	1.084	1.088	11
12	1.052	1.057	1.061	1.066	1.071	1.076	1.081	1.085	1.090	1.095	12
13	1.056	1.061	1.066	1.071	1.076	1.081	1.086	1.092	1.097	1.102	13
14	1.059	1.065	1.070	1.076	1.081	1.087	1.092	1.098	1.103	1.109	14
15	1.063	1.069	1.075	1.081	1.086	1.092	1.098	1.104	1.110	1.116	15

E-3. (continued)

	p										
n	2.1	2.2	2.3	2.4	2.5	2.6	2.7	2.8	2.9	3.0	n
1	1.021	1.022	1.023	1.024	1.025	1.026	1.027	1.028	1.029	1.030	1
2	1.028	1.029	1.031	1.032	1.033	1.035	1.036	1.037	1.039	1.040	2
3	1.035	1.037	1.038	1.040	1.042	1.044	1.045	1.047	1.049	1.050	3
4	1.042	1.044	1.046	1.048	1.050	1.052	1.054	1.056	1.058	1.060	4
5	1.049	1.052	1.054	1.056	1.059	1.061	1.064	1.066	1.068	1.071	5
6	1.056	1.059	1.062	1.065	1.067	1.070	1.073	1.076	1.078	1.081	6
7	1.064	1.067	1.070	1.073	1.076	1.079	1.082	1.085	1.088	1.091	7
8	1.071	1.074	1.078	1.081	1.085	1.088	1.091	1.095	1.098	1.102	8
9	1.078	1.082	1.086	1.089	1.093	1.097	1.101	1.105	1.108	1.112	9
10	1.085	1.089	1.094	1.098	1.102	1.106	1.110	1.114	1.118	1.123	10
11	1.093	1.097	1.102	1.106	1.111	1.115	1.120	1.124	1.129	1.133	11
12	1.100	1.105	1.110	1.114	1.119	1.124	1.129	1.134	1.139	1.144	12
13	1.107	1.112	1.118	1.123	1.128	1.133	1.139	1.144	1.149	1.154	13
14	1.114	1.120	1.126	1.131	1.137	1.142	1.148	1.154	1.159	1.165	14
15	1.122	1.128	1.134	1.140	1.146	1.152	1.158	1.164	1.170	1.176	15

E-3. (continued)

n	p = 3.1	3.2	3.3	3.4	3.5	3.6	3.7	3.8	3.9	4.0	n
1	1.031	1.032	1.033	1.034	1.035	1.036	1.037	1.038	1.039	1.040	1
2	1.041	1.043	1.044	1.045	1.047	1.048	1.049	1.051	1.052	1.054	2
3	1.052	1.054	1.055	1.057	1.059	1.060	1.062	1.064	1.065	1.067	3
4	1.062	1.064	1.067	1.069	1.071	1.073	1.075	1.077	1.079	1.081	4
5	1.073	1.075	1.078	1.080	1.083	1.085	1.087	1.090	1.092	1.095	5
6	1.084	1.086	1.089	1.092	1.095	1.097	1.100	1.103	1.106	1.108	6
7	1.094	1.097	1.101	1.104	1.107	1.110	1.113	1.116	1.119	1.122	7
8	1.105	1.109	1.112	1.116	1.119	1.122	1.126	1.129	1.133	1.136	8
9	1.116	1.120	1.124	1.127	1.131	1.135	1.139	1.143	1.147	1.150	9
10	1.127	1.131	1.135	1.139	1.144	1.148	1.152	1.156	1.160	1.165	10
11	1.138	1.142	1.147	1.151	1.156	1.160	1.165	1.170	1.174	1.179	11
12	1.149	1.154	1.158	1.163	1.168	1.173	1.178	1.183	1.188	1.193	12
13	1.160	1.165	1.170	1.176	1.181	1.186	1.191	1.197	1.202	1.208	13
14	1.171	1.176	1.182	1.188	1.193	1.199	1.205	1.211	1.216	1.222	14
15	1.182	1.188	1.194	1.200	1.206	1.212	1.218	1.224	1.230	1.237	15

E-4. Restatement Coefficients for Materials Used When the Average Method Is Practiced (R_{net})*

	p										
n	0.1	0.2	0.3	0.4	0.5	0.6	0.7	0.8	0.9	1.0	n
1	1.001	1.002	1.003	1.004	1.005	1.006	1.007	1.008	1.009	1.010	1
2	1.002	1.003	1.005	1.006	1.008	1.009	1.011	1.012	1.014	1.015	2
3	1.002	1.004	1.006	1.008	1.010	1.012	1.014	1.016	1.018	1.020	3
4	1.003	1.005	1.008	1.010	1.013	1.015	1.018	1.020	1.023	1.025	4
5	1.003	1.006	1.009	1.012	1.015	1.018	1.021	1.024	1.027	1.030	5
6	1.004	1.007	1.011	1.014	1.018	1.021	1.025	1.028	1.032	1.035	6
7	1.004	1.008	1.012	1.016	1.020	1.024	1.028	1.032	1.036	1.040	7
8	1.005	1.009	1.014	1.018	1.023	1.027	1.032	1.036	1.041	1.046	8
9	1.005	1.010	1.015	1.020	1.025	1.030	1.035	1.040	1.046	1.051	9
10	1.006	1.011	1.017	1.022	1.028	1.033	1.039	1.045	1.050	1.056	10
11	1.006	1.012	1.018	1.024	1.030	1.036	1.042	1.049	1.055	1.061	11
12	1.007	1.013	1.020	1.026	1.033	1.039	1.046	1.053	1.059	1.066	12
13	1.007	1.014	1.021	1.028	1.035	1.043	1.050	1.057	1.064	1.071	13
14	1.008	1.015	1.023	1.030	1.038	1.046	1.053	1.061	1.069	1.077	14
15	1.008	1.016	1.024	1.032	1.040	1.049	1.057	1.065	1.074	1.082	15

p = inflation rate, % per period
n = life span, periods
*Assuming zero rate of growth

E-4. (continued)

	p										
n	1.1	1.2	1.3	1.4	1.5	1.6	1.7	1.8	1.9	2.0	n
1	1.011	1.012	1.013	1.014	1.015	1.016	1.017	1.018	1.019	1.020	1
2	1.017	1.018	1.020	1.021	1.023	1.024	1.026	1.027	1.029	1.030	2
3	1.022	1.024	1.026	1.028	1.030	1.032	1.034	1.036	1.038	1.040	3
4	1.028	1.030	1.033	1.035	1.038	1.040	1.043	1.045	1.048	1.050	4
5	1.033	1.036	1.039	1.042	1.045	1.049	1.052	1.055	1.058	1.061	5
6	1.039	1.042	1.046	1.050	1.053	1.057	1.060	1.064	1.068	1.071	6
7	1.044	1.049	1.053	1.057	1.061	1.065	1.069	1.073	1.077	1.082	7
8	1.050	1.055	1.059	1.064	1.069	1.073	1.078	1.083	1.087	1.092	8
9	1.056	1.061	1.066	1.071	1.076	1.082	1.087	1.092	1.097	1.103	9
10	1.061	1.067	1.073	1.079	1.084	1.090	1.096	1.102	1.107	1.113	10
11	1.067	1.073	1.080	1.086	1.092	1.099	1.105	1.111	1.118	1.124	11
12	1.073	1.080	1.087	1.093	1.100	1.107	1.114	1.121	1.128	1.135	12
13	1.079	1.086	1.093	1.101	1.108	1.116	1.123	1.130	1.138	1.146	13
14	1.084	1.092	1.100	1.108	1.116	1.124	1.132	1.140	1.148	1.156	14
15	1.090	1.099	1.107	1.116	1.124	1.133	1.141	1.150	1.159	1.167	15

E-4. (continued)

n	p = 2.1	2.2	2.3	2.4	2.5	2.6	2.7	2.8	2.9	3.0	n
1	1.021	1.022	1.023	1.024	1.025	1.026	1.027	1.028	1.029	1.030	1
2	1.032	1.033	1.035	1.036	1.038	1.039	1.041	1.042	1.044	1.045	2
3	1.042	1.044	1.046	1.048	1.050	1.052	1.054	1.057	1.059	1.061	3
4	1.053	1.056	1.058	1.061	1.063	1.066	1.068	1.071	1.074	1.076	4
5	1.064	1.067	1.070	1.073	1.076	1.079	1.082	1.086	1.089	1.092	5
6	1.075	1.078	1.082	1.086	1.089	1.093	1.097	1.100	1.104	1.108	6
7	1.086	1.090	1.094	1.098	1.102	1.107	1.111	1.115	1.119	1.124	7
8	1.097	1.102	1.106	1.111	1.116	1.121	1.125	1.130	1.135	1.140	8
9	1.108	1.113	1.118	1.124	1.129	1.134	1.140	1.145	1.151	1.156	9
10	1.119	1.125	1.131	1.137	1.143	1.148	1.154	1.160	1.166	1.172	10
11	1.130	1.137	1.143	1.150	1.156	1.163	1.169	1.176	1.182	1.189	11
12	1.142	1.149	1.156	1.163	1.170	1.177	1.184	1.191	1.198	1.206	12
13	1.153	1.161	1.168	1.176	1.184	1.191	1.199	1.207	1.215	1.222	13
14	1.165	1.173	1.181	1.189	1.198	1.206	1.214	1.223	1.231	1.239	14
15	1.176	1.185	1.194	1.203	1.211	1.220	1.229	1.238	1.247	1.256	15

E-4. (continued)

	p										
n	3.1	3.2	3.3	3.4	3.5	3.6	3.7	3.8	3.9	4.0	n
1	1.031	1.032	1.033	1.034	1.035	1.036	1.037	1.038	1.039	1.040	1
2	1.047	1.048	1.050	1.051	1.053	1.054	1.056	1.057	1.059	1.060	2
3	1.063	1.065	1.067	1.069	1.071	1.073	1.075	1.077	1.079	1.081	3
4	1.079	1.081	1.084	1.086	1.089	1.092	1.094	1.097	1.099	1.102	4
5	1.095	1.098	1.101	1.104	1.107	1.111	1.114	1.117	1.120	1.123	5
6	1.111	1.115	1.119	1.122	1.126	1.130	1.133	1.137	1.141	1.145	6
7	1.128	1.132	1.136	1.141	1.145	1.149	1.153	1.158	1.162	1.166	7
8	1.144	1.149	1.154	1.159	1.164	1.169	1.174	1.178	1.183	1.188	8
9	1.161	1.167	1.172	1.178	1.183	1.188	1.194	1.199	1.205	1.210	9
10	1.178	1.184	1.190	1.196	1.202	1.208	1.215	1.221	1.227	1.233	10
11	1.195	1.202	1.209	1.215	1.222	1.229	1.235	1.242	1.249	1.256	11
12	1.213	1.220	1.227	1.235	1.242	1.249	1.256	1.264	1.271	1.279	12
13	1.230	1.238	1.246	1.254	1.262	1.270	1.278	1.286	1.294	1.302	13
14	1.248	1.256	1.265	1.273	1.282	1.291	1.299	1.308	1.317	1.325	14
15	1.266	1.275	1.284	1.293	1.302	1.312	1.321	1.330	1.340	1.349	15

Bibliography

Abramovitz, M., *An Approach to a Price Theory for a Changing Economy,* Columbia University Press, New York, 1939.

———, *The Role of Inventories and Business Cycles,* National Bureau of Economic Research, New York, 1948.

*Accounting Principles Board, *Financial Statements Restated for General Price Level Changes,* Statement No. 3, American Institute of Certified Public Accountants, New York, 1969.

*Aharoni, Y. and T. Ophir, "Accounting for Linked Loans," *Journal of Accounting Research,* Spring 1967, pp. 1–26.

Alexander, M. O. (ed.), *Accounting for Inflation,* Maclean Hunter, 1975.

*Alexander, S. S., M. Bronfenbrenner, S. Fabricant, and C. Warburton, *Five Monographs on Business Income,* American Institute of Certified Public Accountants, New York, 1950.

*American Accounting Association, *A Statement of Basic Accounting Theory,* Evanston, Ill., 1966.

American Institute of Accountants, *Accounting Trends in Corporate Reports,* New York, 1949.

American Institute of Certified Public Accountants, *Accounting and Changing Price Levels,* New York, 1948.

———, *Depreciation and High Costs,* Accounting Research Bulletin No. 43, New York, 1953.

*———, *Reporting the Financial Effects of Price Level Changes,* Accounting Research Study No. 6 by the Staff of the Accounting Research Division, New York, 1963.

*American Institute of Certified Public Accountants and Institutes of Chartered Accountants of Canada, England and Wales, Scotland, and Ireland, *Accounting and Auditing Approaches to Inventories in Three Nations,* 1968.

*American Institute of Real Estate Appraisers, *The Appraisal of Real Estate,* Chicago, 1967.

*Anthony, R. N., "Accounting for the Cost of Equity," *Harvard Business Review,* November–December 1973, pp. 88–102.

Arthur Andersen & Co., "Price Level Depreciation," *Accounting and Reporting Problems of the Accounting Profession,* 1960.

*Asterisks indicate the literature cited in the text.

*Arthur Young & Company, *Measuring and Reporting the Impact of Inflation through Price-Level Accounting,* New York, 1975.

Association of Certified and Corporate Accountants in England, *Accounting for Inflation—A Study of Techniques under Conditions of Changing Price Levels,* Taxation and Research Committee, Gee & Co., London, 1952.

*Babcock, H. A., *Appraisal Principles and Procedures,* Irwin, Homewood, Ill., 1968.

*Backer, M. (ed.), *Modern Accounting Theory,* Prentice-Hall, Englewood Cliffs, N.J., 1966.

*Backer, M., *Financial Reporting for Security Investment and Credit Decisions,* National Association of Accountants, 1969.

*———, *Current Value Accounting,* Financial Executive Research Foundation, New York, 1973.

Backman, J., *Inflation and Price Indexes,* National Industrial Conference Board, 1966.

*Bak, G. G. M., "Financial Reporting under Inflationary Conditions—The Netherlands," in Institute of Certified Public Accountants in Israel, *Critical Problems of External Financial Reporting,* Proceedings of the 2nd Jerusalem Conference on Accountancy, 1974, pp. B-IV-1–11.

Barber, C. L., *Inventories and the Business Cycle, with Special Reference to Canada,* University of Toronto Press, 1958.

*Bauer, J., "Renewal Costs and Business Profits in Relation to Rising Prices," *Journal of Accountancy,* December 1919, pp. 413–419.

*Baxter, W. T., "The Accountant's Contribution to the Trade Cycle," in R. H. Parker and G. C. Harcourt (eds.), *Readings in the Concept and Measurement of Income,* Cambridge University Press, London, 1969, pp. 215–229. Reprinted from *Economica,* Vol. XXII, 1955, pp. 99–112, Revised.

*Bedford, N. M., *Income Determination Theory: An Accounting Framework,* Addison-Wesley, Reading, Mass., 1966.

*Beidleman, C. R., *Valuation of Used Capital Assets,* Studies in Accounting Research No. 7, American Accounting Association, Sarasota, Fla., 1973.

*Bonbright, J. C., *The Valuation of Property,* McGraw-Hill, New York, 1937.

*Bradford, W. D., "Price Level Restated Accounting and the Measurement of Inflation Gains and Losses," *Accounting Review,* April 1974, pp. 296–305.

Brown, E. C., *Depreciation Adjustments for Price Changes,* Riverside Press, Cambridge, Mass., 1952.

———, *Effects of Taxation: Depreciation Adjustments for Price Changes,* Harvard University Business School, Boston, Mass., 1952.

*Bullers, J. K., and P. Niland, *Effects of Taxation—Inventory Accounting and Policies,* Riverside Press, Cambridge, Mass., 1949.

*Burgett, R., "Reservations about 'Replacement Value' Accounting in the Netherlands," *Abacus,* December 1972, pp. 111–126.

*Canadian Institute of Chartered Accountants, *Accounting for Changes in the General Purchasing Power of Money,* July 1975.

*Cargill, T. F. and R. A. Meyer, "Interest Rates and Prices since 1950," *International Economic Review,* June 1974, pp. 458–471.

*Carter, R. N. and W. R. Carter, *Advanced Accounts,* Pitman, London, 1942.

*Asterisks indicate the literature cited in the text.

*Chambers, R. J., *Accounting, Evaluation and Economic Behavior,* Prentice-Hall, Englewood Cliffs, N.J., 1966.

———, *Accounting for Inflation,* The University of Sydney, Australia, 1975.

*Clarke, F. L., "Some Observations on the Indexation of Accounts," *Abacus,* December 1975, pp. 107–121.

*Cost Accounting Standards Board, "Adjustment of Historical Depreciation Costs for Inflation," Proposed Rules, *Federal Register,* Vol. 40, No. 197, October 9, 1975, pp. 57,517–57,519.

*Cotter, A., *Fool's Profits,* Barron's, New York, 1940.

*Cutler, R. S. and C. A. Westwick, "The Impact of Inflation Accounting on the Stock Market," *Accountancy,* March 1973, pp. 15–24.

*Cyert, R. M. and J. G. March, *A Behavioral Theory of the Firm,* Prentice-Hall, Englewood Cliffs, N. J., 1963.

*Davidson, S. and R. L. Weil, "Inflation Accounting," *Financial Analyst Journal,* January–February 1975, pp. 27–31, 70–84.

*———, "Impact of Inflation Accounting on 1974 Earnings," *Financial Analyst Journal,* September–October 1975, pp. 42–54.

Davidson, S., R. L. Weil, and C. P. Stickney, *Inflation Accounting: General Price Level Adjustment for the Accountant and the Financial Analyst,* McGraw-Hill, New York, 1976.

Davis, B. J., *Inflation—Its Treatment in Accounts,* Gee & Co., London, 1953.

Dean, A. H., *Business Income under Present Price Levels,* American Institute of Accountants, New York, 1949.

*Drake, O. F. and N. Dopuch, "On the Case for Dichotomizing Income," *Journal of Accounting Research,* Autumn 1965, pp. 192–205.

Dyckman, T. R., *Investment Analysis and General Price Level Statements,* Studies in Accounting Research No. 1, American Accounting Association, Evanston, Ill., 1969.

*Edwards, E. O., "The State of Current Value Accounting," *Accounting Review,* April 1975, pp. 235–245.

*Edwards, E. O., and P. W. Bell, *The Theory and Measurement of Business Income,* University of California Press, Berkeley and Los Angeles, 1961.

*Fabricant, S., *Revaluation of Fixed Assets, 1925–1934,* National Bureau of Economic Research Bulletin No. 62, 1936.

*Fama, E., "Short-Term Interest Rates as Predictors of Inflation," *American Economic Review,* June 1975, pp. 269–282.

*Financial Accounting Standards Board, *Financial Reporting in Units of General Purchasing Power,* Exposure Draft, Stamford, Conn., December 1974.

*Finley, J. A., *Handling Higher Replacement Costs,* Studies in Business Policy No. 47, National Industrial Conference Board, New York, 1950.

Fitzgerald, A. A., *Current Accounting Trends,* Butterworth & Co., Australia, 1952.

*Fleischer, G. A. and A. Reisman, "Investment Decisions under Conditions of Inflation," *International Journal of Production Research,* Vol. I, No. 2, 1967, pp. 87–95.

*Gak, A. L., "Financial Reporting under Inflationary Conditions—Argentine," in Insti-

*Asterisks indicate the literature cited in the text.

tute of Certified Public Accountants in Israel, *Critical Problems of External Financial Reporting,* Proceedings of the 2nd Jerusalem Conference on Accountancy, 1974, pp. B-I-1–15.

*Goldschmidt, Y., *Information for Management Decisions—A System for Economic Analysis and Accounting Procedures,* Cornell University Press, Ithaca and London, 1970.

*Goldschmidt, Y., and S. Smidt, "Valuing the Firm's Durable Assets for Managerial Information," *Accounting Review,* April 1969, pp. 317–329.

*Goldsmith, R. W., *A Study of Saving in the United States,* Princeton University Press, Princeton, N. J., 1955.

*———, *The National Wealth of the United States in the Postwar Period,* National Bureau of Economic Research, New York, 1962.

Graham, W. J., *Public Utility Valuation—Reproduction Cost as a Basis for Depreciation and Rate-Base Determination,* Studies in Business Administration, University of Chicago, Chicago, Ill., 1934.

*Grant, E. L., and W. G. Ireson, *Principles of Engineering Economy,* (4th ed.), Ronald Press, New York, 1960.

*Gray, S. J., "ED-8: Its Defects and an Alternative," *Accountancy,* September 1973, pp. 40–41.

———, "Price Changes and Company Profits in the Securities Market," *Abacus,* June 1975, pp. 71–85.

*Grinyer, J. R., "Inflation and Capital Budgeting Decisions: A Comment," *Journal of Business Finance and Accounting,* Spring 1974, pp. 149–155.

*Gynther, R. S., *Accounting for Price Level Changes—Theory and Procedures,* Pergamon Press, Oxford, 1966.

*———, "Capital Maintenance, Price Changes, and Profit Determination," *Accounting Review,* October 1970, pp. 712–730.

Hendriksen, E. S., *Price-Level Adjustments of Financial Statements–An Evaluation and Case Study of Two Public Utility Firms,* Bureau of Economic and Business Research, Washington State University, Pullman, 1961.

*———, *Accounting Theory,* Irwin, Homewood, Ill., 1970.

*Herzberg, F., "One More Time: How Do You Motivate Employees?" *Harvard Business Review,* January–February 1968, pp. 53–62.

*Hicks, J. R., *Value and Capital,* Clarendon Press, Oxford, 1950.

Institute of Certified Public Accountants in Israel, "Financial Reporting under Inflationary Conditions—Trends and Prospects," in *Critical Problems of External Financial Reporting,* National Papers in the 2nd Jerusalem Conference on Accountancy, October 1974.

*Institute of Chartered Accountants in Australia, *A Method of Accounting for Changes in the Purchasing Power of Money,* Preliminary Exposure Draft, December 1974.

Institute of Chartered Accountants in England and Wales, *Recommendations on Accounting Principles: XV—Accounting in Relation to the Changes in the Purchasing Power of Money,* Gee & Co., London, 1952.

———, *Accounting for Stewardship in a Period of Inflation,* Research Foundation Publication, 1968.

*Asterisks indicate the literature cited in the text.

*———, *Accounting Principles and Practices in European Countries,* London, 1972.

———, *Accounting for Inflation,* A Working Guide to the Accounting Procedures, Parts 1 and 2, 1974.

*———, *Accounting for Changes in the Purchasing Power of Money,* Provisional Statement of Standard Accounting Practice No. 7, May 1974.

Institute of Cost and Works Accountants, *The Accountancy of Changing Price Levels,* London, 1952.

*Jones, R. C., "The Effect of Inflation on Capital and Profits: The Record of Nine Steel Companies," *Journal of Accountancy,* January 1949, pp. 9–27.

———, *Price Level Changes and Financial Statements: Case Studies of Four Companies,* American Accounting Association, Urbana, Ill., 1955.

———, *Effects of Price-Level Changes on Business Income, Capital and Taxes,* American Accounting Association, Urbana, Ill., 1956.

*Jones, R. H., "Why Business Must Seek Tax Reform," *Harvard Business Review,* September–October 1975, pp. 49–55.

*Keynes, J. M., *A Treatise on Money,* Vol. 1, MacMillan, London, 1971.

*Kirkman, P. R. A., *Accounting under Inflationary Conditions,* Allen & Unwin, London, 1974.

*Kollaritsch, F. P., "Replacement Values in Practice—The Example of Austria," *Management Accounting,* August 1961 (reproduced in National Association of Accountants, *Management Reporting under Inflation,* 1975, pp. 146–157).

Lacey, K., *Profit Measurement and Price Changes,* Pitman, London, 1952.

*Lerner, A. P., *Flation—Not Inflation of Prices, Not Deflation of Jobs,* Quadrangle Books, New York, 1972.

MacDonald, G., *Profit Measurement: Alternatives to Historical Cost,* Accountancy Age Books, London, 1974.

*Marshall, A., *Principles of Economics* (6th ed.), MacMillan, London, 1910.

Mason, P., *Price-Level Changes in Financial Statements—Basic Concepts and Methods,* American Accounting Association, Urbana, Ill., 1956.

Mathews, R. and J. McB. Grant, *Inflation and Company Finance,* Law Book Co., Sydney, Australia, 1958.

*Mathews, R. L. "Price Level Changes and Useless Information," *Journal of Accounting Research,* Spring 1965, pp. 133–155.

May, G. O., *Business Income and Price Levels: An Accounting Study,* Study Group of Business Income of the American Institute of Accountants, New York, 1949.

*McDonald, D. L., "A Test Application of the Feasibility of Market Based Measures in Accounting," *Journal of Accounting Research,* Spring 1968, pp. 38–49.

*McKeown, J. D., "Comparative Application of Market and Cost Based Accounting Models," *Journal of Accounting Research,* Spring 1973, pp. 62–99.

Meij, J. L. (ed.), *Depreciation and Replacement Policy,* North Holland, Amsterdam, 1961.

Mey, A., *On the Application of Business Economics and Replacement Value Accounting in the Netherlands,* International Accounting Studies Institute and Graduate School of Business Administration, University of Washington, Seattle, 1970.

*Asterisks indicate the literature cited in the text.

*Middleditch, L., Jr., "Should Accounts Reflect the Changing Value of the Dollar?" *Journal of Accountancy,* February 1918, pp. 114–120.

*Moonitz, M., "Price Level Accounting and Scales of Measurement," *Accounting Review,* July 1970, pp. 465–475.

*———, *Changing Prices and Financial Reporting,* Occasional Paper No. 3, International Center for Research Accounting, University of Lancaster, England, 1973.

*Morley, M. F.,*The Fiscal Implication of Inflation Accounting,* Institute for Fiscal Studies and Institute of Chartered Accountants in England and Wales, London, 1974.

*Morris, W. T., *Engineering Economy,* Irwin, Homewood, Ill., 1960.

Mueller, G. G., *Accounting Practices in the Netherlands,* International Business Series, Studies in Accounting, University of Washington, Seattle, 1962.

*Mundell, R., "Inflation and Real Interest," *Journal of Political Economy,* Vol. 71, 1963, pp. 280–283.

National Association of Accountants, *Managing Price Level Accounting* (selected reading from *Management Accounting*), New York, 1975.

———, *Management Reporting under Inflation* (selected readings from *Management Accounting*), New York, 1975.

*National Council of Chartered Accountants in South Africa, *Accounting for Inflation and Other Changes in Price Level,* Discussion Paper, May 1975.

National Industrial Conference Board, *Replacement Costs and Depreciation Policy,* Studies in Business Policy No. 27, 1948.

*Okun, A. M., "Inflation: The Problems and Prospects Before Us," in A. M. Okun, H. H. Fowler, and M. Gilbert, *Inflation: The Problems It Creates and the Policies It Requires,* New York University Press and University of London Press, New York and London, 1970, pp. 1–53.

*Parker, J. E., "Testing Comparability and Objectivity of Exit Value Accounting," *Accounting Review,* July 1975, pp. 512–524.

*Parker, R. H. and G. C. Harcourt, *Readings in the Concept and Measurement of Income,* Cambridge University Press, London, 1969.

Paton, W. A., Jr., *Study in Liquidity; the Impact of Inflation on Monetary Accounts,* Michigan Business Studies, Vol. 14, No. 2, University of Michigan, 1958.

*Petersen, R. J., "Portfolio Analysis of General Price Level Restatement," *Accounting Review,* July 1975, pp. 525–532.

*Petrei, A. H., "Inflation and Personal Income Tax," *Finance and Development,* September 1974, pp. 38–41.

*Price Waterhouse International, *Survey of Accounting Principles and Reporting Practices in 38 Countries,* Price Waterhouse & Co., London, 1973.

*Radford, R. A., "The Price System in Microcosm: A P.O.W. Camp," in C. L. Harriss (ed.), *Selected Readings in Economics,* Prentice-Hall, Englewood Cliffs, N.J., 1958, pp. 69–79.

*Ray, D. D., *Accounting and Business Fluctuations,* University of Florida Press, Gainesville, 1960.

*Reisman, A., *Managerial and Engineering Economics,* Allyn & Bacon, Boston, Mass., 1971.

*Asterisks indicate the literature cited in the text.

*Reisman, A. and A. K. Rao, *Discounted Cash Flow Analysis: Stochastic Extensions,* Monograph Series No. 1, American Institute of Industrial Engineers, Norcross, Ga., 1973.

*Revsine, L., *Replacement Cost Accounting,* Prentice-Hall, Englewood Cliffs, N.J., 1973.

*Roll, R., "Interest Rates on Monetary Assets and Commodity Price Index Changes," *Journal of Finance,* May 1972, pp. 251–277.

*Rosen, L. S., *Current Value Accounting and Price Level Restatements,* Canadian Institute of Chartered Accountants, Toronto, Canada, 1972.

*Rosenfield, P., "Accounting for Inflation—A Field Test," *Journal of Accountancy,* June 1969, pp. 45–51.

Ross, H., *The Elusive Art of Accounting,* Ronald Press, New York, 1966.

*_______, *Financial Statements: A Crusade for Current Values,* Pitman, New York, 1969.

*_______, "Is It Better to Be Precisely Wrong Than Vaguely Right?" *Financial Executive,* June 1971, pp. 8–12.

*Sandilands, F. E. P. *Inflation Accounting,* Report of the Inflation Accounting Committee, Her Majesty's Stationery Office, London, 1975.

*Scapens, R. W., *The Treatment of Inflation in the Published Accounts of Companies in Overseas Countries,* Institute of Chartered Accountants in England and Wales, 1973.

*Securities and Exchange Commission, "Release No. 190," *Accounting Series,* Bureau of National Affairs, Washington, D.C., March 1976, pp. E–1–4.

*_______, "Interpretations of Accounting Series Release No. 190," *Staff Accounting Bulletin,* No. 7, SEC DOCKET, March 1976, pp. 295–300.

*Shashua, L. and Y. Goldschmidt, "A Tool for Inflation Adjustment of Financial Statements," *Journal Of Business Finance and Accounting,* Spring 1976, pp. 33–42.

*Shashua, L., Y. Goldschmidt, and G. Levkovitz, *"Revaluation of the Productive Assets in the Kibbutz Sector,"* Working Paper 67/73, Heshev, Tel Aviv, 1973. In Hebrew.

*_______, "Alternative Methods of Estimating the Capital Stock of the Kibbutz," forthcoming in *Issues in the Economy of Israel,* Maurice Falk Institute for Economic Research in Israel, 1977. In Hebrew; forthcoming in English.

*Sprinkel, B. W., "Inflation—Its Cause and Cure," *Financial Analyst Journal,* May–June 1971, pp. 11–16.

*Staubus, G. J., *Activity Costing and Input–Output Accounting,* Irwin, Homewood, Ill., 1971.

*Sterling, R. R., *Theory of the Measurement of Enterprise Income,* Kansas University Press, 1970.

*_______ (ed.), *Asset Valuation and Income Determination,* Scholars Book Co., Lawrence, Kan., 1971.

Stickler, A. D. and C. S. R. Hutchins, *General Price Level Accounting—Described and Illustrated,* Canadian Institute of Chartered Accountants, Toronto, 1975.

*Stickney, C. P. and D. O. Green, "No Price Level Adjusted Statements, Please (Pleas)," *CPA Journal,* January 1974, pp. 25–31.

*Asterisks indicate the literature cited in the text.

*Stigler, G. J. and J. K. Kendahl, *The Behavior of Industrial Prices,* National Bureau of Economic Research, General Series, No. 90, 1970.

*Sweeney, H. W., *Stabilized Accounting,* Harper, New York, 1936 (Renewed, Holt, Rinehart & Winston, New York, 1964).

Terborgh, G., *Depreciation Policy and the Postwar Price Level,* Machinery and Allied Products Institute, Chicago, 1949.

———, *Inflation and Postwar Profits,* Machinery and Allied Products Institute, Chicago, 1949.

*Trienens, H. J., "Some Legal Implications of Current Value Accounting," in M. Backer, *Current Value Accounting,* Financial Executive Research Foundation, 1973, pp. 77–109 (also in *Financial Executive,* September 1972).

*Vos, J., "Replacement Value Accounting," *Abacus,* December 1970, pp. 132–143.

Walsh, F. J., Jr., *Inflation and Corporate Accounting,* National Industrial Conference Board, Business Policy Study No. 104, 1962.

*Weston, J. F. and E. F. Brigham, *Managerial Finance,* Holt, Rinehart & Winston, New York, 1969.

Wilk, A., *Accounting for Inflation,* Sweet and Maxwell, London, 1960.

*Wright, F. K., "Accounting and Price Changes," R. J. Chambers, L. Goldberg, and R. L. Mathews (eds.), *The Accounting Frontier,* Cheshire, Melbourne and London, 1966.

*Asterisks indicate the literature cited in the text.

Index